HUMANIZING TECHNOLOGY

Computers in Community Use and Adult Education

ELISABETH GERVER

Scottish Institute of Adult and Continuing Education
Edinburgh, Scotland

SPRINGER SCIENCE+BUSINESS MEDIA, LLC

Library of Congress Cataloging in Publication Data

Gerver, Elisabeth.
  Humanizing technology.

  (Approaches to information technology)
  Bibliography: p.
  Includes index.
  1. Computers. 2. Computers — Social aspects. 3. Computer-asssisted instruction. 4. Adult
education — Data processing. I. Title. II. Series.
QA76.G436   1986   .004   85-28309
  ISBN 978-0-306-42141-9   ISBN 978-1-4615-9448-2 (eBook)
  DOI 10.1007/978-1-4615-9448-2

Cover photograph reproduced courtesy of
Apple Computer Inc.

© 1986 Springer Science+Business Media New York
Originally published by Plenum Press, New York in 1986

To my father, Don Archibald

FOREWORD

A few years ago, a book of this type and style could not or would not have been written. This is because, until a few years ago, no real in-depth knowledge of computers and computerized equipment was at the disposal of those with a nonscience, nonquantitative background. Some people from other disciplines—including business, the arts, and the social sciences—had been working with such equipment, but they had "gone over" and tended to be even more computer-conscious than those whom they served.

It is only comparatively recently that people like Elisabeth Gerver with a firm arts and adult education background first of all became knowledgeable and then remained true to that background.

To her eternal credit, Elisabeth Gerver, when she became involved, avoided being sucked into the world of the jargon or even that of the thinking of the computer scientists and the electronic engineers. On the contrary, she insisted that she was an educated woman dealing with other educated people, and that they would all speak in the language of everyday discourse. It worked!

One consequence of her experience and her thought is this remarkably lucid and readable book. It will prove to be of immense value to many in the world of adult and community education. But the beneficiaries will run beyond those sectors of society. Other people with a nonscience, nonquantitative background will surely find it of immense value in their early, inevitably hesitant and faulty, grappling with the world of new technology. Indeed, even computer scientists and their colleagues in electrical and electronic engineering will read it with advantage. They will find that they have less difficulty in reading and following Dr. Gerver's book than she and I and others have in reading their work, and they may care to reflect on that—and do something about it.

THOMAS F. CARBERY

Strathclyde Business School
University of Strathclyde
Glasgow, Scotland

ACKNOWLEDGMENTS

Many current developments in the use of computers in community education are unrecorded: especially in voluntary organizations and in informal adult education, staff are often so hard-pressed to meet immediate needs that they find little time to prepare detailed public records of their activities. I am, therefore, indebted to a large number of people in Europe, Canada, and the United States who have patiently let me share their experiences either through conversations or in writing. The names which follow represent only a small proportion of all those who have helped in the making of this book.

Professor Tom Carbery of the University of Strathclyde first tempted me into writing about this area of experience, to which he had already contributed substantially both as Chairman of the Information Technology 82 campaign in Scotland and in many other ways as well. I am grateful for his encouragement and his practical help. I should also like to thank Ken Derham, of Plenum Press, who has given me many useful suggestions, and who then waited patiently for longer than should have been necessary.

The book was made possible by my experience in the Scottish Community Education Microelectronics Project and particularly by the informed help given by Shiona McDonald, Margaret Sutherland, and Gill Gibson on the staff, and Dr. Ethel Gray and H.M.I. Graham Wilson of the Management Committee; I am very grateful to all of them.

Discussions with a number of other groups of people have also contributed significantly to developing the ideas in the book. I am grateful to my colleagues in the Scottish Council for Community Education and its successor, the Scottish Community Education Council, the staff at ECCTIS, the continuing education staff of the BBC, the staff of "microsyster," the members of

Sheffield Computers for People, the adult education staff of the Department of Education in Sheffield, and the senior staff of the community education service in Fife.

I have also learned a great deal from all those people who have politely listened to my papers at conferences and then helped me to develop the ideas further afterwards. Asha Craemer-Kachru, John Dobson, Ann Jones, Linda Lewis, Wendy Miller, Doug Myers, Margaret Shotton, Gillian Skirrow, and John Traxler have all contributed many ideas and much information.

I am also grateful for the tactful and patient help given to me at work by the staff and members of the Scottish Institute of Adult Education and at home by Mrs. Anne Sturrock and Mrs. Marjory Suttie, who have had to bear the brunt of the many hours on which I have worked on my computer in the study.

But above all I am grateful to my own family. My children, Sascha and Miriam, have tolerated gracefully their mother's long absorption in the writing of books, and they have offered much practical help as well. My two sisters, Jean Lawson in Canada and Joyce Archibald in Australia, generously invited the children for a long holiday, while I completed the book, and I greatly appreciate their practical assistance.

The book is dedicated to my father, Don Archibald. Throughout his life, he has combined deep compassion for other people and a profound sense of social justice with a recognition of the need for efficient work. He has always believed, too, in the value of adult education; recently, in his seventies, he learned how to use a computer as a word processor in order to raise funds for a charity. I have tried throughout to reflect his commitment to learning and to the need to work cooperatively for the benefit of the whole community by humanizing technology.

CONTENTS

INTRODUCTION

In the last few years throughout Europe and North America, there has been an extraordinary growth of interest and projects in the use of computers in community education. The development of microcomputers has now brought the power of computers into people's homes, often by way of children's apparently universal enthusiasm for them. Among those who are still employed, more and more people are using computers as part of their professional, technical, and skilled work. The extensive use of computers in formal education in schools, colleges, and universities has created a climate of expectation that computers can be used for learning. The spread of computerization into small businesses has also contributed to the growing recognition that microcomputers can help community organizations to strengthen existing services and perhaps to offer new ones as well.

Above all, there is now a clear and urgent need for everyone to have a general understanding of how to use computers for specific purposes, to recognize their usefulness and their limitations, and to be able to make informed judgments about the implications of computerization on society—to be, using a term now widely accepted, computer-literate. Throughout the developed world, adult educators have responded to this need to such an extent that computer courses for adults now represent probably the fastest growing area of adult education.

The content of both national and international gatherings also reflects an increasing awareness of the use of computers in community education. The connections between adult learning and the new technologies formed one of the major areas for study at the world conference of the International Council for Adult Education in Paris in 1982 and, as this book goes to press, this

1

area will again be an important topic in the next conference of the Council to be held in Buenos Aires in 1985.

European gatherings on adult education also feature the issues involved in computers and the other new information technologies more and more prominently. The European Bureau of Adult Education's conference on "Women's Education and the Crisis of the Welfare State," held in Dusseldorf in 1984, considered the question of women and computers at some length. There are plans for a European conference on Adult Education and the New Technologies to be held in England in 1985; in the same year, a seminar in Scotland will consider the educational issues involved in the under-representation of women in dealing with computers.

In the United States and Canada, too, growing numbers of papers on adult education and the new technologies, including computers, are presented at conferences of adult educators. And, increasingly, at national and international gatherings of computer specialists and of educational technologists, the practices and issues involved in using computers in adult education are raised.

There is already an established body of evidence resulting from investigations into the interaction between people and computers, while educational computing in formal educational institutions and as a form of distance learning is a rapidly expanding field. Introducing people to computer literacy has become a major growth area within publishing, as well as among those who design computerized introductions to computers. Even my own computer, now unfashionably several years old, came with an introductory program that set out in entertaining, brilliantly colored graphics many of the things that I could reasonably expect to do with the machine.

The proliferation of journals, both popular and academic, which deal with various facets of computing, is further evidence of the very large volume of activity that is going on, much of it at neighborhood level with the formation of computer clubs and other computer projects. Even in the small village in which I live in Scotland, the newsagent carries a good supply of computing magazines. In the United States, anyone attempting to read through all of the journals which carry reports of computer projects in, or related to, the community use of computers would quickly drown in the flood of print.

But, like the proliferation of microcomputers themselves, such developments are all very recent. And, as with the promotion of microcomputers in general, claims have often been made about the way in which computers are transforming community education which cannot be sustained in practice: a leaflet issued by one project in England, for instance, claims that "if you want to know how to set about it, want to know where to do it, want to learn it from scratch, want to get better at it, our computer knows it all."

As a consequence of the enthusiastic overpromotion of computers generally and of computer literacy in particular, a sense of disappointment often arises when people actually come to terms with computers. In his study of students who attended adult evening classes in computing in one city in England, Banks (1984) found that "an alarmingly large number of students are unhappy with introductory computing courses." Similarly, the distance-learning courses in computer programming, which were mounted by the National Extension College in England during 1983, had one of the highest enrollment rates, but also one of the lowest completion rates in the history of the College (Freeman, 1983).

In schools, "many see the microcomputer as limited. There have been disappointments as reality has slid over the first dream" (Stevenson, 1984). At home, the major use of microcomputers has not been to transform domestic life but rather primarily to add another media in which games can be played. In the world of professional and commercial applications of computers, books are increasingly being written on the perils and limitations of computing rather than on computers as the gateway to Utopia. There is, indeed, increasing acknowledgment that there are many things which computers can do, but that in many cases there are other more efficient ways of achieving the same end.

The inflated promises of how computers can contribute to a better life for us all, then, are rapidly being replaced by a profound sense of disillusionment about what can actually be done with them that does contribute toward genuine educational and social community development. It is in such a climate of realistic appraisal, but sometimes overly pessimistic rejection of computers, that this book appears. Its appearance is both premature and out-dated. It is premature because many of the useful applications of computers in community education remain possibilities rather than actualities, and some of the uses described here may seem relatively trivial. It is out-dated because, even as it is being written, developments are rapidly changing as projects spring up and disappear; by the time it is printed and read, it may well seem like a faded photograph of times past.

But the book does not try to present a comprehensive account of the ways in which computers are being used in community education in the mid-1980s. Rather, it is a series of reflections about snap-shots of people using computers in various ways in their communities. These reflections are not offered as a professional assessment either of the computer technology involved or of the theory and practice of community education throughout the developed world. Rather, I hope to provide a taste of what is going on, together with a glimpse of the kinds of issues that are raised both by the increasing computerization of our societies and by the uses of computers in adult education and community development.

The book is *not* about computers as such, although Appendix A does comment briefly on several factors that any community educator who is thinking about acquiring a computer might want to bear in mind. Nor is its language intended for computing specialists, who are most likely to be irritated by the general avoidance of jargon. It is, instead, a book intended for all those people who are either interested or actually involved in using computers for community benefit, and for everyone else who believes that machines should be used in such a way.

Throughout, I have tried to avoid any use of computer jargon, except where I could not find any viable alternative; for these instances in which I have failed to avoid jargon, Appendix C attempts to provide an explanation of the main abuses of language. One reason for trying to avoid jargon wherever possible is, if I am honest, purely aesthetic: I find much specialist computer language offensive to my ears and eyes, reminiscent of George Orwell's "Newspeak" rather than of human communication. A second reason stems from my own experience of introductory computer literacy courses where the initial focus lay always on the machine and its capabilities rather than on what people might want to do with such power. By using ordinary language I hope instead to be able to focus more directly on people as they interact with machines for their own purposes. But I have also tried to communicate in ordinary language because I believe that computer jargon can too easily be used as a smokescreen behind which decisions are made to which only an elite can be party, because no one else can understand the words. This book is intended to follow in a more democratic tradition.

Despite its references to work in Europe and North America, the book is not written as a comparative study of the theory and practice of community education in those countries, nor does it attempt to be balanced in its coverage. It is written primarily as the result of my own experience in Scotland, a small country very far away from most of Europe and from all of North America. I have tried to suggest more general patterns where they seem to exist. But I am also very conscious of how limited the wider coverage is, both because of the impossibility of mastering and keeping up-to-date with everything that is going on and because, particularly in Canada and the United States, the decentralization of education has led to sometimes extreme variation in practice.

The main impulse of what follows lies in the years that I have spent as an adult educator and particularly in my experience in the early 1980s as director of the Scottish Community Education Microelectronics Project. This project, which was for obvious reasons invariably called by its acronym SCEMP, began in 1981 as a three-year project to explore the effective use and potential application of microelectronics in community education. Its major aim was to increase general awareness of the potential scope of microcomputers as a community resource for individualized learning and for providing information. It was funded by the Scottish Education Department on the advice of the Scottish Council for Community Education, and in 1984 was extended for a further three-year period by the Scottish Community Education Council.

SCEMP tried to see if and how the power of computers could be harnessed to meet the needs of the whole community rather than merely helping those institutions and individuals who can afford to purchase or lease their own computers. Its roots thus lay deep in the theory and practice of community education and development, and its collaborative, cooperative methods of working were also those characteristic of community adult education. During the years since 1981, SCEMP has generated a great deal of experience both in computer literacy and in the uses to which computers could be put in community organizations. It is on these experiences that most of this book has been built.

The emphasis of the book lies primarily on ways in which community education can take advantage of computers and the reasons why it should do so. Precise definitions may be rather more of a hindrance than a help in what is essentially a pragmatic look at the realities, the potential, and the problems in the interaction between communities and computers. Nevertheless, I am very conscious of the accusation that "the word 'community' is one which has the power to inspire a reverential suspension of critical judgment in the minds of adult educators" (Brookfield, 1983). There are, therefore, a few distinctions which I should like to make.

In the first place, this book does not presuppose consistently any pure model of community education as liberal or as liberating. It recognizes the existence of serious disparities and conflicts within communities and groups, but it does not always insist that adult community education has necessarily to lead to significant social change. It does, however, always see adult learning as taking place within a social context, whether that context consists primarily of the domestic circumstances which shape the lives of most adults or whether it also includes neighborhoods and wider forms of social relatedness and responsibility.

Within the range included in the concept of community education—and with apologies to Brookfield (1983), whose categories I have adapted and probably distorted—it seems to me that there are at least four different ways in which adult education relates to communities of people. The book is partly concerned with adult education *for* the community, with the kinds of traditional liberal nonexaminable courses for adults, such as those in computer literacy, which are provided by university extra-mural departments, voluntary organizations, such as the Workers' Educational Associations, community colleges, educational broadcasters, and so on.

Secondly, it includes the idea of adult education *in* the community, where, especially in trying to work with people who are economically and socially disadvantaged, adult educators support the goals and modes of learning experiences which students choose for themselves, as in work in adult basic education which more and more includes basic computer literacy. Thirdly, the book includes adult education *by* the community, where neighborhood resources are used informally by groups of people for the benefit of those communities, as in the development of community computer literacy experiences.

Finally, and perhaps most importantly of all, the book includes adult education *of* the community—those elements in community education which aim to better the quality of life of individual people, specific groups in the community, or the community as a whole. Many voluntary organizations form part of this kind of community education, and many adult educators also see such community development as among their long-term goals. The effects of computerization on our society are far-reaching and, if unchecked, the introduction of computers in a competitive society can reinforce and exacerbate the injustices within that society. The most important focus of this book, therefore, lies on the ways in which community education might, by using computers, try to better the quality of life in an increasingly computerized society; it is this emphasis which leads directly to the title *Humanizing Technology*.

However, there is one major section of our communities that the book does not consider to any significant extent—our children. There are several reasons why I have chosen not to consider them in any great detail. One reason is that there is already such an extensive literature on the ways in which children interact with computers. Another reason is that children's responses to computers tend to be so different from those of adults that the length of the book would virtually have doubled had I tried to include their interactions as well. The third reason is that, on the whole, certain issues in the interaction between adults and computers simply do not exist for most children. Where adults are often wary of computers, almost all children are attracted to them and, indeed, tend on the whole to be more familiar with them than do adults; as an IBM advertisement for a personal computer put it, "your kids will teach you how to use it."

While children are, therefore, rarely considered, this book does attempt to see what kind of world we are creating for them to grow up in. So far, computers have mainly been used to create ever more destructive weapons, to enhance the profit especially of multinational corporations, and to increase the power of those individuals and groups who already have more than a fair share of resources of all kinds. I do not pretend that community educators can redress that enormous balance against social and economic justice. Rather, I shall look at some ways in which computers have been, and can be, used to the benefit of communities in specific, even if limited, ways.

Because I have tried to focus on people rather than on machines, the book does not contain the normally obligatory account of what computers consist of, the theory behind them, how they are made, and all the different ways in which they are used. For those readers who wish to pursue such matters in any depth, Appendix B suggests further reading among the wide choice of literature available. Meanwhile, I shall usually concentrate on microcomputers as being the kind of equipment which community educators are most likely to use. At times, however, I shall range more widely over larger computers, particularly in discussing the general effects of computerization and in considering the publicly available computer-based systems which community educators might also want to use.

Chapters 1 and 2 will set the scene for the issues raised in the book. Chapter 1, "The Paradox of Computers," will consider some of the major paradoxes which appear in using computers, including the often yawning gap between their promise and their reality. Chapter 2, "Computers and Gender," will discuss the specific problem of the apparent reluctance of many women to interact with computers, and will describe and analyze several ways in which adult educators have tried to overcome the gender imbalance in the use of computers.

Chapters 3 and 4 are intended to provide the major discussion of current developments and issues in using computers in community education. Chapter 3, "Computers and Informal Learning," will argue that computer literacy has become an essential element in the basic education of all adults. It will consider the ways in which adult educators now can make use of computer programs and the variety of ways in which community educators have tried to encourage people to become "computer-literate." Chapter 4, "Using Computers in the Community," will present a series of case studies of the use of computers in community development and will try to reach some general conclusions about the efficacy of computers in this area.

Chapters 5 and 6 will take, respectively, a narrow and a wide view of using computers in community education. Chapter 5, "Cooperating with Computers," will concentrate on the practical realities of using computers in different kinds of community organizations and will argue for a model of cooperative development. Chapter 6, "Promises and Pitfalls," will look critically at the promises of a golden future of computerized learning and will try to assess the real value of computers in community education.

1

THE PARADOX OF COMPUTERS

"To see a world in a grain of sand . . . " William Blake, *Auguries of Innocence.*

Depending on their context and their purposes, computers have a bewildering variety of characteristics and effects. Their power is matched only by their frailty. The highly competitive ethos in the computer industry sits oddly beside the claim that the use of computers encourages collaborative and cooperative patterns of work. And the grandeur of visions of how computers may transform the ways in which we think and learn becomes ironic in the light of the banal and trivial realities of many of the computer programs currently available. Paradoxical characteristics and effects such as these shape how community educators and adult learners perceive computers and determine the quality and quantity of the contribution that computers can make to adult learning and community development.

For community educators, however, perhaps the most important characteristic of computers—and the source of their often paradoxical effects— is their neutral power, through which human purposes can be significantly enhanced or deformed. The computer is a "mindless tool with infinite use" (Radcliffe and Salkeld, 1983). Where such a tool is used to extend the possibilities for learning and for community service, it can enrich the quality of people's lives, while learning how to use computers can empower people in many different ways.

At this point, most books about the impact of computers in almost any field contain one chapter on the theory and construction of computers, followed by another containing the history of the development of a particular computer application. I shall not follow this course. There are many works which already provide such surveys, some of which are noted in the section on further reading. But much of the technical detail and history of how computers work are simply irrelevant to community education: as Boden (1977) has commented, "computers are metallic machines of intrinsic interest to electronic engineers but not, as such, to many others." My concern lies rather with those characteristics of contemporary computers which seem to affect the ways in which they could and should be used to humanize technology in community education.

This chapter will, therefore, explore some of the paradoxes of computers before looking at what seem to be the dominant characteristics of the machines as they affect their users. I shall also probe some of the particularly sensitive, even perhaps diseased, facets of computer use. Finally, in the light of the previous discussion, I shall argue that community education can and should use computers for the benefit of both local and wider communities.

But why should community educators—particularly those who are concerned with adult learning—want to think seriously about computers in the first place? There are, I should like to argue, educational and educative, as well as some purely pragmatic, reasons why they should do so.

In the first place, the diversity of the learning styles and circumstances of adults makes the possible use of computer programs as an educational medium particularly attractive. Computer programs can respond to individual differences and can be finely tuned to fit individual circumstances, such as physical disability or distance. Moreover, computer programs can allow students to experiment with situations that are too dangerous or too distant to encounter in reality, and the use of computer simulations can also encourage learners to recognize the ways in which the many parts of a complex system are interrelated.

Even more important than the educational potential of computers is their educative force. The use of computers can encourage adults who usually do not seek educational experience to try new ways of learning. Also, using computers to store large amounts of information can increase access to education by making information about learning opportunities more widely available.

More important still is the argument that community educators need to help their communities to come to terms with computers—at least to avoid being disadvantaged by the increasing computerization of society and, at best, to take advantage of the enormous power of computers. The need for computer literacy is ubiquitous, as may be seen in the remarkably high figures for public responses to programs which help people learn about computers.

Indeed, the strong public interest in using computers forms a powerful pragmatic reason why many community educators are now exploring ways of learning by and about computers. The evidence for this interest is so widespread that it has become almost banal. It is now a truism that courses in learning about computers are likely to be oversubscribed; computer exhibitions can almost be guaranteed to produce queues of eager users; the market for books about computers seems almost inexhaustible. As the discussion below will often suggest, this enthusiasm may sometimes be ill-informed and ill-placed. But the very fact that computers seem to be so attractive to so many people—in Britain alone over one million microcomputers are sold every year—should be sufficient in itself to make community educators alert to ways of building on such popularity.

POWER AND FRAILTY

Computers, as they have been presented through advertising and in other public representations, are often surrounded by an aura of reliability, if not infallibility, in their capacity as perfect slaves. Indeed, assuming that there are no faults in the design and manufacture of the equipment itself, a computer will do exactly as its programs tell it to do: it does not misread figures; it does not forget how to carry out particular procedures, or indeed, anything else that it has been programmed to remember and which is entered in its memory in a permanent form. In fact, much of the justification for introducing the computerization of many processes is that it can eliminate the kinds of human errors which arise from tiredness, distraction, emotional involvement, impatience, and so on.

The rate at which computer systems tend to break down stands in striking contrast to this emphasis on absolute reliability. Evidence of this fallibility is ubiquitous, even if there is often pressure not to report it widely. A number of projects trying to promote greater educational use of computer-based videotex systems in both Canada and Britain have reported relatively high rates of failure of the equipment itself. In a Canadian study of Telidon, "while participants were very pleased by their ability to access databases on distant computers, many reported difficulty in getting or staying on the system" (Wilson, 1984); in Britain over 20% of those replying to a questionnaire about using an analogous system, Prestel, felt that the equipment had not been reliable (Kania, 1983). In the use of computers in one training scheme in Canada, there was a complete failure of the system on 30% of the days involved (Loyer, 1983), while on a training scheme in Britain "terminals frequently collapsed and died" (Deakin, 1984).

The kinds of technical difficulties which users often experience with new computer equipment will be illustrated at some length in case studies in Chapter 5. But the frailty of computers appears to be ubiquitous, with a failure rate that seems to run between 25% and 30%. A further indication of the extent of the problem with the equipment itself may be seen in the fact that 27% of people who received the widely praised BBC computers in the first year found that the machines were defective (BBC, 1983). In North America as well, the general experience has been that "no other feature of human engineering elicits so little praise or so much condemnation as the reliability of computer systems" (Champine, 1978).

Computers themselves, then, may be defective in design or manufacture. To this deficiency must be added the kinds of human error which can often have disastrous consequences for the physical operation of the machine itself. Many personal computers are now casually carried from place to place; Figure 1 shows how one project for using computers in the community involves carting the computer around on a motorbike. Computers tend to withstand this kind of rough treatment remarkably well. Nevertheless, a few drops spilled from a cup of coffee on to a computer keyboard can disrupt the entire system.

Such paradoxes are multiplied many times over when one takes into account not merely the machines themselves but also the physical character-istics of their programs, especially when they are stored on tape or disks. As McWilliams (1982) comments, "it is hard to duplicate, using ordinary meth-ods, the efficiency and effectiveness of a computer. It is equally hard to duplicate, using ordinary methods, the degree of devastation and disaster possible on a computer." Many otherwise minor ordinary incidents can have disastrous consequences for computer programs: the placing of a computer disk near a magnet can destroy its contents; in many older microcomputers, a sudden power surge or failure can instantly destroy all the information held on the computer; even smoking can interfere with the accuracy of the infor-mation which is put into and taken out of a computer; and a mislaid computer disk contains a far larger amount of information than any one mislaid sheet of paper.

There is now a large repertory of anecdotes about how vulnerable com-puter programs are to human error and, more menacingly, about how open they are to deliberate breaches of security for various purposes, including fraud (Whiteside, 1978). The blunt fact is that no computer system is wholly secure or free from human error or malice; as Laver (1980) recognizes from

Figure 1. The itinerant computer: a community education worker in central Scotland prepares to travel. Photograph reproduced by courtesy of *The Scotsman*, 1984.

his experience as a computer specialist, "given time and sufficient motive a determined computer expert can penetrate the security of the most complex system." In the mid-1980s, the spate of incidents involving unauthorized access to military information in the United States confirms the assessment (for one example among many, see *The Scotsman*, 1983).

Human error in the operation of computers also has consequences which range from the merely irritating—as in the demand to pay a computerized account which has already been settled—to the seriously inconvenient—such as the denial of credit to a customer because of an erroneous computer entry on a database. Most ominous of all, however, is the possibility of a global nuclear conflict brought about by accident because of the combined effect of shortness of response time and human error:

On November, 1979, a 'war game' scenario was accidentally fed into the early warning sensing system, the simulated missile attack being read as a 'live launch.' It took six minutes to discover the mistake, in which time fighters from bases in the U.S. and Canada had taken off, and missile and submarine bases had been placed on a higher level of alert. . . . Of course such alarms present no problem provided they can be identified as false alarms. But in times of crisis, with weapons systems already on alert, there is less than eight minutes available to decide if an attack is underway (Smoker, 1984).

The scale of the problem has been exacerbated by the use of increasingly computerized systems of military communication and control; by the beginning of 1983, such "false alerts" were occurring at the rate of two every three days (ibid).

THE TRIVIAL USES OF POTENTIAL POWER

It is probably inevitable—at least in largely market-oriented economies— that much of the enormous power of microelectronics in general and computers in particular has been harnessed to essentially trivial purposes. There has been a seemingly endless stream of computer-based gadgets that do not obviously fulfill any human need beyond that of conspicuous consumption. Probably the major use to which home computers are now put, for instance, is the playing of games. And, as we shall see later in this chapter, many computer-based applications have been developed where the apparent criterion is based on Dr. Johnson's sardonic assessment of a woman's preaching as being "like a dog's walking on his hinder legs. It is not done well, but you are surprised to find it done at all." As Chapter 2 will suggest, both the sexist attitude, as well as the delight in machines for the novelty rather than the value of what they can do, are highly characteristic of many computer applications.

But a more significant variant of the paradox of harnessing powerful computer equipment to less than impressive programs appears in the general emphasis on the equipment itself rather than on what is actually done with it. What happened in trials of Telidon in Canada is characteristic of the attitudes of many governments toward promoting the use of computer-based applications: "The emphasis in government funding has been focussed on the development and deployment of hardware and operating systems support (i.e. terminals, communications networks, the computer programs to create, store, and display content . . .). The actual design and creation of content to display on the hardware/network configuration have received the lowest funding priority" (Wilson, 1984).

In Britain, too, most government funding to promote the use of computers in education has been directed toward providing the equipment itself rather than being spent on the development of good programs. In Scotland, for instance, the Scottish Community Education Microelectronics Project received substantial funding for the purchase of computers but very little for the buying of programming time, despite the fact that the major need in the field was not so much for the machines themselves as for discovering and providing good educational uses to which they could be put. The evaluation of SCEMP concluded that "resource provision, in order of importance, is required in human, software, and hardware terms. The order of provision has certainly been the reverse. The project was provided with hardware, software was then purchased and staff have always been overstretched" (Laidlaw, 1984).

It is only fair to note that not all governments have responded in similar ways. In France between 1970 and 1976, at a time when the costs of computer equipment were proportionately much higher than in the early 1980s when SCEMP began, pilot schemes to introduce computers to secondary schools spent about 70% of their budgets on staffing costs, including teacher training and programming (Hebenstreit, 1983).

Overall, however, in much of the developed world, the focus has lain on the equipment itself, and there continues to be considerable disparity between what the machines can do and what they are actually used for. Some of this disparity arises simply from inappropriate use. As McWilliams (1982) has realistically commented about the role of computer programs in managing personal finances, "computers will accurately record, add, and subtract a row of checking deposits and debits, but doing it 'the old-fashioned way' is faster, easier, and cheaper." But most often the paradox arises, as we shall see again below, because of the enormous pressure of marketing computer systems.

INTENSE RESPONSES TO EMOTIONAL NEUTRALITY

Part of the paradoxical quality of computers lies in the intensity of the responses that many people have to them. As Chapter 2 will discuss in greater detail, the responses of men and women to computers tend to be very different from one another; indeed, as we shall see later in the present chapter, among those who are most infatuated with computers—the so-called "computer junkies" or "compulsive programmers"—there are scarcely any women. Among men and women working with computers, the case study described by Deakin (1984) seems to be typical:

> Nora soon found that on the many occasions when the service men came
> out, most willingly and helpfully, to get the machine going or sort out some

problem, they wasted hours following up some different and irrelevant matter which fascinated them but merely delayed the solution of the problem in hand. They loved the computer for itself, whereas she loved it only for what it could do.

It may be that such a highly utilitarian attitude on the part of many women is one of the factors behind the apparent reluctance of many women to become involved with computers; as we have seen above, computer equipment often promises much more than computer programs actually deliver. Regardless of the possible reasons, however, the fact remains that, particularly in Britain but also to a noticeable extent in most of the rest of the developed world, far more men than women tend to respond to the lure of computers: at open public computer exhibitions in the United States, for instance, women formed only about 15% of those attending (Loop, Anton, and Zamora, 1983). As Chapter 3 will discuss further, both adult students and tutors also tend to have relationships of love or hate with the computers which they use for educational purposes.

As well as inviting intense responses, the emotional neutrality of computers also seems to encourage greater honesty in the responses elicited from users, particularly in those areas of personal experiences about which people tend to feel some reticence. One hospital in Edinburgh has reported that, in responding to questions posed by a computer, people will confess to drinking 30% more than they have told their doctors (Menzies, 1982), while another study in Glasgow found that patients who were suspected of being alcoholics admitted to drinking 50% more alcohol to the computer than to highly trained consultants (Evans, 1979). There is also some evidence that, when they are taking part in interviews conducted by a computer system, "patients can strike up a surprising rapport with the computer, particularly in sensitive areas as such as those involving psychosexual or emotional problems" (Evans, ibid).

THE LOWLY ART OF USING HIGH TECHNOLOGY

Most of the high-pressured advertising currently directed to potential purchasers of computers tends to emphasize their appeal to decision-makers. A common expectation is that a computer system can improve the decision-making within an institution or organization because of the way in which it can present all the necessary information immediately at the touch of a finger on the keyboard, a pen on a touch-sensitive screen, or a mouse moved in the right direction. In practice, however, once the technology is actually installed and fully working in most noncomputer organizations, "a common experience is that clerks, typists, and secretaries have got more out of the system than expected and management has got less" (Goodman, 1984).

One reason for this apparently paradoxical outcome is simply that the skills of using an old-fashioned QWERTY keyboard, which is the form of most computer keyboards and typewriters, may become transient as computer technology replaces them with alternatives, but remain necessary for the efficient operation of most computers. One study in England recently found that the skill which most employers who used computers and most computer specialists saw as being most essential for using high technology was, simply, the skill of accurate typing (Glyn-Jones, 1984). Indeed, the once-lowly skill of typing, which many managers have seen as being unnecessary except for typists and secretaries, is now becoming an essential prerequisite for many clearly nonsecretarial jobs: "no fire brigade control officers will be recruited in Devon in future unless they can type" (ibid). Increasingly, professional people who request additional secretarial help are being given word processors instead. In a number of American firms, senior management are now using electronic mail across the world and are expected to be able to use their computer keyboards to send such messages directly themselves.

Where the use of computers in many respects tends to decrease the amount of skill needed in many activities, paradoxically it increases, at least for the present, the need for most users to acquire the skill of typing. Over and over in a survey in Britain, employers commented about how education could best help their potential employees: "I wish the schools would teach them typing instead of computing" (Glyn-Jones, 1984).

FRIENDLY WORDS AND UNFRIENDLY LANGUAGE

Many of the words used in the world of computing sound friendly. Mice, fields, bugs, trees, turtles, and echo have connotations of the natural world. And we use in everyday life terms such as network, boot, memory, string, port, write, read, wrap, trace, track, bus, address, stack, sort, queue, and pack, even if they are rarely used in connection with one another. Words such as these—and there are many others like them in computing—therefore sound immediately familiar and accessible. Many of the names given to computer equipment or programs make them sound very friendly indeed, and again are often reminiscent of the natural world: Apple, Peachtree, Apricot, Pet, Rainbow, Lotus, Tulip, Tangerine, Acorn, Sage.

But the friendliness of this world is often surrounded by forbidding barricades of noncommunication. Like any technology, computing requires a specialized use of language. The problem for many newcomers, however, is not that the terms are unfamiliar, and that, therefore, a new vocabulary needs to be learned. Where the terms are unfamiliar, they can fairly readily be learned as one would learn the working foreign language of any new activity. The language problem in computing arises paradoxically because so many of the words are familiar, but the meanings are strange; it is often difficult to know whether apparently ordinary words are being used in a highly technical way or not.

But the communication problems go well beyond merely those of new learners who need to become familiar with the language. Many people encountering computers for the first time are bewildered by the often gratuitous use of technical terms, acronyms, and abbreviations, where standard English terminology would have done just as well. And, perhaps even more seriously, people who try to learn to use computers for their own purposes are very often frustrated by the fact that nearly all of the manuals which try to teach how to use the equipment and programs contain inaccuracies and important omissions. Even more deleteriously, manuals seem invariably to start from the premise that the user wants to know about the machine and programs rather than how to use them.

When I first started to use computers, I struggled for some time with an incomprehensible manual, which told me a great deal about the computer itself but not much that I actually felt I wanted to know. It seemed to be impossible that a manual should be so badly written as scarcely to communicate at all, and I believed at first that the fault lay in my own abysmal ignorance. But I then discovered that there really were only a few things which I wanted to do with my computer and its word processing program; so I simply asked someone who already know how to use it, and she was able to show me what I needed to know in a relatively short time. All of the manuals which I have since encountered for other word processing programs have also been organized according to the principle of telling the user what the machine and the program can do, and leaving the user to a large extent to work out for himself or herself exactly how to achieve the final result.

Complaints about the lack of communication in computer manuals are now commonplace; Knowles (1983) provides a similar example. Deakin (1984) reports that "sorting out the instructions and the documentation is the hardest part of using a computer. There is so much of it, all necessary at some point but often not in the first instance, and it is usually badly written . . . . One firm of software writers analyzed all their telephone calls and found that 80% of the calls asking for help were the consequence of bad documentation," in other words, the consequences of the poor quality of all the material written about the program. It is true that, since I first encountered computers in 1981,

` some manual writing has improved. But overall, the paradox remains that the words of computing sound friendly, but for most nonexperts the communication is not.

Here again, the problem lies not in computers themselves but in ways in which people have chosen to use them. In themselves, microcomputers are relatively easy to use, as most children have already discovered. But the tangle of acronyms, slang, and technical jargon with which their use tends to be surrounded has too often made adults feel, unjustifiably, that difficulties in use result from their own failure to understand rather than from the failure of the computer specialists to communicate effectively.

INACCURATE PRECISION

Because of their ability to handle large amounts of information very rapidly, computers provide an attractive way of making decisions where a large number of factors must be taken into account. Computers are, therefore, increasingly used to make diagnoses in fields such as medicine or geology. Their obvious value in such situations, where the factual information is generally unambiguous and can be precisely coded, has led to more speculative developments in trying to use computers for decision-making in less readily specified areas where large amounts of information are also involved.

There are now, for example, proposals to construct computer systems to play important roles in the decision-making procedures that would precede a nuclear war. To the planners of the decision-making procedures that would lead to the launch of a nuclear attack, there would be clear advantages in using such systems, which would be able to make more rapid judgments, taking account of more factors, than could any human being. The problem remains, however, as we have seen earlier, that false alerts, resulting from unpredictable situations, arise frequently in the interaction between computer systems and the real world. Any computer system required to make an absolute judgment in such a situation would have to have been fed with a "prior *exhaustive* characterization of all the circumstances which may affect that judgement" (Thompson, 1984); such an entirely comprehensive picture is, of course, impossible.

Analogous difficulties arise in trying to use computer simulations as a basis for making decisions about other matters in which many interacting factors are involved. Again, because of its ability to handle so much information so quickly and precisely, it appears that the computer could be ideally placed to make a decision that would be better informed and more securely based than those of human beings. As with the question of the use of computers for decision-making in nuclear war, difficulties inevitably arise because of possible errors in the model used for the simulation and the necessarily imprecise nature of at least some of the information fed into it. Computer models of national economies provide an obvious example of the possibilities of large-scale error. At a more mundane level, if I make a typing error in entering information into a computer program which is assessing my liability to a heart attack, I will get as precise a calculation of my risk as if I had entered the correct information; it will merely happen to be wrong.

ECONOMIC PARADOXES OF COMPUTERIZATION

There is, as yet, little agreement about the overall economic consequences of computerization, and I do not propose to indulge in economic forecasting. Among those who do engage in such risky activities, however, the larger number of writers appear to believe that increasing computerization is, at best, unlikely to improve the current high levels of unemployment throughout much of the developed world and, at worst, may well be an exacerbating factor, at least in the short-to-medium term. Thus, OECD (1982) estimates that "only 60% of the direct reduction of manpower demand imputable to technology will be compensated by 1990."

Laver (1980) believes that "we have neither the facts nor the understanding to be able to predict the long-term effects of computers on employment, but short-term increases in unemployment and enforced changes of job seem inevitable." Certainly the evidence in Britain by the mid 1980s appears to be that computerization, combined with at least some indices of economic recession, is an important factor in creating unacceptably high levels of unemployment. At the same time, however, there is unquestionably a rising demand for computer specialists; throughout the developed world, the demand for computer skills seems everywhere to outstrip the number of people who are trained in such skills.

There are many other ways in which computerization already seems to be having paradoxical effects on economic activity and the distribution of wealth. Merely to give a taste of the difficulties that are emerging, I shall briefly examine two of these. In the first place, many analysts now believe that one effect of computerization will be to increase the number of well-paying jobs in high technology, but that low-paid jobs in service industries will increase considerably more. Secondly, computers appear overall to be exacerbating the division between rich and poor, even after one has allowed for the effect of the current cutting back of the welfare state in much of the developed world.

In Britain, Canada, and the United States, all economic forecasts appear to agree that there will be an increased demand for computer specialists in a number of fields. There have been a variety of government initiatives in Britain to try to ensure that there will be an adequate number of qualified people to hold the many jobs that are anticipated in high technology; in 1983–84, for instance, the government financed a 500% increase in places for post-graduate studies in information technology (WNC, 1984). In the United States, the Bureau of Labor's forecast for employment for 1983–1995 predicted that the growth in computer technicians would be over 96%, while systems analysts were expected to grow at the rate of 85%, and computer programmers at the rate of 76% (Harris, 1983). But over the same period the Bureau also predicted that three times as many janitors as new computer systems analysts would be required (Matas, 1983). Meanwhile, in Canada, "the less glamorous skills in the hospitality and fast-food industries are in greater demand than highly skilled computer programmers and technicians" (ibid).

Within the computer industry itself, too, there is already a "wasp-waisted" distribution of employment, with a few well-paying jobs in engineering and management on the top, almost none in the middle, and most on the bottom, in assembling electronic components and performing other repetitive production tasks (Harris, 1983). Both this pattern within the computer industry itself and the more general economic scenarios predicted at least until the end of this century are likely to increase economic and social divisiveness, as the chances of moving from the bottom to the top become less and less.

At the same time that computerization appears to be creating a larger gap between those employed at the top and those at the bottom of the economic hierarchy, there is also some evidence that it may exacerbate existing differences between the rich and the poor. Many commentators have noted that computerization tends to increase the strength of the strong and to weaken the fragile (see, for example, Norman, 1981; Sieghart, 1982). The situation is clearly outlined by Laver (1980):

> The advance of information technology could . . . make the information-rich even richer, and widen the gap between them and the information-poor. This is a troublesome possibility because the information-poor will tend to be those who are deprived economically and educationally, and who are thus most in need of the benefits that better information could bring.

The problem here is partly that computer-based technology—at least in its more serious applications—is relatively expensive. In Canada, for instance, fee-paying schools in Ontario were almost ten years ahead of state schools in installing computers (Menzies, 1982). Libraries, whose services were originally intended to be free, are now often having to charge for the expensive computer searches which they can conduct. The problem then is, as Menzies (ibid) suggests, that "if public libraries . . . turn toward electronic data bases as the major source of research information for the public, the search fee charged could restrict knowledge to an elite or at least impose a severe handicap on those who have to rely only on standard free-access print materials on library shelves."

In Canada, TV Ontario's investigation into the uses of videotex and a comparable study of Prestel in Britain both raised explicitly the serious question of who would be able to afford such a service and whether it should be subsidized and by whom (Wilson, 1984; Kania, 1983). For the poor in the United States, there is simply no access to the increasingly rich world of information available to those who can pay for it. In Britain, as Deakin (1984) suggests, the main reason why girls do not receive the training that they need in the computerized forms of typing and bookkeeping is simply that computers are expensive. The general tendency appears to be for computerization to change information from a resource to a commodity. The "electronic cottage" and the "global village" are nearly complete—but on present indications only the rich will be able to afford to live in them.

SOCIAL PARADOXES OF COMPUTERIZATION

As with the economic effects, it seems far too early to speak about the likely overall social effects of computerization. Chapter 2 will consider in some detail one apparent social effect, that of the sexual divisiveness of computers. In the meantime, I shall explore one area which is already being affected—home-based working with computers as an illustration of the paradoxical, inconclusive effects of computers on social life.

Because of the coming together of advances in telecommunications and computer technology, it is now possible for considerable numbers of people to carry out much of their paid employment while working in their own homes. Such a possibility is cost-effective to the firms which encourage it, as it represents a considerable saving in overhead costs. Its effect on the lives of those who undertake such "remote work," as it is sometimes called, are often contradictory. While somewhat adverse to the use of technical terms, I shall use this phrase of "remote work" to designate such activity, in order to differentiate it from three other forms of work that also take place at home— housework, care of dependents, and piece-work, such as sewing, knitting, assembling, and so on, which is traditionally undertaken by women for very low pay.

Obviously, some of the most important determinants in the effect of remote work are the conditions under which it is undertaken. For someone who has adequate space and sufficient domestic support so that the care of dependents is not a full-time occupation, it can be an attractive option, eliminating the need to travel daily to work, although, of course, most professional computer specialists would need to spend some of their time actually on site. For people who are physically disabled, there are also obvious attractions in being able to lead full working lives without having to struggle with the additional burden of simply getting to work. Remote work can offer attractive flexibility of time, too: the actual hours of a full- or part-time job can be spread throughout a period of time at the discretion and convenience of the worker, who thereby acquires greater autonomy. Indeed, it offers the possibility of integrating personal life with working life; the "electronic cottage" (Toffler, 1980) thus becomes a symbol of the wholly integrated life. And increasing numbers of firms are making such opportunities available: Elling (1984) points to examples from Sweden and West Germany, as well as to more widespread practices of remote work in Britain and the United States.

If one changes the context within which the remote work is being undertaken, however, the quality of the picture changes dramatically. Imagine, for instance, a single parent—probably female—who has to care for young children at home or who is responsible for an aging, perhaps senile relative. Given poor working conditions, and the constant distraction of the care of dependents, such a worker might well choose remote work not for its attractions but simply because she felt that nothing else was realistically open to her. And, if she lacks high professional qualifications in computing, she may well find that she is exploited with poorly paying low-level computer work, without any of the social advantages that would come from doing equivalent work in an office with other people. It is not surprising, then, that an American study has shown that not everyone would necessarily welcome the opportunity of working at home (Laver, 1980). Here, as elsewhere in economic and social life, the paradoxical effects of computers depend on the context in which they are used.

THE IDEOLOGICAL FLAVOR OF COMPUTERIZATION

As well as the effects which computers may have in economic and social life, there appear to be certain characteristic ideologies associated with their use. In the first place, the main tendency of present computer and allied telecommunications technology is toward cooperation, networking in its broadest senses: it appears that the best programs are those created by teams of programmers rather than by isolated individuals, and many educationalists believe that learning by way of an activity based on a computer is enhanced by being shared among at least two people. There are also now many ways in which individuals can work together at a distance through the medium of computers and allied telecommunications—by computer conferencing, electronic mail, shared computer systems, electronic journals, and so on.

Yet the whole ethos of the commercial computer world is highly competitive; indeed, it is so obviously ruthless that many women are deterred from working in it simply for that reason (Deakin, 1984). There is thus a strange ideological clash within the world of computing between the impulse toward cooperative ways of working and the spirit of ruthless competition.

There is also a strange disjunction—or perhaps a fatal similarity—between the rigor of the systematic, logical thought that is needed to work with computers in any professional capacity and the various irrational, even pathological, responses involved in certain attitudes toward computers. Martin (1978), an enthusiastic apologist for a society based on information technology, has written of what he calls "the narcotic spell of programming." An increasing number of other commentators are now coming to believe, with Grant Johnson (1980), that "working with computers requires the user to separate him/herself from the social reality he/she lives in and to shut him/herself off in an artificial world of arbitrary symbols."

In fact, Grant Johnson's careful reference to both sexes is almost unnecessary, as there are virtually no women who fall into the category of the compulsive programmer or the computer junkie. The phenomenon has been described most fully by Weizenbaum (1976):

> Wherever computer centers have become established . . . bright young men of disheveled appearance, often with sunken glowing eyes, can be seen sitting at computer consoles, their arms tensed and waiting to fire their fingers, already poised to strike, at the buttons and keys. . . . When not so transfixed, they often sit at tables strewn with computer printouts over which they pore like possessed students of a cabalistic text. They work until they nearly drop, twenty, thirty hours at a time. Their food, if they arrange it, is brought to them: coffee, Cokes, sandwiches. If possible, they sleep on cots near the computer. But only for a few hours—then back to the console or the printout. . . . They are oblivious to their bodies and to the world in which they move. They exist . . . only through and for the computers. These are computer bums, compulsive programmers. They are an international phenomenon.

There appears to be general agreement about the characteristics of these "computer junkies." In the first place, for them, working with computers takes precedence over, and is often preferred to, relationships with people. Kidder (1982) reports the experiences of a group of men working on a microcomputer project: "By signing up for the project you agreed to do whatever was necessary for success. You agreed to forsake, if necessary, family, hobbies, and friends—if you had any of these left (and you might not if you had signed up too many times before)." As Beer (1983) says, "Computers don't talk back to you, and for some people that's one of the nice things about working with computers. . . . They don't argue. They're less complicated to deal with than people." The same characteristics appear in the comments which Shotton (1984) has collected from "computer junkies": "it's not going to be rude to you or criticise you"; "you don't have to worry about it as you do about humans."

Secondly, working with computers as machines offers the security of a highly structured environment where there are only right or wrong answers:

> Among its tenets is the general idea that the engineer's right environment is a highly structured one, in which only right and wrong answers exist. It's a binary world; the computer might be its paradigm. And many engineers seem to aspire to be binary people within it. No wonder. The prospect is alluring. It doesn't matter if you're ugly or graceless or even half crazy; if you produce right results in this world, your colleagues must accept you (Kidder, 1982.).

For many compulsive programmers, however, getting results often seems to matter less than the intoxication of the process of programming, as Shotton (1984) has found in her conversations with them. The main source of pleasure lies, apparently, in the sense of power acquired by using the machine. One of the technicians cited in Kidder reported: "I'd run a little program and when it worked, I'd get a little high, and then I'd do another. It was neat. I loved writing programs. I could control the machine. I could make it express my own thoughts. It was an expansion of the mind to have a computer." Both Shotton (1984) and Turkle (1982) agree that it is this sense of personal power which appears to be the main factor in such compulsive use of computers.

Equivalent addictions exist among the fanatics in almost any field. It appears, however, as if the particularly impersonalized, relentlessly logical and systematic forms of thinking which are widely found in the world of computers may have a dangerous attraction for people who lack both power and emotional richness in their own lives. Shotton has found that the people who appear to need such power most are those who are most isolated in their personal relationships.

There are, then, a number of paradoxical characteristics and effects of computer use which, left unchecked, carry unpleasant and even ominous portents. In nearly every case, however, the computer is a kind of chameleon that becomes the color of its surroundings, and its characteristic effects are determined to a far greater extent by the purposes for which it is used than by any characteristics inherent in the nature of computers themselves.

Before considering how far it may be possible for community education to use these paradoxical effects of computerization for the benefit of communities, I should like to turn from this overly broad picture to explore one example of the actual use of computers. Because I am most familiar with it and because its use is becoming so widespread, I shall look at word processing in detail to try to see what other effects may result from transferring non-computerized activity to a computer.

USING A COMPUTER FOR WORD PROCESSING

There are two significantly different kinds of purposes for which computers can be used to process text: they can be used by intermediaries, such as secretaries or computer operators, to transfer someone else's text into an immaculate form or many different forms, or they can be used by someone who produces original text, in the form of creative writing, academic research reports, administrative papers, and so on. Because the effects of word processing are, I believe, more pronounced in the second case than in the first, I shall concentrate on the use of word processing for preparing original text.

But first, let us look at some of the characteristics of word processing which are shared by both users. First, one needs to be familiar with a standard QWERTY keyboard so that it can be used reasonably accurately and at a moderate speed. The fact that it is so easy to make corrections, however, means that, in this particular instance of using computers, it is not as important to be wholly accurate in the way in which good typists have been trained to be.

Secondly, one needs to change from paying attention to words as they appear on a page to words as they appear on a screen, usually on a special monitor attached to the computer. There are several potential problems associated with the change from paper to screen, including the fact that it is still generally more difficult to proofread accurately on a screen than on paper, as many computer misprints bear witness. Eyestrain also seems to be more readily caused by staring at a monitor than by looking at pieces of paper, and some concern has been expressed about the possible health hazards of long-term exposure to the minute amount of radiation emanating from computer monitors (Pearce, 1982).

And, of course, all the usual drawbacks of using computers tend to apply. There is a wide variety of word processing programs available. All of them seem to have minor disadvantages and unnecessarily irritating features, and they are supported by instruction manuals which are usually badly written and which often fail to include at least one piece of crucial information. Some programs display on the screen the words as they will appear in the final printed version; others allow for considerable variation between what is seen on the screen and what appears on the page when it is finally printed. The process of getting to the stage at which one can use a computer for word processing, then, takes a little time and may even be frustrating. But all of these disadvantages are greatly outweighed by the advantages.

Many of the advantages are shared by both the creators and the reproducers of original text. Because it is so widely used—about 60% of professional American writers now use word processing (Hammond, 1984)—there is already a substantial literature on word processing, and I shall not try to replicate it here. Perhaps the most striking feature is the enormous flexibility in manipulating text which can be offered by word processing programs. This flexibility transforms the nature of much of what both the originator and the reproducer of text have to do and unquestionably makes dramatic savings of time.

There are, however, also some rather more unexpected effects of using a computer for word processing, particularly for the creator of text. In the first place, as some writers have admitted, anyone creating text on a word processor is tempted to use more words than necessary, simply because of the sheer ease of doing so. As Tom Sharpe (1984) characteristically put it, "because the words are on the screen and can be easily edited, I put a damn sight more words onto it with a damn sight less care. It's not an object, you see, it's simply an image. As a result you can have verbal diarrhoea on the machine, and it doesn't make the slightest difference." Ezard (1984) has justifiably commented that "writers who like automation tend to rave on unquotably for pages—particularly if they are using processors at the time."

While the seductive ease of using word processing can result in verbosity, the opaque quality of the computer screen can also have unexpected effects on the quality of writing. Unlike pieces of paper which can be spread over a surface and related to one another, a computer screen presents only a limited number of lines at any one time; earlier lines are stored in the computer, but one cannot look at them all together. Repetitiveness of phrases and even of ideas is thus harder to avoid unless one reverts to using the computer with its printer as a kind of glorified typewriter, printing out many drafts for careful editing.

Here again, there are paradoxical effects. Despite the temptation to use too many words, the ease and speed of rewriting drafts can help toward more extensive editing and redrafting than might take place where each new draft had to be painstakingly typed afresh. However, the depressing fact remains, as Ezard (1984) suggests, that there has so far been not one outstanding novel written by using word processing. The common characteristic of many books written on word processors seems to be the often astonishing speed at which they were produced rather than depth of thought or careful selection of words. Analogously, the ease of producing word processed documents often means that the electronic office, far from being "paperless," is awash with more paper than ever before.

Word processing offers in many ways a typical illustration of the extent to which the effects of computerization are highly dependent on the purposes and the contexts of the use of computers. It is possible electronically to monitor the speed and efficiency with which a computer operator enters words on to a computer, thereby increasing rigid managerial control over the work process. In such circumstances, a secretary who used to balance her working life among typing, talking, and other forms of work, may well find that the quality of her office life is seriously diminished, not because of the computer itself but because of how her manager has decided to use the power at his disposal. Used for another purpose, precisely the same word processing system can free a secretary from the boredom of routine retyping and can give her more time for more interesting and stimulating work. Unlike Acton's pessimistic assessment of political power, therefore, the power of computers does not necessarily and inevitably corrupt.

JANUS, COMPUTERS, AND COMMUNITY EDUCATION

In both of his symbolic functions, the Roman god Janus is perhaps the closest representation of the paradoxical characteristics of computers. As the spirit of doorways and archways, he embodies the beginning of things; many of the characteristics which have been attributed to computers stem from the very newness of the art, where the potential greatly exceeds much of the actual reality of practice. Janus may thus appropriately stand for the multitude of possibilities which have been created by the use of computers. But his symbol of the double-faced head is also appropriate as a representation of the paradoxical qualities of computers with their enormous power for both good and ill. It is in the light of both of these representations that I should now like to ask what roles community education could attempt to play in using computers.

Community education has often suffered from the accusation or the apology that it has the widest intended scope and the fewest resources of any form of educational provision. If one were to add responsibility for the ways in which computers might be used for community benefit, to a wide scope and few resources, it would merely be adding madness to folly. In the first place, trying to assume responsibility for the whole field of computers would be an advanced form of megalomania: computers are specifically useful for an enormous range of specific purposes, most of which community education is in no position to affect significantly. Secondly, the kinds of resources traditionally most available to community education—scarcity of funds but a substantial supply of the time of voluntary workers—are diametrically opposed to two of the major characteristics of computers, which require substantial funds but relatively few people.

Nevertheless, community educators will feel a need to ameliorate some of the less socially and economically beneficial effects of computerization. The sexual divide in which men deal with computers and women, on the whole, do not, for instance, is clearly one which can be tackled by community educators. And there are many practical ways in which computers could contribute toward meeting some of the needs which community educators identify. Using computers, for instance, can help to attract to adult learning people who otherwise might not be willing participants, and voluntary organizations can computerize many of their functions to work more efficiently. The increasingly widespread use of computers has also created a need and a hunger for computer literacy, which is now becoming as essential for the leading of a full economic and political life as literacy itself was in the last century; here again is territory which is ripe for further development by community educators.

The rest of this book will attempt to discuss some of these ways in which computers can be used by and for community education. The accounts which follow are built on a dual premise. In the first place, I believe that community education has a responsibility to counteract, where possible, the socially and economically divisive effects of much computerization. If community educators accepted this responsibility, they would need to provide greatly enhanced opportunities for adults to learn computer literacy and to develop many more ways to enable women to approach computers. They would also need to seek out and promote ways in which computerized information can be made accessible to those who are now "information-poor," regardless of their economic or social status. Ways of approaching these possibilities will be discussed in Chapters 2, 3, and 4, and cooperative means of working toward the goals will be considered in Chapter 5.

Secondly, I believe that community education should exploit to the fullest the fact that computers can be absolute slaves to whatever purposes people choose to use them for. In providing educational programs and in other ways of empowering adult learners, in relieving much of the tedium of administrative work in voluntary organizations, and in providing access to information about such matters as educational opportunities, computers can already be used as tools to enrich the educational experience of adults and the quality of voluntary work. Possibilities in these areas will be considered further in Chapters 3 and 4, while some of the difficulties of actually using computers for such purposes will be discussed in Chapter 5.

Throughout the discussion which follows, I shall often return to the theme of how the largely neutral power of computers can be used positively for human good. I shall also emphasize how using computers can make it easier for people to work together. But I shall begin by taking a closer look at perhaps the most blatant of the ways in which present uses of computers seem to be divisive and at how community educators can help to ameliorate such a situation. Chapter 2 will, therefore, look at the gender bias of computers as an example of a major problem in the world of computing. The strategies for starting to overcome such a bias may also, I hope, provide a demonstration in miniature of how community educators can work toward obliterating that side of the Janus face of computers that stands against social justice and human equality.

2

Computers and Gender

"Microcomputers offer a golden, and perhaps unprecedented, opportunity to women" Deakin, 1984.

In the initial enthusiastic introduction of computers into various forms of community education in many parts of the developed world, grandiose claims were sometimes made for the beneficial effects that computerization could have on entire communities. It was against such a background of enthusiasm that I started to work in 1981 in the Scottish Community Education Microelectronics Project. Two impressions of that time are particularly vivid. The first is that there was already an extraordinarily high level of interest in using computers for individualized learning and for community information.

The second is that, among the large number of people who expressed interest in the project, there were very few women. As a collaborative venture, the project drew heavily on the help of volunteers to create computer programs to demonstrate some of the possibilities of using individualized learning in community education. Nearly all of the volunteer programmers were men and boys. The project also required the help of voluntary organizations to coordinate and manage computer exhibitions which would give ordinary people a chance to experience the machines for themselves. Nearly all of the individuals who offered to help with these exhibitions were men. At that time, there were no women among the senior staff and computer programmers employed by the government-funded project to introduce computers into schools in Scotland, a project with which SCEMP was closely associated, and most of the visitors to both projects appeared to be men.

When the public exhibitions of computer programs began, their most notable feature at first was the large number of young people who wanted to use the equipment, and who often had to be tactfully or even bluntly steered away so that the adults, for whom the exhibitions were primarily intended, could also sample the programs. Almost all the young people were young and adolescent boys, and most of the adults for whom they made way were young men. Yet, the exhibitions were intended as an educational experience for adults, and in Britain, as in most of the developed world, most of the students in adult education are women.

At first glance, then, the phenomenon was puzzling. The programs used in the exhibitions were intended to have a reasonably wide appeal; they included programs on managing personal finance, assessing one's current state of health, chooosing well-balanced meals, answering quiz questions about road safety, and a number of programs illustrating the kinds of educational games which children often played at school. Several exhibitions even included a program designed to help women make well-informed decisions about whether to breast or to bottle feed their babies! On the face of it, then, there was no explicit appeal primarily to male users.

Yet the users were predominantly male. At about the same time, I attended a conference for providers of computer literacy courses in support of the BBC Computer Literacy Project, which was expected to, and did, rouse a great deal of public interest in computers. Again, despite the fact that there are many female tutors in adult education, nearly all of those present were men.

The next evidence of the strangely single-gendered world of computers was visual. The overwhelming impression created by all the computer magazines and advertisements for microcomputers in Britain in the early 1980s was that this was a world only for men and their sons. "Son, where's my Epson?" demanded a happy father in an advertisement, as his school-age child sheepishly hid the computer behind his back. Early figures for sales of the extraordinarily popular BBC Computer indicated that over 90% of the purchasers were male (BBC, 1983).

Printed material for the computer hobbyist or for the serious computer educationalist seemed to assume that its reader would be a man. In magazines in 1983, there were about ten males to every one female, and she was usually there in a decorative capacity (Gerver, 1984). Even in the Open University, which usually avoids explicitly sexist material, the original leaflet for a course for teachers to learn about computers depicted far more men than women (ibid). These visual impressions are confirmed by Bernstein (1984), who has found that there are three types of advertisements for computers: "men as decision-makers; women as attention-getters; and family-oriented ads which do not include the whole family." Those women who are included in advertisements portraying family life are shown only as being in charge of young children. Where the children are older, women tend to disappear, and girls, where they are depicted at all, are merely shown as watching the boys admiringly.

Advertisers are now beginning—more so in the United States than in Britain—to include women more often as users of computers. Deakin (1984) cites one advertisement on television in Britain in which a mother and father were shown as creeping down to use the home computer when they thought the children were not around. The commercial need for new markets for computers means that the representation of women in advertisements for computers is likely to increase, as women form 50% of the potential market. But until the mid-1980s, the message of most computer advertising was that computers were for men and boys, an assumption which is ironically turned on its head in Figure 2.

The phenomenon seemed to me not merely striking, because unexpected, but also very dangerous, because it appeared to be so little noticed in the world of community education. Attention had already been drawn to the underrepresentation of women in the field of computing as a whole (Simons, 1981), but the largely male tutors of computer courses and the male observers at computer exhibitions seemed not even to notice that the great majority of the participants were men. Since then, increasing attention has been paid to the single gender of computers in publications (Deakin, 1984; Gerver and Lewis, 1984, among many others), at international conferences on the new information technologies, in action groups, and in many projects which have been started to try to redress the sexual balance in this field. Before considering the various ways in which adult educators and feminist groups have been trying to address the problem, however, I should like first to sketch the dimensions of the situation which has caused so much concern.

GENDER BIAS IN LEARNING ABOUT COMPUTERS

The land of computing is a frontier country, and, as in the development of most frontier territories, there are many more men than women. Indeed, it appears that at all levels of learning about computers—in school, in higher education, in further education, in training, in adult education classes, and in independent learning—women tend to be strikingly underrepresented. The extent of their underrepresentation varies from sector to sector and to some extent from country to country, but the fact of it is so ubiquitous that the

Figure 2. One woman's view of the male world of computing. Drawing reproduced by courtesy of Quillan, 1984.

evidence tends to become monotonous. The statistical evidence that follows gives an indication of the scope of the problem, but it does not attempt to cover the phenomenon at all comprehensively.

Anyone observing the use of computers in schools in Britain and the United States will find many male teachers and students—and few females—among the enthusiasts. Even in the recently developing use of computers in primary school, there is already evidence in Britain that "girls are failing to seize the opportunity. There seems to be a preponderance of boys even in the more imaginative and exciting courses . . . designed for primary schools and intended to stimulate children before there is any firmly recognizable division of activities according to gender" (Deakin, 1984). In the United

States, the pattern appears to be that seen in California, where at elementary school both sexes participate nearly equally in using computers, but by the time of junior high school, girls form only 37% of the users (Beyers, 1983).

In courses in computing in American secondary schools, males outnumber females by nearly 2:1 in a pattern that remains remarkably similar over a number of states (PEER, 1983). In Britain, the sexual bias in computing in schools may be seen in the finding that computer studies are assumed by many schools to be boys' subjects, along with nearly all the other sciences (Rogers, 1983). At the most senior level of work in computer studies in schools in England and Wales—that of A level examinations in computer science—the ratio of boys to girls is 4:1 (EOC, 1984).

In the more informal uses of computers in schools, the same pattern is evident. In Britain, "there are a few schools where an imaginative teacher has managed to stimulate girls into using computers, but in general there is a distressingly low take-up" (Deakin, 1984). The situation described by Deakin in one school is emblematic:

> At one north London comprehensive school, the current fifth-year computer studies group has no girls at all. The current fourth year shows an improvement with six girls, but alongside them are seventeen boys. . . . A computer was available in the library, and here again boys tended to dominate. In the opinion of the deputy head, this was because 'girls were not assertive or confident enough to resist the boys' "helpful" suggestions about programming and gradually the girls would be eased out. . . .' Girls would not join the lunchtime computer club.

At the university level of study, in 1970–80 in the United States, only 30.3% of all first degrees in computer and information sciences were earned by women (National Science Foundation, undated). In the same year, only 20.9% of all masters degrees in the same subject were awarded to women, while at the doctoral level, the figure falls to 11.2% (ibid). In Britain in 1979, women formed only 27% of all the applicants for computer science undergraduate courses at the university level (Simons, 1981).

The pattern is not restricted to the level of undergraduate work. In Britain, where the shortage in computing skills led the government to fund a 500% increase in places for post-graduate studies in information technology in 1983–84, only 10% of those qualifying in 1984 were women (WNC, 1984). The low percentage is unexpected and striking, especially as some of the new courses are "conversion" courses for graduates with degrees in the arts or social sciences and, therefore, could have offered women an opportunity to change direction and to enhance their chances of employment.

In computer courses within adult education, the pattern at first seems encouragingly less sexist: in Britain in 1982–83 the proportion of males to females in enrollment in adult education classes in computing appeared to be about only 2:1 (Banks, 1983; Gerver, 1984). In 1983–84, there was an encouraging increase in the number of women in computer classes in at least one local authority area, where the proportion of women rose to 43% (Banks, 1984). These figures, however, need to be treated with some caution. They should be seen in the light of the fact that, whereas there are roughly equal numbers of boys and girls in the school population, far more women than men traditionally take part in adult education classes, so that the population, from which such an apparently encouraging proportion of women is drawn, does not consist equally of men and women.

Among the providers of education in computers, there appears to be an even more pronounced male bias. Within schools in Britain, most work with computers is carried out by teachers of mathematics and physics, by far the great majority of whom are male. In 1983–84 in Britain, no woman was among the "new blood" university appointments in information technology.

Within the field of training unemployed people for new careers, the same pattern seems to persist. In Scotland in 1983, for instance, there was a striking difference in the numbers of unemployed men and women who completed training in higher level computer skills: 83% of those completing courses in computing at higher levels were male (Gerver, 1984). At the new Information Technology Centers, which have been established in Britain to provide skills in computing for school-leavers, there are far more young men than young women: in 1984, less than one-third of the trainees at these centers were women (WNC, 1984). The manager of one such center reported that he "is rather concerned about the lack of female applicants. . . . Girl[s] . . . are just not interested enough to apply" (Deakin, 1984).

As noted in Chapter 1, among those who are addicted to working with computers—the "compulsive programmers" or "computer junkies"—there appear to be no women. Research being currently conducted into the social pathology of computer addiction, has so far failed to uncover any examples of women who fall into this category (Shotton, 1984). In the United States, the compulsive programmers described by Weizenbaum (1976) are all "bright young *men* of disheveled appearance."

At the level of leisure pursuits, there is ample evidence that fascination with computers is largely a male phenomenon. Almost all the users of computer-based games are boys and young men, and the games appeal primarily to traditionally male preferences. In a review of computer games on the market for sale at Christmas in Britain, Hetherington (1984) noted that "all of the games have heroes, not heroines, and are in other ways oriented toward boys. This unfortunately reflects the current market, which apart from a few patronizing 'games for girls' is almost entirely aimed at boys." The predominantly male appeal of most leisure computer magazines is overwhelmingly evident. The articles, written mainly by men, assume that the reader is male; the advertisements sometimes verge on being offensive to women; the illustrations are primarily of men using computers, with women occupying a lesser, mainly picturesque, role.

Studies on the use of computers at home also show a pronounced sexual imbalance. Beyers (1983) reports that interviews with typical computer-owning families in the United States "indicated that sons used the machine most. They spent an average of two to three hours a day playing and programming games. The father used the computer regularly for business, while the mother did not use it at all."

In the informal learning that takes place in computer camps, where learning about computers is chosen purely as a form of pleasure, there are fewer girls than boys in Britain (Deakin, 1984) and in the United States (Beyers, 1983). In American computer camps, in 1983, "boys outnumbered girls by three to one. The proportion of girls in beginning and intermediate classes was 27 percent. This dropped to 14 percent in advanced programming classes and to 5 percent in higher level courses teaching assembly language" (ibid).

In the setting of the public library, whose users tend to be female, it has been shown by Yeates (1982) that far more men than women will use computer-based systems to provide information. At central lending libraries in Britain, the ratio of users of Prestel (a computer-based information system) was seven men to every three women, while at reference libraries the gender imbalance was even more pronounced, with nearly four men to every one woman.

Such an apparently ubiquitous gender imbalance in the use of computers cries out for systematic research which would allow informed speculation about the reasons as a firm basis for trying to redress the imbalance. The field of computing is relatively new, and the studies which directly address the very complex problem of the reasons for the imbalance are scattered. Nevertheless, sufficient evidence has already been accumulated to provide indicators of some of the major factors at work.

FACTORS IN THE GENDER IMBALANCE OF COMPUTER USE

In trying to assess the major sources of the difficulties here, one might be tempted to look at the world of employment as the overriding factor, and at the ability of girls and women to use computers effectively as a second major factor. As I shall suggest, however, both of these approaches lead to blind alleys, and one has to seek elsewhere for possible explanations.

At first sight it appears as if the situation in employment is one of the chief factors: women are significantly underrepresented in employment at most levels of working with computers. At the lowest levels—that of merely entering data into computers—there are far more women than men. In 1980 in the United States, women formed 78% of those employed as keypunchers or computer operators (Wider Opportunities for Women, 1983), while, in Britain of the same year, a survey showed that between 75–100% of all workers at the lowest level of computing were women (Simons, 1981).

At the more advanced levels of working with computers, in the United States in 1980, only 29% of computer programmers and 22% of systems analysts were women (Wider Opportunities for Women, 1983). In Britain, the gender imbalance was even more dramatic: females comprised only between 5 and 15% of all computer programmers, and less than 5% of systems analysts (Simons, 1981). In Germany in 1979, female systems analysts, programmers, and sales staff comprised only 18% of the total employed in these areas of computing (Simons, 1981).

But there is evidence that companies involved in the computer industry, far from discriminating against women, are trying actively to encourage their participation. Moreover, there are certain characteristics of working with computers which make such work particularly attractive to women who place a high value on their domestic roles. In Britain, the Women's National Commission (1984) has found that:

> The new technology industries are the least resistant to the employment of women at all levels, provided qualified women come forward. Some companies have made special efforts to make their recruitment literature attractive to women. Companies like 'F International' which employ women computing experts as 'home workers,' together with women managers of this now large-scale operation, show that skills in computing can offer women a special kind of compatibility between home and work responsibilities; isolation is also alleviated by the high-powered nature of much of the work and the need for periods of working contact with the client firm. Many women working for such companies have been able to make geographical moves following their husband's career without jeopardising their own; levels of work commitment can be varied over time, and there are opportunities to take wider responsibilities for managing others.

In the United States, evidence adduced in the mid 1970s suggested that the computer industry represented a relatively favorable employment environment for women (Simons, 1981), and the position appears, if anything, to have improved since that time. In varying degrees, throughout the developed world, women still suffer from multifarious patterns of stereotyping and of direct and indirect discrimination, and their progress up the hierarchy of the world of computing is often as tenuous as it is in many other fields. But, as Simons (1981) suggests, "compared with other, older industries, it is arguable that women have done well in data processing"; indeed, as Chivers (1984) reports, "some of the large high technology companies in computing and electronics . . . have actively supported the very able women technologists entering their ranks."

It appears, then, as if the reasons for the underrepresentation of women at all levels of computing do not stem primarily from discriminatory practices within the computer industry itself. Perhaps, then, women simply have less ability to use computers? There often appear to be connections between using computers and using mathematical ideas, and women and girls seem to perform less well at mathematics than men and boys. Perhaps, then, the problem lies in the lesser mathematical ability of females?

So far, nearly all the evidence available seem to suggest that women have abilities to work with computers which are at least equal to those of men. As Deakin (1984) points out, "computing is a discipline that requires some (but not necessarily great) mathematical ability, logic, . . . and a grasp of the principles of language systems and communication methods."

But even the assumption that girls and women are "bad" at mathematics needs further investigation. More females than males do say that they are afraid of mathematics and of technology, but there is evidence to suggest that such anxiety is a learned rather than an innate response. At primary school level, it appears that girls and boys perform almost equally in mathematics. It is only after elementary school that there appears to be a decline in the aptitude and achievement of girls. Thus, girls' attitudes toward mathematics tend to take a turn for the worse during the years of their early adolescence, at a time when they tend not to want to compete with boys. It has been shown that, in the United States, where mathematically gifted boys often take advanced courses, mathematically gifted girls are reluctant to do so because of their fear of social rejection (Stanley, 1973).

From Britain, there is a growing body of evidence to suggest that, when girls are taught mathematics in single-sex settings, their academic results are at least equal to those of boys taught in mixed-sex groupings, where boys have consistently been shown to be superior to girls in their results in mathematics. In a cautious review of the evidence in Britain so far, Smith (1984) concluded that "secondary school girls are likely to do better at maths when segregated from boys." This finding was confirmed in an experiment in England at Stamford High School, where a single-sex setting for the teaching of mathematics appeared to have a pronounced beneficial effect on the final marks of the girls during the two years in which it operated. It appears then, that, at least in mathematics, the performance of girls is at least as good as that of boys. The factors affecting the apparent decline in secondary school appear to be social rather than innate.

But the significant dropout of girls from computer courses discussed above seems to imply that they may have less ability at working with computers than boys. In the United States, as Rossen (1982) shows, girls have been doing slightly less well than boys on computer programming tests. However, when they have good exposure to computers, the girls perform as well as, or better than, boys (ibid). Here again, as in the question of mathematical performance, social factors rather than innate abilities appear to be the main cause of the apparent lesser performance by girls. There is now a mass of anecdotal evidence to suggest that girls will be discouraged from computing by the attitudes of their male peers. In one American high school, for instance, adolescent boys harassed the girls in order to discourage them from registering for the after-school computer courses. The boys admitted that they were doing this deliberately to limit enrollment, so that they could have more computer time for themselves (Rossen, 1982). In Britain, the EOC (1983) has graphically depicted one example of a ubiquitous problem with mixed-sex teaching of computer courses in secondary school:

> Because the number of boys in the course far outweighed the number of girls, the girls felt as though they were interlopers, and that they had fewer rights than the boys when the computers were being used.
>
> There was not enough time in class for adequate programming on the computers. The boys compensated for this by using the computer room at other times, but they did this in a way that forced the girls out or discouraged them from entering at all. This caused many girls to drop out of the course as they felt they had little or no chance of completing their project work. The sheer size and power of the average boy, determined to take more than his fair share of computer time, gradually forced the more timid girls to give up altogether.

It appears, then, that the factors involved in the underrepresentation of women in computing can be traced neither to the beginning of their formal learning at school nor to their employment at the end of their formal education. Instead, the first of our clues may lie in the interaction that takes place between girls and computers at school.

GIRLS AND COMPUTERS

Even where girls do choose to take part in computer studies and in other ways of using computers at school, they have a particularly pronounced dropout rate. In one local education authority in England, for instance, twice as many girls as boys failed to take the final, qualifying examination in Computer Studies (EOC, 1983). As we have already seen, the ways in which boys effectively exclude girls from using the few machines available in many schools clearly contribute to such a wastage rate; competition between boys and girls for what is still a relatively scarce resource is likely to benefit those who are more aggressive and competitive. But other factors seem to interact with such sexist exclusion to create a situation in which girls choose to exclude themselves from the specific opportunities that are available to them.

A number of features about the way in which computer studies are presented in school seem to alienate girls. Indeed, it appears that some of the same characteristics are at least partially responsible for the extent to which many women also feel alienated from the new information technologies, including computers.

In the first place, work with computers in schools often focuses primarily on the machine itself, the theories behind its functioning and the electronics that implement those theories. The Deputy Director of the Microelectronics Education Programme in England and Wales, for instance, believes that Computer Studies should emphasize "the concepts which underlie electronic systems, electronics, and the binary logic of a system" (EOC, 1983). Since many local authorities in those two countries depend on MEP for in-service training and advice in using computers in schools, such an emphasis will presumably be reflected in practice at the grass roots level in the schools themselves.

The fact that computing studies tend to be taught, at least in Britain, by teachers of physics and mathematics reinforces the tendency to emphasize the theory and the electronics of the technology itself, and may contribute to the speed at which girls, who tend to have much less affinity with machines as a whole, often opt out of such courses. Moreover, the problems set for pupils to solve by using computer programs tend to be mathematically based, and may thus create gratuitous difficulties for girls who are insecure about their mathematical abilities in the first place.

Other possible reasons for girls' withdrawal from computers emerge from the responses given by girls in England who had chosen Computer Studies at the end of their third year in secondary school. EOC (1983) cited some typical answers to questions which the girls were asked:

> Q. Has the course been of use to you? Why?
> A. Yes, it helps me practise my typing.
> Q. Do you think the course was aimed mainly at boys, girls, or both equally? Explain why.
> A. Boys—all the teachers are men. . . .
> Q. Has the course turned out as you expected? (Explain fully).

A. No. I expected to be taught more practical use of the computers; more lessons on actual programming.

Q. Can you suggest any changes in the course which could have helped out?

A. 1. More practical programming. 2. The present course is very dull. A more active lesson would create greater interest on the pupil's part.

Q. Has the course been of use to you. Why?

A. No, I have found the majority of the work uninteresting and the concepts difficult to understand and grasp.

Q. Can you suggest any changes in the course which would help you?

A. More explanation and practice of computer language and terms.

This sample of pupil responses draws unflattering attention to the effect of the quality of teaching in work on computer studies. Because computer studies form a new area of academic study—an area where in many cases teachers are not even a single step ahead of their more able pupils—it is perhaps inevitable that standards of presentation may not be as high as in more traditional subjects. There is now evidence to suggest, however, that this apparent lack of high quality does discourage more girls than boys.

Why? Here again there seem to be a variety of interlocking factors. In the first place, boys seem to have a much stronger motivation to engage with computers for their own sake and will, therefore, probably be more tolerant of difficulties placed in their path, such as poor quality teaching. Girls, with their stronger practical bent, will often wonder what the point of it all is, when, in many cases, the power of the computer is used to perform trivial tasks which could be carried out more efficiently by hand or by using a calculator. Indeed, as McClain (1983) has shown, while men are more interested in computer games and graphics, females tend to see the computer as a tool—a means to an end. Where they fail to find sufficient evidence of the efficacy of the computer as a tool, girls are likely to lose interest quickly.

Secondly, much of the material actually available to children in connection with computers is oriented primarily toward boys. Textbooks for Computer Studies in Britain tend to present a world in which computers are mainly for men and boys. The graphics in one textbook, for example, contained ten men to every woman, while those in another contained eleven men to the one woman, a barely clothed girl on a screen (EOC, 1983).

But children both at home and at school tend to use computer games far more than computer textbooks. And, as we have seen, those games tend to be for boys only. The noneducational games have titles like "Armageddon," "Dracula," "Space Invaders," or "War Games" (after the film of the same name in which an adolescent boy nearly destroys the world as a result of breaking into a computer defense system). Nearly all girls are repelled by the violence in both the concept and the actuality of these games. Descriptions of two recent games from a review of them illustrate their typical characteristics:

> Along with a nimble fire-button, you also need a keen sense of strategy, if you're to survive in its alien universe. You are a trader who will deal in anything in order to buy weapons and defenses to defend you from anything from galactic pirates to the police.
>
> The atmosphere is created by the spoken start of the game when an evil voice welcomes you with the chilling words, 'Another visitor, stay awhile, stay forever!' This voice belongs to [a man] . . . who will destroy the world unless you crack his security code, but to do that you will have to outwit the most fiendish robots (Hetherington, 1984).

But much of the imagery used in educational programs is also either boring or unattractive to girls. Zimmerman (1983) reports on a game used to teach fractions to young children, which showed an arrow piercing a floating balloon when the pupil made a correct answer. "The girls, unlike the boys, did not care much about popping the balloons. When the reward image changed to a little puppy, girls' scores rose significantly."

A further difficulty often arises because most computer games foster a spirit of intense, often speed-ridden competitiveness either between the individual and the machine or between two individuals. There is a considerable body of evidence to suggest that females tend to view competitive success as dangerous (Whiting and Pope, 1973; Maccoby and Jacklin, 1974; Pollak and Gilligan, 1982; Gilligan, 1983, among many others). Games that appeal primarily to competitiveness rather than to the pleasures of interpersonal relationships may, therefore, tend to alienate girls and women.

Other social factors in girls' experience are also likely to alienate them from engaging with computers at school, as at home. It appears that many teachers and careers advisers still perceive science and technology, including computing, as subjects predominantly for boys. In the United States, for instance, women have consistently reported that the careers counseling which they received at school not only failed to encourage their participation in nontraditional fields but, in many cases, actually attempted to discourage them from study that would lead to mathematical and scientific careers (Luchins and Luchins, 1980). In Britain, concern about an analogous problem about careers counseling of girls led in 1984 to the establishment of the WISE campaign, designed to increase awareness of opportunities for girls in science and engineering, including the new information technologies.

All of these factors which contribute toward the alienation of girls from computers at school may also be found in the experiences of many women, with an even more pronounced adverse effect. Women have less money and less time to spend on themselves than men; many social factors conspire to make it more difficult for women to advance upwards in careers; the computer world itself tends to be composed primarily of young men rather than of middle-aged women. All of these factors make it unlikely that women will, of their own accord, contribute fully to the world of computing.

Does this relative exclusion matter? Well, there are compelling arguments that can be made about the need for our economies to use to the fullest the talents of both men and women. The moral arguments in favor of gender equality are becoming more generally accepted. But there are also specific reasons why the participation of women in the world of computing is necessary both for that world and for the economic position of women themselves. It is to these that I shall now turn, before considering some of the ways that have already been found to enable women to interact more fully with computers.

REDRESSING THE GENDER IMBALANCE

It is essential to encourage more women to engage in computers, both for their economic survival and for the ways in which their greater participation may help to make computers more responsive to human needs. Throughout most of the developed world, computerization seems to be having an apparently contradictory effect on employment: many new jobs are created in the new information technologies, at the same time as the demand for many older skills appears to be decreasing. To an even greater extent than men, women are trapped by this contradictory effect. The situation in Canada, as depicted by Menzies (1981) in Figure 3, seems to be replicated in most other developed

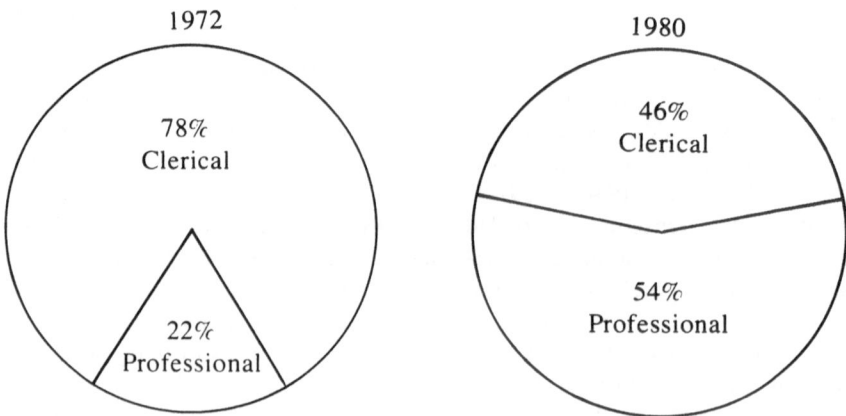

Figure 3. Clerical and professional employment in the information services of a large corporation, 1972 and 1980. Chart reproduced by courtesy of Menzies, 1981.

countries: "informatics is creating new work and employment, but largely in the professional and technical ranks where men predominate and women are still in a minority." In particular, Menzies argues, there is likely to be an "alarmingly high rate of structural unemployment among female clerical workers . . . unless appropriate measures are taken by governments, employers, and women."

The same conclusion appears elsewhere in the growing literature of this field. Thus, Feldberg and Glenn (1982) find that "the expansion of computer-related occupations has increased the total number of jobs and created some new higher paid occupations. However, the workers displaced by automation do not appear to benefit: the new jobs are technical level and largely held by males." The finding is substantiated by Menzies, who cites the fact that, in the Canadian corporation which she examined, only 2 out of the 130 workers displaced from clerical work moved upwards to professional or managerial level.

The extent of the potential wastage of female staff may be seen in the fact that "in most industrialized countries . . . the reduction of staff predicted in offices and banks is in the region of 30 to 50 percent" (Trudel and Belanger, 1982). By far the vast majority of these workers are women, and, as Menzies bleakly notes, "the supply of clerical labour is projected to outstrip demand."

But it is not only the quantity of female jobs which are affected adversely by computerization. There is also evidence that the quality, particularly of the kinds of clerical work traditionally undertaken by women, may be suffering in the process. Examining four representative fields in which computerization has affected work—a large, broadly diversified corporation, an insurance company, banking, and supermarkets—Menzies concludes that:

> The continuing standardization, streamlining, and fragmentation of work functions, which was observed in all of the case studies, suggests that clerical work is becoming more like an assembly line. . . . Monitoring tends to place quantity of output over sophistication of input, and thereby subtly degrades the scope of the work involved. . . . The operation of a word processor terminal does not require a great deal of skill on the part of the operator.

As a homely illustration, my word processor makes it possible for me no longer to need traditional typing skills: I can readily correct the many errors that arise from inaccurate typing before I print out a final version; I can, if I wish, use a spelling program to indicate to me words that I have unwittingly misspelled; indeed, the only loss may be stylistic, in that my computer cannot tactfully suggest where I have communicated unclearly in the way that a sympathetic typist might have done! The final result is to upgrade my incompetent typing skills and thereby to devalue the skills of a conventional typist, whose speed, accuracy, and neatness are largely redundant. Thus, Feldberg and Glenn (1982) conclude that "women have been differentially and more negatively affected than men by changes accompanying office automation." The clerical skills by which many women have earned their living, then, are no longer likely to ensure their economic survival.

But there are other reasons why women need to engage more readily with computers. The fact that some computing firms are actively recruiting and supporting their female staff is not altruistic. In certain respects, women tend to make better computer programmers than men. Women's traditional ability to master languages with apparent ease extends also to the mastery of computer languages, and women's tendency toward linear logic also stands them in good stead in this field. McClain (1983) has found that women are more likely to write good computer programs with the user in mind. Women's tendency to ignore extraneous factors and to concentrate on the task at hand also leads to good programming technique. Indeed, there is a considerable amount of evidence that, while males tend to be more curious and more likely to take risks, females are better able to screen out irrelevancies, carry out tasks, and be better problem-solvers under stress (Weitzman, 1975; Safran, 1983; among others). All of these qualities again are conducive to good computer techniques.

The advantages that women bring to computing have also been spelled out by the course tutor in a computing school (WNC, 1984). She noted first that women provided a disproportionate share of the really able and most tenacious students and that they demonstrated an ability to serve industry well. In particular, she reported that women "frequently showed a clear advantage over men as project managers/systems analysts, as they communicated better with non-computing staff, an absolute requirement of the future."

Deakin (1984) notes that women are often as good as, or better than, men at selling computers. She analyzes her own experience as a sales consultant:

> Now that I work as a sales consultant, I still feel that there are some ways in which I have something special to offer by being female. I think that I have been able to advise and assist the male customers particularly well because they do not feel threatened by me, because I have learned to communicate and because I am concerned with the practicalities of their needs rather than the beauty of any particular machine. As one person said, I am 'into customer solutions.' This may not be the preserve of women, but it is their very special contribution and one which the whole industry needs. This is one reason why it is as important for men as it is for women that women become more involved in computers and computing.

Although such comparisons are probably invidious, there are also snippets of evidence that women may be perceived as better than men in teaching computing to adults. Banks (1984) found that nearly half of the students whom he interviewed about their experiences of computing courses for adults did not consider their tutor to be a good teacher but that "generally students were less critical of female tutors than male." Salkeld (1983) has also suggested that the few female tutors on introductory computer courses for adults seemed to be particularly popular as teachers. Any rash hypothesis that most of the students were male and, therefore, preferred to have women tutors is nullified by the fact that nearly half of the students interviewed by Banks were female.

Finally, simply because of their traditional proficiency in clerical skills—especially in typing—women have a distinct advantage in using computer keyboards. Familiarity with the QWERTY keyboard and accuracy in pressing keys are practical skills, the lack of which are often disadvantageous to male users, particularly male users who wish to use computers for practical applications rather than to write programs or design computer architectures. It is largely for such male users that various devices such as the "mouse" have been designed, but, for sheer practical ease, using the keyboard remains the most efficient way to harness the power of a computer. And more women are better placed than most men to do so.

For their own economic good and for the economic good of the computer industry, then, there are clear advantages in a closer interaction between women and computers. Beyond these economic considerations, however, a more far-reaching case also exists for the need for more women to become involved in computing.

As Chapter 1 has shown, at least part of the world dominated by computers is pathological—obsessed by power and ruled by instrumental reason. There are many reasons why such characteristics have emerged. The relative scarcity of women in computing is probably only a minor factor in creating a situation where computers are used primarily for military purposes and commercial profit rather than to help to meet the real needs that people have to find out more about their local communities, to keep in touch with each other and their compassionate desires to help one another, and to nurture the young, the handicapped, and the frail. As later chapters will suggest, computer applications can provide valuable help in all of these traditionally "female" areas of concern. It may be, then, that when women play a substantially increased part in computing, greater attention will be given to ways in which computers can actively help people.

Many of the characteristics that women currently find so alienating about computers are not inevitable in the technology itself. There is no absolute reason why using computers has to be accompanied by smokescreens of jargon or delight in the machines themselves: women have used automatic washing machines for decades without feeling any need to worship the object which replaces unpleasant physical labor. Most women, too, bring to computers a hard core of common sense, based on a lack of time to waste. They tend to recognize that, just as there are many tasks which can be performed more efficiently and effectively on a computer, so there are many more which can be performed, but which are not worth performing. If women were to play an increased role in using computers, then, it is possible that a more humanly balanced view of the uses and nonuses of computers might result.

Despite these arguments for redressing the gender imbalance in using computers, however, strong counter-arguments have been advanced against any greater involvement by women. Some radical feminists in particular believe that technology is not simply a neutral means whereby individuals, groups, and societies can achieve their goals.

In the first place, the argument runs, women throughout the world are often exploited by computer technology, particularly in Third World countries where they tend to be employed in the production and assemblage of computer and microprocessor equipment. And there appear to be certain dangers to women's health when they are required to use computer terminals for long periods of time. In these ways, women are seriously disadvantaged by computer technology.

More broadly, radical feminists argue that:

> Women must not forget that the range and nature of a society's technology is a reflection of the dominant socio-economic system. And in the Western culture that means that it is a process guided by the values of the various patriarchies and one which owes its very existence to the requirements of the military–industrial complex. At its furthest development their argument challenges the whole nature of technology and the societies that spawned it, asking the . . . question: can feminists use technology as it stands at all, or does using it involve fatal compromise and collusion with the forces of patriarchy (Women and Computing, 1981)?

Such a stance, however, involves the acceptance of premises that are not shared by all feminists. I should like to argue, more pragmatically, that women who exclude themselves from learning about and using computers risk experiencing even greater vulnerability in a world that is increasingly dependent on the power of computers and telecommunications. In a similar belief that education and training, rather than withdrawal from the world of technology, are more likely to empower women, many individuals and organizations are now responding to what they see as the need to help women to use computer technology for their own ends. During the 1980s, there has thus been a dramatic growth in the number of opportunities which have been created for women to learn about computers.

WOMEN LEARNING ABOUT COMPUTERS

We have already seen that girls' mathematical and computer performance tends to increase when they are taught in single-sex settings. And, as Chapter 3 will discuss, women tend to use computers in greater numbers in women-only groups. Most of the opportunities currently being created for women to come to terms with computers, therefore, tend to be for women only and, more frequently than not, taught by women only. The one major exception to the general pattern—that of the BBC's Computer Literacy Project—appealed more or less equally to men and women, partly because it was careful to show that all ages and both sexes could use computers with equal facility and efficacy (Radcliffe and Salkeld, 1983), but also possibly because the television programs could be watched at home rather than in adult education classes composed predominantly of men.

The range of courses to enable women to learn about computers is wide, encompassing formal training courses, as well as formal courses in educational institutions and nonformal adult education classes. They seem clearly to be meeting a felt need: the demand for them almost invariably exceeds provision. Three case studies of courses in Britain, the United States, and New Zealand may illustrate the range and suggest some of the essential characteristics of successful courses of this type.

"Computers for Women" in New Zealand

In 1984 in Wellington, New Zealand, a course called "Computers for Women" was organized, according to one of the women course leaders:

> To provide a 'safe' environment where women can happily expose their ignorance and try things out and ask elementary questions without being or feeling put down. There has certainly been a lot of interest and a good response from a wide variety of women. We have pointed out to all enrolling that this is indeed a course for absolute beginners, and if they know *anything* about computers they are too advanced for the course. The usual response is 'Oh good, that's just what I want—I've never even *seen* a computer'. . . . We hope women who become interested through our courses will go on to take others in special fields of their own choosing. . . . Once they know a little, they can cope better with the 'male expert' syndrome and feel less inadequate faced with all that jargon (Else, 1984a).

The attractively elementary nature of the course would be very likely to appeal to women who feel uneasy about coming to terms with computers.

Following the completion of the course, an analysis of completed question-naires showed that participants:

> Appreciated the friendly supportive atmosphere and the availability of an all-women class. They liked feeling able to ask any questions at all without feeling threatened or put down. They liked the variety of speakers arranged and the exchange of ideas between course members and lecturers; also the chance to hear about others' problems with computers. They enjoyed the hands-on experience. . . . Three stated their approval/enjoyment of the way political issues to do with women, computers, and society were raised, as well as the technical points. . . . On the whole, the response was one of positive enjoyment and enhanced confidence (Else, 1984b).

The difficulties experienced were largely those created by this being the first course of its kind in the country:

> It was clear that we had not really broken down the initial instruction sessions into small or simple enough chunks for some people. We were still using too much jargon in places or moving too quickly over basic points, e.g., use of keyboard. We needed one more person to help the participants when all were present and using the computers, and should also have provided more written material as simple manuals and hand-outs. There were also some problems with the [computer equipment] breaking down. Not everyone liked politics being in-cluded—they would have preferred a straight technical approach. Time was a constant problem (ibid).

The crucial element in this course was clearly the provision of an all-female environment in which women felt free to start from the very beginning. The second characteristic is that of utility, with an emphasis on what the computer can be used for rather than on the details of what exactly it is in itself. For many women, however, such a course may have created practical problems, both because it was relatively expensive, and because it made no provisions for the care of their children. Both of these issues have been directly addressed in Sheffield, England, in a new scheme designed to introduce women to computing.

A Women's Technology Training Workshop in Britain

The purpose of this workshop, which is funded jointly by the City Council and the European Social Fund, is:

> To provide basic and more advanced training in microelectronics and com-puting fields, where women are underrepresented. The training . . . is intended for women over 25 who are unemployed, threatened with unemployment, or wishing to return to work after a period of child-rearing. The courses are specif-ically tailored to suit unskilled women who have been unable to take advantage

of existing training facilities in the field. To this end . . . there are no formal
entry requirements; the courses are part-time; child-care allowances are available;
the courses are administered by, and taught by, women (Sheffield City Council,
1984).

As soon as the course was advertised, despite the fact that its initial
intake consisted only of 28 places, there were thousands of telephone enquiries
which provided evidence of an unsuspected scale of demand for such training
(Miller, 1984a). Over 500 women completed application forms, and trainees
were selected primarily on a quota system of age, status, ethnic origin, and
"social need". Over two-thirds of the women had no qualifications at all
(Miller, 1984b).

The course which the women are following has four main components.
The "Return to Work" component aims "to develop confidence and to provide
support for the new training environment" and "to provide a critical appreciation of the social impact of New Technology." The "Computing" component aims to enable trainees "to gain familiarity and confidence in using
both mini- and microcomputers, to gain an understanding of programming in
a high-level language (BASIC), to gain skills in using software packages . . . , to become computer literate." The Microelectronics part of the
course develops a range of technical knowledge and skills. Mathematics,
ranging from basic numeracy to certificate standard, is also taught to enable
the students to understand fully the technical course components (Miller,
1984b).

By late autumn of 1984, the response of the trainees, who began in
March, was seen as "extremely encouraging. All the trainees, including those
with small children, have not only shown considerable enthusiasm and ded-
ication while attending the Workshop, but have also specifically requested
that homework be set and assessed on a regular basis, despite the fact that
this was not intended to be a requirement of the course" (ibid).

However, an analysis of the course has indicated that, while lack of
formal qualifications has been no bar to satisfactory performance, some women
who lacked numeracy and literacy skills have been unable to grasp essential
background concepts. The course organizer has accepted that "these basic
skills cannot be taught concurrently with main courses. Moreover teaching
of these skills is both a specialized and lengthy process and cannot always
be done on an intensive basis. Accordingly, literacy and numeracy must figure
in the criteria for admission to the course" (ibid).

This problem is not dissimilar to that which emerged from the course in
New Zealand, where the initial concepts were not simple enough for some
people. Indeed, the Sheffield findings reflect elements in the experience of
some girls in computer studies in schools, where they reported that "the con-

cepts [were] difficult to understand and grasp" and that the course was "much more complicated, detailed and theoretical than I imagined" (EOC, 1983).

This issue of the interrelationships between computer literacy and more traditional forms of literacy and numeracy also arises in the use of computers in nonformal adult basic education, and is obviously a matter to which much more thought and research needs to be addressed. It is already clear, however, that women, disadvantaged as they often seem to be in numeracy, may also be disadvantaged in coming to terms with computers unless ways can be found of tackling the combined problem of computer illiteracy and general lack of numeracy.

Meanwhile, it appears as if the prospect of enhanced employment and training opportunities at the end of the course, together with the provision of child-care arrangements and the payment of training expenses to the trainees, have been significant factors in the overwhelming demand for the course. The Women's Technology Training Workshop appears to have demonstrated that, once socio-economic factors are taken realistically and sensitively into account, women are very willing indeed to come to terms with computers.

The Women's Computer Literacy Project in the United States

This project to enable women to acquire computer-literacy was set up as "an alternative to the computer classes many women found alienating" (Marohn, undated). As one of the organizers of the courses saw the situation, "many women have an approach-avoidance attitude toward computers, . . . and most men are not very good at teaching women. We've heard all kinds of horror stories about classes at city colleges and computer stores where smart women have been made to feel stupid and have been given the sense that they can't do it" (Marohn, undated).

The Project offers two-day, full-time, and four-week part-time courses in San Francisco and two-day courses in New York "for those who know nothing about computers and prefer to learn in a woman-centered environment." As are the course in New Zealand and that in Sheffield, it is highly practically oriented, as the leaflet proclaims:

> At the end of the course you will know what microcomputers can and cannot do; you will be able to operate a microcomputer with confidence; and you will be able to read and understand most operations manuals for computer hardware and software systems. You will also understand the differences between various microcomputer systems so that you can shop for the correct system to meet your personal, business, or organizational needs.

Unlike the course in Sheffield, however, the American course, like most others in the United States, has to be self-financing; it is expensive, at least for women who do not have much money at their disposal. Clearly, however, it meets considerably more needs than the courses in programming in BASIC which formed the staple diet of computing courses for adults in Britain and other countries in the first years of using microcomputers (Gerver, 1984).

Other Ways of Encouraging Women to Use Computers

Even where no computer is actually provided as part of an introduction to the new technologies, there is now substantial international evidence that women will respond in large numbers to events and material which are prepared specifically for them about computers. In Israel, NA'AMAT, the largest women's organization in the country, chose "Women and Technology" as the theme for its annual Status of Women Month in 1983. The movement designed a portfolio designed to give women a feeling of familiarity with computers, selected films showing high technology at work in various fields, and used both print and television media to reinforce its message about ways in which women could link up to the new technology. The result was that, even though they themselves were not providing computer experiences or training opportunities, they received more enquiries than they could handle (NA'AMAT, undated). The same experience of demand exceeding supply has been almost invariably repeated in other countries.

As well as burgeoning opportunities in education and training, there have also been a number of important developments in other ways for women to use computers. The WISE Campaign in Britain exemplifies campaigns designed to encourage girls to choose computing as a career; groups to support women in computing have mushroomed in the past few years throughout the developed world; and books and conferences are increasingly addressing the question of the underrepresentation of women in computing.

As its logo in Figure 4 suggests, the Women into Science and Engineering (WISE) Campaign promoted by the Equal Opportunities Commission in Britain in 1984 aimed to encourage girls themselves to consider positively the opportunities for careers in science and technology, including particularly information technology. The EOC's (1984) booklet "Working with Computers" exemplifies the approach, in its careful selection of biographies of women who have achieved significant success in the world of the new technologies. Throughout, its approach is one of demystifying. It points out, for example, that for one girl, "the key to coping with computers for her was much more to do with being able to use the English language than to do with

Figure 4. A British program to encourage greater female participation in computing and other male-dominated subjects. Figure reproduced by courtesy of Equal Opportunities Commission.

maths" ; it draws attention to various cooperative ways of using computers and it highlights women who have come into the field from apparently unrelated disciplines and interests.

Such an approach to girls and women to help themselves in coming to terms with computers is likely, of course, to lead to only very limited change. WISE has placed great stress on what can be achieved "simply by a change to more positive attitudes by all concerned. . . . Girls leaving school simply need the interest and energy to find out and fully appreciate the many incentives and opportunities available in engineering and science" (WISE, 1984). As the discussion throughout this chapter has suggested, however, the matter cannot be resolved merely by altering the attitudes of girls, who, in many cases, are merely responding adversely to characteristics of the world of technology which are genuinely alienating.

Other organizations in Britain and the United States are trying to use the technology itself to offer more concrete help to those women and girls who feel they would like to use computers but are not sure how to go about it. One of the best examples of such supportive use of computers for women who feel that they may want to use computers may be seen in Microsyster, a London-based organization which was set up in 1982 (and which is considered in greater detail in Chapter 5).

Microsyster "aims to encourage women to think about positive ways of making computers work for women. We are aware that many women feel alienated and excluded by new technology and are worried by the threat they do pose to our jobs and privacy. We not only want to provide a service for women, but also to open up these debates in the Women's Liberation Movement" (Microsyster, 1984). Microsyster, therefore, aims to "provide computing services to women and women's groups; make contact with and support other feminists working in computing; provide a feminist perspective on new technology; to introduce the skills and knowledge necessary for women to benefit from and critically assess new technology" (ibid).

As with the computer courses offered by women for women, so also the computer services offered by Microsyster are highly practical. They offer advice about whether a computer would really help an individual or a group; they help determine the system that would be most suitable and they even help with the writing out of the applications for grants to buy it. They also offer to help to set up systems and to teach women how to use the software packages which they have bought or acquired; as Chapter 1 has already indicated, the presentation of information in most computer manuals makes such informed help mandatory!

Support for women who want to use computers and for women who might want to use them if they were presented in a nonthreatening way has also come from an increasing number of books and conferences which, in the mid-1980s, have addressed the problem directly. In Britain in 1981, Simons' account of *Women in Computing* aimed "to encourage a search for constructive policies on the part of managers, employers, politicians, and others." Deakin's *Women and Computing: The Golden Opportunity* (1984) looks "first at the special benefits that exist for women in computing and then . . . at the ways in which the arrival of microcomputers can be a heaven-sent opportunity for them." Both books rely heavily on illuminating case studies of women who have successfully made careers for themselves in the world of computing.

Academic investigations of the problem of the underrepresentation of women in the new technologies generally and in computing in particular have multiplied during the 1980s. Work has been particularly concentrated on the adverse effects of computerization on the employment of women (Menzies, 1981; Rothschild, 1982; Werneke, 1983, among many others). The educational implications of the underrepresentation of women in computing are attracting European concern. In 1984, at least two European conferences devoted a substantial amount of time to the question of women and new technology, and there are plans to consider the subject in at least four conferences to be held in Britain in 1985. The awareness of the subject in the United States is also indicated by the growing numbers of academic publications on the topic (Gerver and Lewis, 1984). The International Council for Adult Education, which is based in Canada, also has plans to investigate the topic.

Those adult educators who feel that there is an overwhelming case for making it possible for more women to engage with computers are thus, at least in the mid-1980s, well supported. But much much more remains to be done, as the enormous over-subscription fo the Women's Technology Training Workshops in Sheffield suggests.

One potentially worrying development is that the current pressures on higher and further education throughout most of the developed world are likely to exclude more and more women from formal study. One indicator of the full extent of the emerging problem may be seen in a report from the Computing School of Thames Polytechnic in London, England. In 1980–81, women formed 25% of the intake to courses in computing. In 1983–84, women formed only 16.9% of those admitted, and applications from women were down to 18%. The course tutor speculated that "the main reason was the increasingly competitive entry to courses . . . which activated women's diffidence, dislike of competition, and belief that a high-powered prestigious profession was 'for men only' " (WNC, 1984).

As places in higher education continue to be cut back in many developed countries, so one can safely predict that this pattern in London will be replicated many times. The onus will, therefore, lie even more heavily on those who provide informal education in the community. Adult educators need to become more aware of the extent of the problem, its main causes, and their possible solutions, so that they can offer greater gender equality than that which presently exists in most educational experiences involving computers.

3

COMPUTERS AND INFORMAL LEARNING

"Computer literacy is now the birthright of every citizen" Megarry, 1983.

The first two chapters have argued that community educators need to respond to the challenges of computers in order to try to counteract the tendencies of the new information technologies, if unchecked, to lead to political, economic, and particularly social divisiveness. Seen from this perspective, the gender bias of computers is only one facet of a wider problem which confronts all those who care about the educational well-being of their communities. The rest of this book will try to suggest some of the ways in which community education can respond to these challenges of humanizing technology. I shall describe and analyze specific projects, trying to tease out from the mass of particular details those general approaches and techniques which seem to have been effective. The discussions show only too plainly that there are many unresolved paradoxes and unsolved serious practical difficulties for community educators as they try to meet the challenge of computers in their local communities. But there is already an impressive amount of evidence about the actual and potential value of attempting to meet the need.

The major contribution which community education has to make here lies, I believe, in its specifically educational function, in helping people to learn *by* and, perhaps even more importantly, *about* computers in informal settings. The term informal is used here as a convenient way to refer to all those forms of purposeful, deliberate, and systematic learning which are voluntarily undertaken by adults outside of designated educational institutions, such as schools, colleges, and universities. Its range includes traditional liberal adult education classes as well as "outreach" programs, noninstitutionally based vocational initiatives for the unemployed as well as leisure learning for both children and adults, formal distance learning schemes as well as private self-directed study.

Distinctions in all forms of adult and community education are becoming increasingly blurred, so it is impossible to draw absolute lines of demarcation. From time to time, therefore, I shall refer to courses which lead to formal academic qualifications and to activities which seem to be purely recreational. But as a general rule of thumb, the educational experiences considered below will exclude those which lead adults—whether young, old, or middle-aged— to formal qualifications and those which are, although often included within the umbrella of "community education," basically recreational.

Beyond the general reasons which have been suggested in earlier chapters, why should community educators want to encourage informal learning by and about computers? Although the reasons overlap, the question needs first to be divided into two parts: why learn by means of computers, and why learn about computers?

WHY LEARN BY COMPUTERS?

Even during the short time in which microcomputers have been available, there is already overwhelming evidence that most children are so attracted to computers that they will use them for anything, even for learning. The fact that computers are apparently so highly motivating for children has encouraged community educators to use them in informal settings for children. Here too, the drawing power of gleaming machines and exciting graphics is indisputable: computer exhibitions almost always have to make special arrangements to cope with the enthusiasm of the children for the machines (Loop, Anton, and Zamora, 1983; Gerver, 1984). While many educators may have serious reservations about the educational dimension of such computer experiences— particularly about the value of computer games—there is no doubt that children are attracted to computers as a learning medium.

But this enthusiasm does not appear to such a degree among adults, and the reasons for choosing to give adults opportunities to learn informally with computers require deeper investigation. Leaving aside for the moment the question of whether adults might prefer to learn by computers, there are still substantial reasons why community educators should take seriously the potential of computers for adult learning.

In the first place, there seems to be a good fit between some of the ways in which adults learn and some of the characteristics of computers which were noted in Chapter 1. Adult learners are probably best characterized by their diversity of circumstances, purposes, and learning styles. Because it can offer such a wide range of options, a computer program can more nearly match this diversity than can a single tutor with a group of perhaps fifteen or twenty students. Using a computer, each student can progress at his or her own speed, concentrating on those parts of the learning experience that he or she finds of greatest value rather than being constrained by the needs and wishes of the other members of a group. As a form of distance learning, the use of computer programs can help to overcome adults' often very diverse constraints of time and place.

Time is usually very valuable for both adult students and tutors, and computer-based systems can provide immediate responses or at least responses that are swifter than those which most hard-pressed, part-time tutors could probably manage. There is some evidence, too, that certain kinds of learning may be accomplished more quickly by using a computer than by more traditional forms of instruction.

Another important characteristic of adult learning is that it appears to be unattractive to certain groups of people, particularly to educationally disadvantaged young men of lower socio-economic groups (ACACE, 1982a). There is growing evidence that it is particularly to such young men that computers appear to be attractive as a learning medium and that some men may even undertake learning experiences by way of a computer that they would not have sought in any other medium (Gerver, 1984). Some of the most vivid experiences of the observers of computer exhibitions in Scotland were watching educationally unqualified young men who had chosen to wrestle with alien concepts and unfamiliar symbols as they were presented in computer programs.

There is already some evidence that educationally disadvantaged children may be motivated to learn by using computer programs (Lally and MacLeod, 1983; O'Shea and Self, 1983); one young man at a Boys' Club in California observed, "If they had computers when I was in school, I'd probably still be there!" (Loop et al., 1980). The limited evidence that exists for educational disadvantaged groups of adults strongly suggests that they too can be reached by computer programs, where conventional means of learning are less attractive to them (Gerver, 1984).

A second group of reasons why computers have substantial potential for community education stems from their ubiquity throughout the developed world. Computers are now used in such a variety of settings and for such diverse purposes that they do not have the kind of immediately didactic associations which books, formal classes, or other educational media may have. Community educators who are trying to reach out to people who have traditionally not participated in adult education may find computers a more neutral and, therefore, more effective means of attracting their interest.

The fact that large numbers of people now have access to some kind of computer is a further reason for community educators to take seriously the potential of computers. In Britain, the Open University has found that 48% of its students have reliable access to a microcomputer (O'Shea, 1984). Access to the equipment itself appeared rarely to represent a problem for any of the mushrooming adult education courses in computing which were offered in England and Wales during 1982–83 (ACACE, 1984). The mass sales of microcomputers, computer programs, and magazines throughout the developed world also indicate how ubiquitous computers have become.

The growing use of computers as a learning tool for adults in formal education adds further weight to the argument that community educators need to take advantage of the educational potential of computers. The growth of computers as learning tools in colleges and universities throughout the developed world—particularly in the United States and to a lesser but still important extent in Britain and Canada—has been rapid and pervasive. The examples which follow are merely indicative of a major trend in further and higher education today.

In the United States, the establishment of the Apple University Consortium has greatly encouraged the use of computers in many of the leading liberal arts-oriented universities: Apple expects that more than 50,000 of its Macintosh computers will be on campus by the end of 1984 (Van Gelder, 1984). The uses to which the computers are likely to be put at first include mainly word processing, information retrieval, and electronic mail, but academics are developing programs to help, for instance, with music composition, the translating of complex demographic statistics into graphics, commentaries on *The Divine Comedy*, and simulating the conditions facing a Filipino rice farmer (ibid).

Also in the United States, the Electronic University, based in San Francisco, offers a wide range of computerized courses, including private tutorials in school subjects for children, adult education in astrology, ballet, nutrition, and accredited courses given in association with certain American universities. Students generally use preprogrammed learning packages on their computers at home, but can also schedule live sessions with their tutors by computer.

A number of Canadian institutions of higher education are also developing educational uses of microcomputers. The British Columbia Institute for Technology plans to offer computer disks containing exercises in accounting and economics, while the Faculty of Extension at the University of Alberta has a learning center which offers a variety of computer-based courses for adults in the community. The University of Calgary's Faculty of Education provides remote learners with computer terminals, so they can make use of the course materials stored in the University computer (Burge, Wilson, and Mehler, 1984).

In Britain, the Open University has since its inception made use of computer-marked assignments for some of its courses, and using a computer terminal has played an important part in many of the science, mathematics, and technology courses, as well as, to a lesser extent, in the other faculties. More recently, it has been developing new ways of using microcomputers both to train teachers in their use and as a means of teaching a variety of subjects.

Courses offered for adults in other universities in Britain have been slower to develop computer-based learning in subjects other than teaching about computers, but there have been several more extensive developments, including those described by Bostock and Seifert (1984). They describe uses of computer programs in the social and the natural sciences, including one program that produced a hierarchical classification of ecological samples, another which analyzed the floristic composition and historical status of parish hedgerows, and computer models of the national economy which were used in teaching macroeconomics.

Finally, there is some evidence that adults may actually like learning by computers. Virtually all of the evidence from specific groups of adult learners in various countries suggests that they enjoy using computers for learning. In Canada in a project at Alberta College, 92% of the hearing-impaired students who used a computerized learning system reported that they were "very enthusiastic" about their experience (Loyer, 1983). In England, in Aylesbury Prison, young offenders markedly preferred using a computer to other methods of mastering literacy and numeracy (Home Office, 1983). Providing computerized marking for student assignments in courses offered by the National Extension College in Britain seemed virtually to eliminate dropout rates in a correspondence course in numeracy (Freeman, 1983). In Sweden, students on an elementary English course for adults preferred computer-assisted communication for correction and commenting on their assignments to that offered by traditional correspondence tuition (CRASH, 1984a).

All of these reasons—particularly the fact that adults actually seem to enjoy the experience of learning with computers—combine to form a powerful case that community educators should consider seriously the potential of the computer as a tool for adult learning. But the reasons for learning about computers are, if anything, even more persuasive, and the growth in this latter area over the past few years has been one of the most striking developments in adult education in Europe and North America.

WHY LEARN ABOUT COMPUTERS?

Let us start not from where we, as educators, would like people to be but from where they actually are. The oversell of computers, particularly as educational and leisure-time pursuits for the home, has meant that many people, having once acquired a machine, simply do not know what to do with it (beyond playing games) and would like to learn both more about their particular machine and more about computers in general. Some community computer camps in Scotland, for instance, cater especially to "people who already have computers but don't know what to do with them" (McCann and McKay, 1983).

There is now ample evidence that, for this reason, as well as for many others, the demand for learning about computers has considerably outstripped the supply in the mid-1980s. As with much of the evidence in this chapter, the following specific examples are, I believe, indicative of a general trend.

In England and Wales in 1983, the Advisory Council for Adult and Continuing Education conducted a survey among the providers of adult education. The intention was to ascertain the extent of provision and demand for courses about computers and for courses which used computers as a means of teaching other subjects. The results indicated that there had been, until then, "very little experimentation in the adult education sector with microcomputers as tools to assist adult learning in different subject areas or with specific groups in the adult population" (ACACE, 1984).

For courses about computers, however, the picture indicated that "the current supply of courses is not matching the growing size of the demand for them" (ibid). This picture of a growing number of courses failing to meet an even greater growth in demand is confirmed by the experience of many providers of courses linked to the BBC Computer Literacy Project: Salkeld (1983) has reported that these classes were oversubscribed two and three times over. Evidence of how great the gap may be between provision and demand also comes from applications to the Women's Technology Training Workshop in Sheffield: in the first year, over 500 applications were received for 28 places (Miller, 1984a). Houser (1984) also speaks of the "huge imbalance between demand and supply for courses. . . . Computer holidays have become a growth industry."

A microcosm of how provision has mushroomed in an attempt to meet the apparently insatiable demand for learning about computers may be seen in the experience of the community education service of Fife, a region in the east of Scotland. Before the academic year 1981–82, the only provision for adults to learn informally about computers in the region was at "Micros for Parents" courses offered at a few schools. During 1982–83, 23 computer literacy classes were formed, with a total enrollment of 368 people (Urquhart, 1983). During 1983–84, there were 30 such classes, with a total enrollment of 441; the actual number of hours spent in learning about computers had in some cases increased from 16 hours per course to 32 hours, however, so the growth in the amount of systematic learning is even greater than the figures at first indicate (Metcalfe, 1984). During the autumn term alone in 1984–85, 20 courses have taken place, with an enrollment of 313; again, a number of these courses last for 32 hours (ibid).

A similar picture appears to emerge in every detailed study. In Leeds in England, Banks (1984) has traced the rise of classes in introductory computing from 11 in 1981–82 to 39 in 1983–84. Throughout Scotland, between 1983–84 and 1984–85, the numbers of courses related to computing doubled (Grace, 1984).

But figures such as these underestimate the amount of provision in Britain. There are now many additional courses provided to help adult tutors and community education staff to feel at home with computers. The main reasons why there are not still more courses are that both the equipment and the available teaching staff in this area tend to be, at least for the present, fully committed.

The same picture appears everywhere such courses on computer literacy have been offered. In Canada, TV Ontario's first courses, called "Academies," in Health and the Environment and the Music of Man attracted 700 paying participants throughout Ontario. The Parents' Academy, which followed, attracted 2,000 (Sharon, 1984). The first Academy on Computers, however, attracted over 10,000 registrants (Burge et al., 1984). The same pattern of mushrooming provision to meet demand may be seen in the spread of the computer literacy learning experiences known as ComputerTowns. Beginning with a single location in 1979, by 1982 ComputerTowns had over 100 affiliated sites throughout the United States, Canada, Britain, Germany, and Poland (Loop et al., 1983). Computer literacy is without doubt the new "growth" area of adult and community education.

The reasons why so many people want to learn about computers are, as we shall see in greater detail later in this chapter, highly varied. ACACE

(1984) found that courses about computers fell into two main categories—"those concentrating on the practical use and application of microcomputers and those dealing with a general awareness of microtechnology and its societal implications." Most of the courses were of the former type. But the fascination with computers as a medium for knowledge and information is often so great that educational experiences designed to focus on what could be learned from computers have sometimes resulted in a focus on what could be learned about the computing system itself. In Canada, for instance, experiments with the computer-based system of videotex resulted in the terminal being "used mostly for learning about the technology, rather than to learn with it" (Wilson, 1984).

In the area of learning about computers, then, the main task for many community educators is not that of trying to attract sufficient numbers of potential learners to be able to offer systematic and purposeful learning experiences for them. Rather, the question is how best to try to meet the present, apparently insatiable demand for learning about computers, so that adult learners can make informed judgments about how computers can serve their needs and those of their communities. Some of the ways in which community educators have tried to meet these demands are discussed below. Before we take a closer look at samples of provision in the mid-1980s, however, there are a number of general cautions which we will want to bear in mind.

A CAUTIOUS APPROACH TO COMPUTER LITERACY

The diversity of the needs and characteristics of adult learners combine with the diversity of computers to create a potential explosion or an entirely inert substance. In the first place, both as learners and as tutors, any one group of adults will tend to have diametrically opposed views about using computers. In one Open University trial of a computer-based electronic blackboard, known as CYCLOPS, four tutors dropped out of the trials because they felt that the system was incompatible with their teaching styles, while the remaining eighteen recorded very favorable responses (Sharples and McConnell, undated).

So far, evaluation of the responses of adult users to educational computer programs has tended to focus on the relatively strong preference for using computers (Gerver, 1984). Little attention has been given to the smaller but important percentage of users who equally strongly prefer not to use them. Although there have been investigations into why certain teachers and pupils in schools prefer not to use computers (EOC, 1983), there has been little investigation of the reasons why particular adults prefer not to use computers for learning, apart from those studies which speculate on why women in particular may be alienated from them (Deakin, 1984). The fact that some adults remain seriously alienated from computers, however, is one cautious reason for not providing overenthusiastically for learning by and about computers.

A related constraint on the provision of computer literacy is the fact that people's reasons for wanting to learn about computers are extraordinarily diverse. In his investigation of computer literacy courses in England, Banks (1983) found that the students on such courses gave a remarkably wide range of reasons for their interest in computers. Different students wanted to learn to use the computer as an educational device for the family, as a business tool, as a way of keeping up with modern technology, and simply to broaden their outlook. Their interests included worry about the unemployment created by computerization, concern about access to computer information, interest in the home-based office, and interest in the effects of computers on education. In Scotland, Gartside (1982) investigated the variety of participants on computer literacy courses. They included "a gentleman of 62 wishing to keep up with his son at university, a farmer keen to know the best programs to help with the operation of his farm, unemployed people . . . , hobbyists."

The difficulty of trying to meet such diverse interests in computer literacy is compounded by the fact that many participants "do not have sufficient knowledge about the range of subject matter contained within the scope of the word 'computing' to be able to specify that their particular needs are in the area of programming skills, thinking skills, advice about careers, or even a diffuse generalized interest in a new subject for the sake of the subject alone" (Banks, ibid).

A further inhibiting factor is the observation that, while both children and adults are greedy for opportunities of learning how to use computers, the two groups have very different, often conflicting responses to using the machines and very different approaches to learning in general. Children simply have more time at their disposal in which to learn in and out of school than do most adults, and they can better afford the luxury of devoting some of that time to playing than adults can. Children also tend (or have been conditioned) to prefer highly competitive modes of learning and of playing games, while traditional adult education has tended to avoid formal public competition.

Moreover, children are already more familiar than most adults with much of the potential and the reality of computers. It is not simply chance or modesty which allows many writers of books about computers to acknowledge their debt to their children. Computer camps for both children and adults are often founded on the premise that the children will be able to teach the adults at least some of the things they will find useful (Houser, 1984; McCann and McKay, 1983).

Extensive programs for introducing children to computers at school are

currently underway in the United States, Canada, Britain, France, and are
beginning in other European countries as well. It is thus likely that children
will continue to know more about computers than their parents or other adults;
in computing one is far removed from the conventional situation in which
adults are expected to know more than children. The organizers of Computertown USA! have found, therefore, that:

> The literacy approaches outlined for kids don't necessarily follow those for
> adults. . . . Most kids appear to be comfortable with the technology. Some kids
> possess an amazing awareness of microcomputers and technology in general. Kids
> prefer to learn, as quickly as possible, how to control and direct the machine
> using the available programming languages. They also like to play games on the
> computer (Loop *et al.*, 1983).

Adults, on the other hand, tend to have more serious purposes: they often
want "a chance to take the first steps toward a career change, share a skill or
hobby with others, or overcome shyness in the face of a new technology"
(ibid).

The fact that children and adults tend to learn in settings very different
from one another also means that much of the computer material currently
devised for school children will simply not be attractive or relevant to adults.
Offering "rewards" of pictures of teddy bears or opportunities to shoot at
passing missiles will rarely appeal to adults using computers as a way of
learning! Most of the educational computer programs so far are for children,
and are often specifically related to particular parts of school curricula.

The most serious constraint of all, however, is not merely that most of
the educational computer programs so far available are for school children
but that nearly all educational computer programs are of poor quality. The
literature of educational computing is full of similar judgments. Preece and
Jones (1984) note despairingly that "one of the most pressing problems for
teachers wanting to get to grips with microcomputers is the lack of good
educational software." O'Shea (1984) also points to "the very poor educational
quality of the computer-based learning software packages generally available
both in the British and the American educational systems." Glyn-Jones (1984)
says that "the complaint is universal . . . that the available software is inadequate to the objectives envisaged" (see also Hawkridge, 1983).

The most successful of the projects considered below have, therefore,
taken a cautious approach to teaching adults by and about computers. The
potential value of using computers—particularly in adult basic education—
and of teaching computer literacy to adults, however, is so great that the
organizers of such projects have judged that the difficulties suggested here,
while making for caution, should incite to imaginative action rather than
leading to inertia.

COMPUTERS AND ADULT BASIC EDUCATION

As discussions earlier in this book have suggested, computers are already being used for a wide range of learning experiences for children both in and out of school and for adults in formal education. Both as a "spin-off" of these uses in formal education and as a response to the widely perceived need for adult computer literacy, the use of computer programs in community education is steadily increasing; the latter part of this chapter will suggest what appear to be some of the more promising ways ahead. Unquestionably, however, in informal adult education in the United States, Canada and Britain, the most frequent use of educational computer programs for adults has been one of the components in basic education. The widespread use of the PLATO Basic Skills programs in North America and the many local experiments currently taking place in Britain are, I believe, only the first manifestations of what looks like one major use of computers in community education.

There are a number of reasons for this interest in the possibilities of using computer programs in adult basic education. Before speculating about these, however, I should like to define how I am using the term "basic education," as it is a concept with often widely differing connotations. Bown (1983) has defined the objectives of adult basic education succinctly. It "has to provide a survival kit, the essential skills and knowledge to enable an individual to function in his/her society and for the society itself to function reasonably smoothly as a whole." It is, in other words, a process defined by its objectives, which have been described helpfully by Noor (1983) as:

> The imparting of skills to communicate; skills to improve the quality of living; and skills to contribute to—and to increase—economic production. The communication skills, at the minimum, include literacy, numeracy, and general civic, scientific, and cultural knowledge, values and attitudes. The living skills embrace knowledge of health, sanitation, nutrition, family planning, the environment, management of the family economy, and creation and maintenance of a home. The production skills encompass all forms of activity directed towards making a living or producing goods and services at whatever level of economic sophistication.

Computer-aided learning, with its emphasis on the acquisition of skills and information, has appeared to many community educators to offer a great deal of potential for developing skills in all of these areas, although such programs are always used as only one element in a variety of learning experiences. A number of factors contribute to their interest: the specific characteristics of computer-aided learning programs, the apparent drawing power that computers have for educationally and socially disadvantaged adults, and the fact that computer literacy is becoming an important goal for all adults who wish to make a living in the developed world.

Just as they are used widely in training adults in many fields (Dean and Whitlock, 1983), so also computer programs can offer a wide variety of educational possibilities to adults who are learning skills at a basic level. There are clear advantages in using a computer to present material which has to be learned and practiced in a variety of ways so that the skill involved is fully mastered: many programs have, therefore, already been developed to teach the various stages of literacy and numeracy, and some of these are considered more fully below. Many of the areas included in health education— such as nutrition, alcohol use, smoking habits, and the effects of exercise— are also readily adaptable to computer programs. Well-designed computer programs on health can allow individuals to relate their personal experience to more general rules and can, the evidence so far suggests, even encourage individuals to be more honest in self-assessment of their lifestyles than they might be otherwise. Some examples of programs of this sort are also discussed below.

But computers offer a wider range of possibilities for adult basic education than merely those directed toward the acquisition and maintenance of specific skills. Many of the ways in which computers can be used in community development, which will be discussed in Chapter 4, are also ways in which computers can empower individuals in their own lives. The use of the computer for word processing, for example, can enable adults who are uncertain of their ability to express their ideas in conventionally acceptable sentences to experiment with many possible words and structures before finally printing out a finished version.

Evidence about the efficacy of using computers in basic education is still tenuous. There is some evidence from Israel that computer-aided instruction can lead to substantial gains with students who have learning disabilities or who are disadvantaged (Osin, 1981). American research has shown that high school students needing remedial work in mathematics can make important advances by using the PLATO computer system (Poore, Qualls, and Brown, 1979), while Alderman (1979) reports that, in the United States in mathematics and English composition, students in community colleges who completed courses under the TICCIT computer-based program generally achieved higher scores than similar students in conventional lecture-discussion classes.

There have, indeed, been a number of enthusiastic American reports about the dramatic increases in educational performance which have been achieved by using computers to teach literacy and numeracy, but most British educators remain sceptical about the direct advantages (Hawkridge, 1983). In summing up the conclusions of extensive testing of the PLATO system generally, Alderman, Appel, and Murphy (1978) concluded that it had not "reached the potential so long claimed for this form of instructional technology. The PLATO system met wih favourable reactions from teachers and students, but it had no significant impact on student achievement."

Moreover, the improvement in mathematics and writing which characterized the outcome of the TICCIT project in the United States was accompanied by very high dropout rates: in mathematics, for instance, the course completion rate was only 16% compared with 50% in conventional courses (Alderman, 1979). A recent trial of computerized literacy and numeracy teaching among young offenders in Britain concluded that there was no significant overall difference in the educational performance of learners taught by the computerized system as compared with those who underwent conventional forms of instruction (Home Office, 1983).

Overall, the widespread use of computer-based training in colleges in the United States, where developments have probably been more extensive than elsewhere, has apparently yielded three advantages. After analyzing the results of 59 evaluations of computer-based college training in the United States, Kulik, Kulik, and Cohen (1980) concluded that the use of the computer provided small but significant contributions to student achievement; produced positive but small effects on the attitudes of students toward instruction and the subject matter; and reduced substantially the time needed for instruction.

But far more important than any specific educational advantages of using computer programs for adult basic learners is the way in which using computers appears to draw adults to learning and to sustain their interest in it. Indeed, the number of commentators who praise the motivating power of computers for disadvantaged learners is almost as great as the number of those who condemn the quality of the programs! One example, characteristic of many others, comes from England, where the Adult Literacy and Basic Skills Unit (ALBSU) set up an advisory group to examine the use of microcomputers in basic education. The group was initially more impressed by the disadvantages associated with the use of microcomputers. In the end, however, "many of the Group's original fears and reservations about the use of microcomputers in basic education were allayed after seeing the students using microcomputers. Having seen . . . their motivating power . . . , there emerged a feeling . . . that microcomputers, although still only an aid to learning, were qualitatively different from other 'aids' " (ALBSU, 1982).

In the United States, it has been claimed with some justification that the use of the PLATO computer system of Basic Skills "has sparked intense interest among students who previously had no motivation to learn" (Control Data, 1981). The use of anglicized PLATO Basic Skills programs with young offenders in a prison in England showed conclusively that the prisoners overwhelmingly preferred to learn with the computer (Home Office, 1983) rather than by conventional methods. Field workers in adult basic education regularly report that students enjoy computers (Traxler, 1984; *Microwave Band,* 1984, among many others).

From all levels of work in adult basic education there is ample evidence of the fact that computer literacy is now becoming one of the fundamental skills needed for survival in the modern world. Bown (1983) has made the case:

> If the future does hold a world in which 'computer literacy' is essential for almost any sort of job, for creative leisure and for the exercise of political rights, here is another challenge for adult basic education. Just as a non-literate·person is at a disadvantage in any society with a number of literates, so a person unable to work with a home computer terminal will be at a disadvantage in the Europe of the very near future. If the adult basic education curriculum does not include computer literacy, it will leave adult learners in a situation of helplessness and society divided and unequal in a degree we can hardly conceive.

Because of the computer's potential educational value for people who lack basic skills, because of its ability to motivate adults who prefer it to other forms of learning, and because of the imperative need for general computer literacy as a basic skill—for all of these reasons there is a growing use of computer programs for basic education, especially in literacy, numeracy, and health education. Many projects have also sprung up to try to bring computer literacy particularly to adults who lack basic communication, social, and economic skills. I hope that the following account of programs and projects in Britain and North America may throw light both on the immense potential of computers in basic education and on the current constraints in realizing that potential.

Using Computer Programs in Adult Literacy

A number of adult basic education tutors in Britain believe that computers may be much more useful for helping adult basic learners with literacy rather than with numeracy, because computers can encourage a creative approach to literacy where numeracy at a basic level is far more fixed and rigid (Twyman, 1983). Even where the available programs fall short of such creative ideals, tutors still find that they can be used as one part of the learning experiences offered to their students. Most of the programs in literacy which have been developed specifically for adults or with adults as potential users tend to offer drill and practice rather than the development of more creative skills. But the acquisition of basic skills in reading and writing does require the systematic presentation and reinforcement of often repetitive material which needs to be directed toward specific learning disabilities and which can be adjusted in the light of student responses. For such purposes, well-designed computer programs can help in teaching students to improve their reading and writing.

Indeed, the lure of the computer appears to be so great that students will accept material by that means which they might reject from any other. One worker in basic education bluntly says about using the computer for such drill and practice: "Where it really comes into its own in adult basic education is in dressing up simple, repetitive exercises designed to reinforce what has already been learned" (Stevenson, 1983). Two examples of the kinds of freestanding programs of this sort in current use in Britain may give a flavor of the approach used.

"Happenings" (TECS, 1984) is one example of a computer program for learning to read which has been designed specifically for adult users. It contains twenty brief story lines which grew out of students' actual talking points; titles include "The Garage," "New Baby," "The Washing Machine," "My Lad's Mice," and "The New Phone." These story lines appear on the computer screen in different ways, so that the learner can practice reading at various speeds, undertake the recognition of whole words, test his or her comprehension, rearrange anagrams to their correct form, or reassemble jumbled sentences, and so on. One of the sample story lines is "My little lad keeps mice. I can't stand the things. Once he let two of them loose in the kitchen. I screamed for ages. In the end I made him get rid of them all" (*Microwave Band*, 1984).

Another program "Keyboard Skills" (SMDP, 1984) has been developed with 14–16 year-old children with moderate learning difficulties in mind, but is eminently suitable for adult users as well. Its intention is to encourage users to learn the location and use of the computer keys with increasing speed and accuracy by playing a series of colorful games of typing skill. In one of the games, the QWERTY keyboard appears on the screen. One number or letter is highlighted in a different color from the others, and the user then has to press the corresponding number or letter on the keyboard. In a variant, the user has to press on the keyboard the single letter that appears on the screen. Another game asks the user to type three- or four-letter words which appear on a stair on the screen. If the entry is correct, a new word appears on the next stair up; if the entry is incorrect, the word appears on the next stair down. Here, as in the other games, the object is to improve the accuracy and speed of using the keyboard by competing against oneself.

Where handwriting skills are needed, it is possible that computer programs originally developed to assist school children with learning how to write well-formed letters could also be used with adults. Lally and MacLeod (1983) describe a computer system which includes a special pen whose movements can be monitored by the computer. Students are offered varying amounts of help, depending on their ability, in tracking a series of line segments ranging from individual strokes to whole words.

Unlike these examples of individual computer programs, the Basic Skills programs available on PLATO in North America and to a limited extent in Britain, cover comprehensively most of the skills required in basic reading and writing. The program packages in basic reading skills include the fundamentals of word structure, fundamental vocabulary development, and basic comprehension skills, while those in basic language skills include basic language structure and word usage, sentence and paragraph structure, and the mechanics and conventions of writing (Control Data, 1980).

All of these programs for reading, writing, and using the computer keyboard are, of course, limited primarily to a drill and practice model based fundamentally on a model of behaviorism that many adult basic educators (and many others too) find distasteful, empirically unjustified, and philosophically unacceptable. The rejection of this kind of model among workers in artificial intelligence—notably Papert (1980) and his followers—has brought into existence many new ways in which children can use computers for basic exploration of structures and concepts particularly through learning the use of computer languages, such as LOGO (Papert, 1980; O'Shea and Self, 1983). Such general exploration may, however, be of less value for adults, who tend to have less time and more specific needs than children. How, then, might community educators who prefer not to use behaviorist models use computer programs for adult literacy?

The possibilities are endless. Even the realities of using present-day computers and programs can offer creative experiences for adults who are learning how to read and write. For instance, simple word processing programs can be used by both children and adults who have difficulty in expressing their ideas on paper and who grow impatient over the need for constant corrections. The prospect of being able to print only a single immaculate version of something that has had many drafts is an obvious spur to creative writing. Producing a community newsletter by way of simplified word processing may be equally attractive for a group of basic learners. Writing or drawing with a special pen on a tablet attached to a computer and having the marks that one makes appear on the computer screen can also stimulate creativity rather than rote learning.

Work in artificial intelligence has also produced a number of fascinating possibilities for children which could well be adapted for use with adult students who want to improve their use of the English language. Sharples (1981), for example, refers to a program which provides a computer aid for helping with spelling in creative writing. After the student has entered part of a story on the computer, the program interrupts the typing to query any apparent misspellings. Several commercially available spelling programs, although more complex to use, may also be helpful in this respect for more advanced adult basic learners.

As many of the articles in Chandler (1983) suggest, the use of the computer in teaching language skills needs to be seen only as an adjunct to good language teaching that is already going on. But well-designed programs can provide potentially significant insights into language, as Adams and Jones (1983) show in their account of programs for building stories, for creating descriptions, for writing poetry, and for experimenting with the layout and organization of material. And, as we shall see in more detail later in this chapter, the use of the computer to teach basic programming concepts may also play an important part in enlarging and liberating adults' perception of their own thought processes.

Meanwhile, the value of programs that teach highly practical applied literacy skills must not be underestimated: filling out forms is one example of a skill which can readily be taught by a computer program, and which requires severely practical training rather than creative thought! Learning English as a second language is also clearly amenable to being taught partially through computer programs, at least for students who are already familiar with the English alphabet; researchers at the Friends Center in Brighton, England, are, therefore, working on a computer program for the development of English language skills using cooking and diet as their main topic (Traxler, 1984b).

Finally, the fascination and delight at being able to use a computer may also mean that adult basic learners simply get more pleasure and perhaps a greater feeling of confidence from reading on a computer screen precisely the same words as they would read in a book. As Stevenson (1983) comments, "it is both an enjoyable and a great confidence boosting experience for adults who might have difficulty with literacy . . . to realise that they can operate a computer."

Using Computer Programs in Adult Numeracy

Partly because computers were originally used primarily for processing numbers, a large number of educational programs concentrate on teaching numeracy and numeracy-related skills. Included in such programs are skills such as budgeting, dealing with bank accounts, reading calendars and time-tables, and many of the other skills of applied numeracy that most adults tend to take for granted, but which are not self-evident either to children or to some adults. Nearly all of these areas appear to be ideally suited to the development of educational computer programs, as they tend to need repetition and reinforcement of material which directly addresses an individual student's specific problem. Moreover, apart perhaps from the managing of personal finance, where there is a clear element of individual, subjective judgment, numeracy and related skills nearly all allow for only one correct answer, but require different responses from the tutor depending on the nature of the errors that are made.

There has, therefore, been an explosion in the numbers of computer programs—both freestanding and as part of more comprehensive packages—which have been developed to teach numeracy and related skills to children. With the exception of the PLATO Basic Skills package, there has not been such a dramatic development in computer programs to teach numeracy to adults. Many programs originally designed for children, however, have proved adaptable for adults as well, and there have been several important developments in computer programs that allow highly detailed individualized responses to students' answers to questions in arithmetic.

To an even greater extent than in using computer programs for literacy, however, there has generally been a sense of frustration that the potential which computers have for individualizing presentation of material and responses has not yet been fully developed in programs in numeracy. Comments contained in a recent evaluation in Brighton, England (Swinfield, 1984) of the use by adults of a number of commercially available programs designed to teach numeracy give an indication of how undeveloped the potential still is. In one option in one program, for instance, "the user was driven along answering a times table with a time limit on each question and no feedback until the end of a session of twenty questions. It was generally disliked. . . . Students found themselves forced to go through drill they did not need and feedback and explanations were lacking." Other comments on other programs included:

> "Option 1 gave a demonstration picture but didn't explain anything, including how to choose tasks."
> "Some of this program seemed to be missing. It did not work at all."
> "It was graphically impressive but provided no explanation whatsoever."

Not surprisingly, the evaluation concluded that "many of the programs and packages available (and the pedagogic ideas which underpin them) are of little value for work with adults."

Against this judgment, which is by and large supported by other assessments of numeracy programs used by adults, must be set the fact that many of the basic education students who were using these programs liked them, despite the serious reservations of the evaluator. Individual students liked the competition against the computer which played a part in certain programs. They also liked and found useful a program which provided drill in simple addition, subtraction, multiplication, and division, the reward for each answer being a move forward in a racing game; the evaluator had judged this package as poor, because it provided no instructions or feedback. Students found useful another program which tested their competence at gauging values in a linear scale, although the evaluator had reservations, because it did not give them enough time to reflect on mistakes and gave no second try after mistakes.

Such a substantial difference in evaluation between students and professional educators is often found to an even greater extent with programs used with children. After observing public use of educational computer programs in Scotland, for instance, Barrett (1982) found that "in coping with the problems, younger users were more flexible, and, if something went wrong, they were happy just to try again, or try something else; older users tended to be less resilient, wanting to be told clearly what to do and less tolerant of poor user guidance." The experience in Brighton, however, suggests that in adult basic education, students' enthusiasm for using computers for numeracy is so great that, despite the fact that "most programs do not come through this evaluation with flying colours" (Traxler, 1984a), the experience of learning numeracy through computer programs is both useful and enjoyable.

Because of the enthusiasm among adult basic learners for using computers for numeracy, there is now a plethora of programs in use for both numeracy and for numeracy-related skills. The variety of the programs currently being developed by the Scottish Microelectronics Development Programme for pupils with special educational needs is indicative of the range in Britain today. The entire list of programs covers a much wider range than those which might be helpful in adult numeracy, but the titles and descriptions are promising. They include "BANK," which "offers a simulated bank account facility. . . . Pupils may deposit cash, write cheques, and use a cashcard." "CLOCKS" gives "practice with clockfaces and telling the time. [It] uses both digital and longhand descriptions [and] introduces 24-hour times." In "JOURNEY (ROUND 2)," the user is "introduced to direction, grid references, and simple street maps and can plan and make a journey." "SURVIVE" is "a decision-making game testing the . . . ability to budget on a given weekly income," while "SUMMER HOLIDAYS" presents a simulated travel agency for booking package holidays at various European resorts (Nash, 1984).

Some of the reservations expressed about the actual programs in use in adult numeracy in Britain do not apply, of course, to the much more comprehensive PLATO Basic Skills system, which has been developed over a longer period of time. PLATO's Basic Mathematics Skills include modularized packages for basic number concepts, basic arithmetic operations, including numbers, fractions, and decimals, and special applications topics involving ratio, proportion, percent, geometry, and measurement (Control Data, 1981). The presentation is also far-ranging, including tutorial lessons, remedial help sequences, review activities, and diagnostic, mastery, and retention tests (ibid). For many tutors in adult basic education, however, systems such as PLATO remain inaccessible simply because of their relatively high cost, whereas the comparative cheapness of popular microcomputers with educational programs remains a more practical option.

Within this framework of using popular microcomputers with purpose-made programs for helping adults with numeracy, one of the most effective forms of computer-supported learning in Britain, as in other countries, appears to be the use of a computer for correspondence courses in which students receive individual letters in response to the specific answers which each gave to multiple-choice questions in numeracy. One good example of such a system in operation is MAIL (Micro Aided Learning) at the National Extension College in Cambridge, England. In this system, the student on the correspondence numeracy course, "Make it Count," posts his or her answers to multiple-choice questions to the College and shortly receives back an individualized letter which offers detailed comments on each answer, and, in particular, analyzes any wrong choice and suggests ways of reaching the right answer the next time round. As with a similar system in Canada (Sharon, 1984), students have expressed great enthusiasm about it: virtually all of the students who used this option completed the first run of the course in England in 1983 (Freeman, 1983), while in Canada 90% of students reported that they enjoyed receiving the computer-generated responses.

To give a flavor of what such a system is able to do, in the course "Make it Count" in 1983, a sample question was: "A family had 28, 33, 26, and 35 bottles of milk in the four weeks of January. The number of bottles of milk they had in January was (a) 100 (b) 102 (c) 112 (d) 122." A sample reply to the incorrect choice of (a) was:

> The correct answer is D, 122 pints. Your answer was A, 100. How did you get this? First put the four numbers neatly in columns with the tens under each other in one column and the units under each other in another. Then add the units $8 + 3 + 6 + 5 = 22$. But 22 is 2 tens and 2 units ($22 = 20 + 2$). Put 2 units in the units column and carry the 2 tens to the tens column. Now add the tens; $2 + 3 + 2 + 3 + 2$ (the 2 tens carried) $= 12$. So the answer is 122. Check for yourself. Try this: $29 + 24 + 36 + 42$ (NEC, 1983).

Clearly it would take an individual tutor a very long time—probably an uneconomically long time—to write individual responses in this kind of helpful detail, and there would be considerable frustration for a tutor who had to write detailed but often repetitive comments in reply to each student's work. The MAIL system thus uses the capacity of the computer to provide faster, more individualized and more detailed feedback than would be possible for a tutor who had to mark all the assignments laboriously by hand.

Such a system does not, of course, directly teach the student by a computer program but rather uses the computer as a way of providing more useful feedback than might otherwise be available. It is, thus, a good illustration of the use of the computer as one specific element in the educational process rather than as the dominant feature, and, as such, represents a promising direction in which providers of numeracy for adults are likely to move more and more.

There are also other directions in which there are promising but not yet fully realized developments for future work with adult basic learners. These developments also originate in the field of teaching mathematics, but they go so far beyond conventional ideas of numeracy that they may best be considered as part of the process of helping people to develop their problem-solving abilities. These developments, largely stemming from applied work in artificial intelligence, are already being widely applied in the education of children but have not yet been extensively used in adult basic education. They will, therefore, be considered below as promising indications of future development rather than as tools immediately available to adult basic educators.

Using Computer Programs in Health Education

As well as being applied in adult literacy and numeracy, computer programs are being increasingly used in adult basic education for the development of the skills needed for healthy living. The stimuli for developing educational programs in this area have come from a variety of sources. In the first place, the use of computers has been particularly well developed in medicine, and medical practitioners have been receptive to the possibility of developing and using computer programs with patients in many different ways, such as the maintenance of records, investigation and diagnosis of conditions, and monitoring. Secondly, as we have already seen, there is evidence that confirms the common sense expectation that people are more willing to give honest responses to a computer than to another person, particularly in health matters about which they feel sensitive, such as smoking, the use of alcohol and other drugs, and sexual matters.

A further incentive for developing computer programs for health education has arisen from the fact, confirmed in many different projects in which the public has been given access to computers, that men of lower socio-economic groupings, who tend to be conspicuously absent from most forms of adult education, are particularly attracted to the possibility of interacting with computers. Finally, health educators have been attracted by the ability of computer programs to enable people to explore the implications of their own life-styles or the accuracy of their own beliefs about health: once people have entered details about themselves on a computer, a carefully designed program can then assess the impact of the stated practices and beliefs.

In the United States, Canada, and Britain, a substantial number of computer programs have, therefore, been developed to provide one useful form of health education. In the United States, a series of "Health Awareness Games" (Ellis, 1981) has allowed users to assess their liability to a heart attack, the risks posed to health by smoking, the implications of their eating and exercise habits, and the likely health consequences of their life-styles. In Montreal in Canada, a project called Télé-Santé offers to the general public computer-based information about specific illnesses, good health, and health management generally. At the Ontario Science Center in Canada as part of an experimental project involving the use of the Canadian videotex system, Telidon, a quiz game was created about good first-aid practice, which attracted considerable attention (Wilson, 1984).

Through the Scottish Community Education Microelectronics Project (SCEMP), a number of health education freestanding computer programs have been developed. Although there has been no formal analysis of their effectiveness—such an analysis would be both methodically and practically very difficult to conduct—the following account of some of the experimental programs gives an indication of current developments in computer programs for community health education.

Two experimental programs have been developed specifically for use with women. One of these, "Breast or Bottle" (Wright and MacLeod, 1981), was developed by psychologists who had recently conducted extensive investigations of the infant feeding practices of a group of mothers. Their program offered users a chance to think about the implications of choosing to breast feed or to bottle feed their infants. It covered the kind of topics that pregnant and nursing mothers are often anxious about, such as how long women who breast feed are likely to continue to do so, how often babies might want feeding, how to determine whether a baby is being fed enough, whether age has any effect on breast feeding, and so on. It also presented the reasons, as given by women themselves, why breast or bottle feeding is chosen, and summarized the advantages and disadvantages of each.

Another program, "Planning a Well-Woman Centre" (Greater Glasgow Health Board Health Education Department, 1983), asked women about their own priorities in the services that can be offered by such a center and encouraged them to bring pressure to realize the type of center they desired. A record was kept of the plans suggested so that it could help in future health planning (SCEMP, 1984).

But these programs remain experimental and are not part of the ones which SCEMP makes generally available to community educators in Scotland. Other, publicly available programs have been designed to help with problems especially associated with those young people who would not normally take any part in adult education. SCEMP has created, or had created for it, programs on drinking, smoking, glue-sniffing, general health assessment, and nutrition.

The approach of the program on "Alcohol and Health" (Argyll and Clyde Health Board, 1983) is characteristic of the way in which these programs offer health education. It attempts to educate the user about how much alcohol he or she—the amount of alcohol that can be safely consumed varies greatly between the sexes—can drink while still remaining healthy. It also aims to teach some of the basic effects of the over-consumption of alcohol on the stomach, liver, nerves, and brain. The main approach is to encourage the user to answer multiple-choice questions about the effects of alcohol abuse and how best to avoid any ill-effects. It assumes that its users will want to drink, and therefore encourages "healthy happy drinking" by staying within the limit for one's age and sex and by occasionally having a complete rest from alcohol.

There has been no serious evaluation of the efficacy of these programs; indeed, because using any one program would represent such a small, probably trivial part of the health experience of any individual, the overall effect would be negligible, if it could be measured at all. Nevertheless, even where the programs are unadventurous as computer programs—the one on "Stopping Smoking" consists mainly of using the computer as a page-turner—they have attracted a great many users and much favorable public comment. Despite the difficulties which SCEMP (1983) has noted in satisfying in a single program the very different criteria desired by health educators, computer programmers, and the general public, the implication is clear that this is territory ripe for further development in adult basic education.

Other Uses of Computer Programs in Adult Basic Education

If we turn our attention to the groups of people with whose needs adult basic education is concerned, the ways in which computers can be used suddenly start to multiply. As ACACE (1979) noted, it is true that the need for adult basic education remains a personal and individual matter. But certain groups of people are more likely to contain individuals for whom a basic education should be provided. ACACE identified these groups as: socially disadvantaged communities, which usually also contain a high proportion of people who suffer from economic disadvantage; ethnic minorities whose needs include basic language skills and knowledge about their host society but also range much more widely as well; the unemployed; the handicapped whose needs may include physical or mental handicap or both; people at particularly stressful moments of their lives, such as young single parents; and those in penal establishments.

Ways of using computers to help those who are socially and economically disadvantaged are considered, either implicitly or explicitly, throughout much of this book, particularly in the following two chapters. People in such groups share with those who are unemployed a great need for computer literacy if they are not to become still further disadvantaged; indeed, as I shall suggest below, training in the skills of using computers may be one valuable way to open up new possibilities of employment for them. Ways of using computers in helping with language skills have already been mentioned, while the contribution which computer literacy can make to ethnic minorities is considerable, as Traxler [1984b] suggests. The amount of help that might be offered by computers to people at particularly stressful periods of their lives seems necessarily extremely limited, although Deakin (1984) cites many persuasive examples of women who have combined heavy domestic commitments with new careers in computing.

Computers, however, have already been shown to be of particular value in penal establishments and in helping individuals who are physically or mentally handicapped. Evidence has already been cited about the preference expressed by young offenders in England for learning skills of literacy and numeracy by way of computer systems. In Scotland, an experimental project conducted by SCEMP in a prison in Edinburgh, which will be discussed further in Chapter 4, suggests that there is substantial enthusiasm among offenders for learning to program computers. Given sufficient support, prisoners are keen both to learn programing and to turn their newly acquired knowledge to social use in creating programs for possible use in adult basic education (Sutherland, 1984). Clearly, there is considerable potential in this area which might well be exploited by those adult educators who work with prisoners.

But it is in the area of computer-assisted help for the handicapped that there have been perhaps the most dramatic successes and some of the most promising developments. Here, to an even greater extent than in many of the other uses of computers, there are sometimes major financial obstacles. It is often technologically feasible to design and build communication aids which enable individuals to overcome specific handicaps, but there is simply not a mass market for such developments in the way that there is for programs for word processing or keeping accounts. Nevertheless, the development of computer-based communication aids for the disabled is now a rapidly expanding area, with a growing literature devoted to it (Perkins, 1983). I shall therefore merely skim the surface of some of the developments currently underway in Britain in order to give an idea of the range of possibilities.

In Britain the Open University has been particularly active in helping blind students to use computers in order to expand and enhance their academic communication. A blind student can now, for instance, type his or her essay in braille on a specially adapted computer keyboard, and the program will convert the text to standard print for a sighted correspondence tutor to read and mark (Vincent, 1983). Developments elsewhere in reading machines and other uses of synthetic speech mean that people who are blind can now feed ordinary printed material through such machines so that they can hear it read aloud (ibid).

A blind learner has the enormous advantage of being able to learn to use a computer keyboard. Men and women who do not have the free use of their hands are more obviously restricted in using computers to communicate. Here, too, however, a number of ways have been developed to enable people to bypass their physical limitations. Some computers are now specially programmed so that they can be operated other than by the conventional keyboard: merely switching a stick back and forth, for example, can allow the user full access to the computer keyboard and thereby to its many functions.

There is also a steadily growing literature which refers to the apparent advantages of using computer programs with learners who are mentally handicapped. Virtually all of the work in this area has been concerned with children rather than with adults (Geoffrion, 1983). The positive results that have been so far indicated suggest that the use of specially designed educational computer programs can significantly help children who are mentally retarded, hearing-impaired, or autistic (ibid). Geoffrion reports of one computer program designed to teach initial reading to children with poor language skills that "most handicapped children greatly enjoy the activity and are gradually learning the vocabulary. The responses of autistic students have been especially interesting. They were highly enthusiastic and worked with sustained concentration, although each chose to interact with the computer in ways different from that intended when designing the computer program." Goldenberg (1979) has also described examples of using the computer language LOGO with severely mentally handicapped individuals; in one particularly striking case, an autistic boy spoke his first clear words while he was using the computer.

The uses made of computers for educational purposes by hearing-impaired students have also been promising, and, again, represent areas for possible future development within nonformal adult education. At a project involving the use of the PLATO Basic Skills system at Alberta College in Canada, 92% of the hearing-impaired students reported that they were "very enthusiastic" about their experience (Loyer, 1983). The DAVID system being developed at the National Technical Institute for the Deaf in Rochester, New York, teaches lip reading to college students by using computer-controlled videotape. Initial evaluation studies showed that it is an effective and enjoyable means of improving speech-reading skills (Sims, Vonfelt, Dowaliby, Hutchinson, and Myers, 1979).

Each of these developments—and there are many others like them—represents an important possibility for using computer programs to try to meet the needs for basic education among many diverse groups of adults. Standing behind all of them, however, is the even wider need for computer literacy. It is here that community education faces perhaps the most directly challenging task of all, as it tries to encourage children to become more aware of the wider implications of computerization, and as it tries to help all adults—both those in need of other forms of basic education, as well as those who have long since mastered many other skills—acquire a new skill and to achieve a new understanding of how computers are transforming our economic, social, and intellectual landscape. For in the matter of computer literacy, we are all—both students and providers—basic learners together.

COMPUTER LITERACY

The extent of the need and the demand for computer literacy has already been suggested. As Chapter 1 attempted to show, computerization has widespread effects and implications for our economic, social, and political lives. The crucial argument here has been formulated by an eminent specialist in computers, Laver (1980): "computers are not the only, nor are they necessarily the most troublesome, of the new technologies which will affect our daily lives. However, the economic, social, and political decisions which our use of them will require us to take are too important to be taken in ignorance, nor can they safely be left to experts—of whatever kind." For groups who are already disadvantaged in our society, their disadvantage is likely to multiply if computer illiteracy is added to other disadvantages, so here the case for computer literacy is perhaps even more urgent and compelling.

But what is meant by the term "computer literacy" which it is so generally agreed that we all ought to acquire? Most adult educators accept that it includes, as a minimum, "awareness of computers and appreciation of their power and limitations" (Burge *et al.*, 1984). Beyond this basic awareness and appreciation, there is a clear need for someone who is computer literate to be able readily to learn how to use specific computer programs designed for nontechnical users and probably, indeed, to be able to handle a computer keyboard; as has been suggested earlier, it may well be that typing, far from becoming a redundant skill, is actually an important element in using computers.

Computer literacy should also include "comprehension of and the ability to discuss computing concepts, applications, and issues intelligently" (Bostock and Seifert, 1983). Above all, "true computer literacy is not just knowing how to make use of computers and computational ideas. It is knowing when it is appropriate to do so" (Papert, 1980). The computer literate is therefore likely to differ considerably from the computer enthusiast. Where the latter will be fascinated merely by the fact that a computer can do certain things, the computer literate will make sterner assessments of whether such uses offer any serious advantages over alternative methods.

At the other end of the spectrum, many educators—particularly those who have come from a computing background—believe that computer literacy includes the ability actually to program computers at a basic level. This argument has been particularly potent in Britain, where most courses in computer literacy have tended to focus primarily on learning elementary programming. Thus, the BBC's Computer Literacy Project has been based on the premise that "the route to computer literacy is through 'hands-on' experience. Some of this may be through ready-made programs, and some through do-it-yourself programming" (Radcliffe, 1983). The BBC therefore followed its initial introduction to computers in the television series, "The Computer Programme," with an introduction to the basic principles and practices of programming in the second series, "Making the Most of the Micro"; an important element in the project was the provision by the National Extension College of courses in programming some of the most popular microcomputers in Britain. In its survey of computer courses offered for adults in England and Wales in 1982–83, ACACE (1984) found that most courses were aimed at the practical usage of microcomputers; in Scotland, Gartside (1982) found a similar situation.

In the United States and Canada, concepts of computer literacy, as expressed in the content of courses, tend to place greater emphasis on a general understanding of computers and to prepare their participants to be able to take advantage of the practical applications of computers in ways that are directly useful to them. The course, "The New Literacy," which is offered by the Southern California Consortium for Community College Television

and by TV Ontario, for instance, does not attempt to teach programming.
Rather, it is designed to:

- provide a comprehensive overview of the computer: what it is, what it can and
  cannot do, how it operates, and how it may be instructed to solve problems;
- familiarize learners with the terminology of data processing;
- examine the application of the computer to a broad range of organizational settings
  and social environments;
- prepare learners to understand and utilize computers in both their personal and
  professional lives ("The New Literacy," 1983).

Indeed, rather than trying to meet as many needs as possible within a
single course, computing courses for adults in the United States tend to be
divided into four main types: general introductions for the newcomer to computers, hardware or equipment courses, software or application courses, and
programming courses (Schmidt, 1985). Courses which lead to qualifications
in Britain are, of course, already highly specific, and it may be that the
American model of carefully distinguishing the purposes for which people
want to learn about computers will finally be adopted widely in Britain, too.
      Meanwhile, the demand for the courses available in Britain and North
America is, as we have seen, far in excess of almost any other demand in
adult education in the mid-1980s. In 1981, the BBC concluded that "the
amount of interest shown in computer applications cannot be stressed too
much." Its judgment was amply vindicated in the public interest subsequently
expressed in the televised programs and the computer and the courses which
were linked to them. About seven million adults saw some part of "The
Computer Programme" during its first broadcasts, and this figure increased
to nine million for the follow-up program, "Making the Most of the Micro;"
the popular appeal of the computer programs associated with the series is
suggested in Figure 5. During 1982, *The Computer Book,* which was published
by the BBC as an introduction to computers for nonexperts, sold "at a level
more usually associated with popular best selling novels" (Radcliffe and
Salkeld, 1983). An indication of the mass interest in the United States may
be seen in the estimate that in 1984 Americans will have spent $180 million
learning how to use microcomputers (Schmidt, 1985).
      Popular interest in the more general implications of the effects of com-
puters on our social, political, and economic lives has also been strikingly
high, as may be seen in the flood of books dealing with these wider issues
(Evans, 1979; Burkitt and Williams, 1980; Forester, 1980; Norman, 1981;
Jones, 1982, among very many others). The BBC found, however, that its
potential audience was far more interested in the applications than the implications of the new computer technology (BBC, 1981), and the relative
sparseness of courses which deal with the wider issues of computer literacy

Figure 5. The BBC's approach to computer literacy: the wise owl which encourages people to use BBC computer programs. Figure reproduced by courtesy of British Broadcasting Corporation, © BBC Publications.

would seem to confirm this finding. There appear to be few such courses offered in North America. In Britain in 1982–83, for every course that concentrated on general awareness, there were at least three with purely practical aims (ACACE, 1984). It may well be that this wider element in computer literacy will become even less significant as the effect of market forces becomes increasingly prevalent in adult education in Britain; certainly, where courses are offered at substantial fees in North America, the wider issues seem to not have surfaced to any great extent.

But any discussion of computer literacy for adults needs to take account of the fact that the development of such learning experiences may well be a short-term expedient. Throughout much of the developed world, governments and commercial interests are concerned with introducing computer literacy at least to all secondary schools and in some cases to primary schools as well. There are the "10,000 Microcomputers plan" in France, the Microelectronics Education Programme in England and Wales, the Scottish Microelectronics Development Programme, and many often commercially funded projects in the states and provinces of North America. These initiatives are likely to ensure that, within the next ten years, the need for providing at least young adults with a minimum of computer literacy may well no longer exist; as a representative from IBM commented, "with children and young adults adapting so easily eventually the problem of educating mid-life adults in first-time computer use will cease to exist" (Lean, 1983).

But unless community education in its many forms is able to meet the challenge for those who did not use computers at school—and most adults now as young as twenty have not encountered computers at school—and for those who do not learn to use computers as part of their professional development, it will have failed most adults. Let us, therefore, look at some of the ways in which various providers of community education are attempting to meet this need through courses, exhibitions, drop-in centers, camps, and other informal learning experiences.

Computer Literacy Courses

Most adults probably try to acquire computer literacy by following a systematic course of much the same kind as they would take throughout the whole range of "evening," "correspondence," or "leisure" courses. Because many adults, and many providers of community education, believe that computer literacy has significant economic advantages, however, the courses available in this field tend to extend well beyond the conventional range of nonqualification classes. Indeed, the European Economic Community has been very active in part-funding courses which aim to train disadvantaged adults, especially women, in the new technologies in general and computers in particular. In discussing computer literacy courses for adults, therefore, we need to take into account the current expansion in this form of provision, as well as that in more conventional informal education.

Let us start from perceptions of the needs of the learner. In Britain, the Open University has found that, among adults who want to acquire computer literacy, "the biggest need was not for mastering technical details or learning to be an accomplished computer programmer, but simply that of crossing the confidence barrier in actually using the microcomputer" (OU, 1984). The Open University, therefore, designed an awareness course for teachers which aims to enable the user to operate a specific computer at an elementary level, to use educational material on the computer, to evaluate the educational potential of the computer, and to understand enough computer jargon to be able to ask for help and advice as necessary (OU, 1984). Here, then, is one good example of a course specifically designed with the needs of a particular group of learners in mind. By the end of the course, teachers will be reasonably at home with most of the major ways in which computers are currently being used in classrooms in Britain—for simulation, demonstration, problem-solving, programming, information-retrieval, control, programmed learning and for games—and they will have gained practical experience through actually using a particular computer for specific, limited tasks.

Particularly in adult basic education, where learning has traditionally taken place in less formal and structured ways, a very different approach has sometimes been advocated. The Scottish Adult Basic Education Unit, for instance, has suggested that:

The acquisition of computer awareness and computer skills depends on the demystifying effect of having-a-go at a time and place where we can relax, take our time and make mistakes without the pressure of 'experts,' other students, or a formal class setting. Once we overcome our initial anxieties through practical experience, we can begin to decide what it is we want to learn and how we want to do it. We can then make demands for more access to computers, more training, and the development of more appropriate software (CRASH, 1984b).

But most courses, particularly those for adult basic learners, have discovered that it is often very difficult—if not impossible—to learn enough about computers in such a casual fashion. Most providers claim that a more structured approach works more effectively, even where they have first attempted more informal methods. Indeed, EEC-sponsored training schemes for adult basic learners to acquire computer literacy have found that, even where they started with a highly structured and systematic approach, if anything, their students found it necessary for yet more structure to enable them to break down the often complex concepts into more manageable parts.

Actually learning any significant amount of even elementary programming demands a highly structured rather than a casual approach. Thus, Traxler (1984b) comments about the experience of introducing adult basic learners to the rudiments of learning a computer language: "like learning any language, it needed practice, repetition and usage; like learning a game it required an ability to assimilate and use a set of apparently arbitrary rules, and like learning maths it needed an ability to assemble ideas in an orderly arrangement, and to subordinate detail within an overall plan." It is also notable that in the Women's Technology Training Workshop in Sheffield, which has already been described in Chapter 2, students expressed appreciation of the highly structured approach and even wanted to do the kind of homework more often associated with unwanted school work (Miller, 1984b)!

The actual experience of adults trying to acquire computer literacy in Britain thus seems to confirm Bown's (1983) judgment that adult basic educators "will be betraying the adults whom we are trying to assist to learn unless we provide them with hard knowledge and new skills." For at least some of the adults involved, the acquisition of "hard knowledge and new skills" in computing has resulted not only in their becoming more confident in using computers but also in their developing more generalizable and transferable intellectual skills. In one of the courses in Brighton:

The work of writing programs and understanding why they work has necessitated useful concepts, such as variables and logical operations. In writing these programs, the adults have developed their study and problem-solving skills. . . . All these areas . . . reinforce the non-passive role of the student with the computer. They also identify the computer as a machine—a highly flexible tool. This under-

lines a whole strategy for adults; that they are controlling a process. . . . Once
equipped with this information and confidence, these adults are approaching a
position where they can take realistic and informed decisions regarding working
with the area of new technology (Traxler, 1984b).

Although it is often difficult to do so, courses in computer literacy also
need, it appears, to take account of the diversity of motivations with which
students come to them. The extent of this diversity has been noted above.
Particularly in computer literacy courses in Britain, which often teach both
programming and computer applications, providers have sometimes found
that there may be a "major split between those students who were enjoying
computer programming and those whose major interest was in learning the
applications of computer software" (Traxler, ibid).

For certain aspects of learning about computers—at least for those for
which no actual use of a keyboard is necessary—distance learning or individualized learning seems to be particularly well suited. Thus, as part of its
Computer Literacy Project, the BBC's televised programs about computers
allowed viewers to watch one or more of a series of ten programs and then
served as a gateway for further systematic study by way of the National
Extension College or the many local courses which were offered by adult
education providers throughout Britain to support the series.

More than probably any other offering in the field of computer literacy,
the BBC's Computer Literacy Project was prepared on the basis of extensive
research (BBC, 1981), and its progress has been thoroughly documented
(BBC, 1983; Radcliffe and Salkeld, 1983). Its outstanding success appears
to be due to a number of factors, all of which have implications for other
intending providers of computer literacy. In the first place, it has provided
many paths toward computer literacy, so that the learner can start with a
general introduction and then follow his or her specific interests. Secondly,
the first program series, "The Computer Programme," started from the point
of view of a presenter who appeared to be new to the subject and who asked
experts the kinds of questions that most newcomers wish to know about.

Thirdly, it appealed across the barriers of age, sex, and social class which
often divide adult learners from one another: it showed both men and women
of all ages and in a large variety of occupations using computers not just
because the machines existed but because they had discovered how computers
could be used for their own purposes. Finally, unlike many of the computing
courses in Britain (Banks, 1984; EOC, 1983), the standard of the teaching
and presentation was extremely high.

Banks's (1983) study of local computer literacy classes for adults in
England has given further support to the idea of offering a central point at

which to begin and then making various options available once an informed choice could be made. He suggested that providers might "view introductory computing classes as a place where students can be acquainted with a whole range of issues within the panorama of computers and computing, so that they can focus their generalized interest into a discrete area which has relevance to themselves. Stemming from this 'sampler' core, perhaps it is possible to generate a whole compass of courses/packages, each package being tailored to a specific audience." As we have seen above, this strategy of specific courses for specific interests within computing is already widely used in the United States.

The strategy of providing many paths toward computer literacy has recently been carried still further by the BBC, while the sales of the first two television series throughout much of the developed world suggest that the model is highly acceptable outside Britain as well. During 1984, the BBC continued to transmit the two original series, but has also presented further series which aimed to explore more specialized aspects of computing for more narrowly defined audiences. "Computers in Control" aimed to "introduce viewers, many of whom will have microcomputers of their own, to the principles behind their use in monitoring and controlling the physical world" (*Computerfax,* 1984). Meanwhile, "The Electronic Office" has explained and explored the revolution in office technology, while "Will Tomorrow Work?" provided "an examination of the fundamental problems of unemployment and recession in the Western World, viewing the current economic situation as a transitional post-industrial period in which it is essential to consider the role of technology and the nature of work in the future" (ibid).

For 1985, the same strategy will apply. There are plans for television series on "The Learning Machine," which aims "to give parents, teachers, children, and other users, a better understanding of how computers can assist learning, and to help develop an informed approach to the choice and use of educational software" (ibid). There is also likely to be a series on "Technology and the Handicapped."

An analogous strategy underlies some of the work on computers and computer-related technology in the newly developed "modules" being offered by the 16–18 Action Plan in Scotland for the first time in the autumn of 1984, and intended to be made available to adults, as well as to younger students. The module on "Social Implications of Computer Technology" specifies that the student should "identify the effects of microelectronics in the world of work" and then allows a choice among identifying the effects of microelectronics in the home, in leisure, or of information technology on society. The specification of the learning outcome for identifying the effects of microelectronics in leisure may not necessarily appeal to all adults, as it is suggested that "the student should use and study a variety of computer games but select one particular area for study in depth"; possibilities specified for detailed study include fruit machines, space invaders, and video games (SED, 1984). But the overall strategy of starting from a beginning common to all and then providing a choice of paths is likely to remain attractive to adults seeking to acquire computer literacy.

Computer Literacy Exhibitions

The pressure of the search for new markets for computer equipment and programs has ensured that there are frequent public computer exhibitions designed to encourage buyers. For a number of obvious reasons, these purely commercial exhibitions contribute little to general computer literacy; rather, they tend to raise public expectations that computers are glamorous and desirable objects to be sought for their own sake, and that buying a computer can answer most human problems.

The strategy of making computers available in public places for casual users to try their hand at the new technology, however, has been used effectively in a number of projects and is about, as this book goes to press, to be implemented on a wide scale throughout the province of Ontario in Canada. In Canada, the Ontario Ministry of Citizenship and Culture has started a project to open a total of 30 community-based computer centers, in places such as schools, public libraries, YMCA buildings, and in the United Chiefs' Council building on a native peoples' reserve. The centers are intended to foster computer literacy in the province; it is hoped that they will "speed up the process of familiarizing children of every age, their parents, and anyone else in the community with microcomputers" (McLean, 1984). The multiple computers in each location will run programs including LOGO (a programming language which will be discussed later in this chapter), word games, music construction, and various writing aids, but they will not contain the sophisticated programs which are essential for serious business use. Access to the computers will be free for children for at least two hours a day, but fees may be charged for access by adults. The fact that the sponsoring community organizations are required to keep "evaluative records of use and success of the centres" (McLean, ibid) may mean that after some time it will be possible to assess the outcomes of such a provision in a more comprehensive way than has been possible with other community computer exhibitions in Britain and the United States.

Since 1979, however, there have been extensive experiments with public computer exhibitions. In the United States, perhaps the best known of these have been those mounted by Computertown USA, the computer literacy project which received funding from the National Science Foundation to enable it to experiment with providing computer literacy in local communities. Since 1982 in Scotland, there has been a series of computer exhibitions mounted by the Scottish Community Education Microelectronics Project (SCEMP); while they have not been rigorously evaluated, observations made at these exhibitions have led to some general conclusions about the possible value of such an approach to computer literacy. There have also been series of public exhibitions of computer-based videotex equipment in both Britain and in Canada which have been more systematically evaluated; because they are primarily concerned with providing computer-based information, they will be discussed further in Chapter 4.

Meanwhile, let us visit some neighborhood forms of computer literacy. A ComputerTown had been defined as "any public access computer literacy project. It is a group of individuals, adults and children, helping each other become informed citizens of today's information society. A ComputerTown's goal is to offer an informal educational opportunity for everyone in the community to become 'computer literate'" (Loop et al., 1983). The organizers hoped that adults who want access to microcomputers but who have no idea of where to begin their search, would be able to move through the stages of computer literacy, which they characterized as "Computer Comfort," "Computer Awareness," and "Computer Tool Use" (ibid).

The project organizers believed that there are four main things which people learn in free-access computer exhibitions in their own neighborhood:

> First, people discover that computers don't bite—they don't explode, and spit fire as in the science fiction portrayals, and they don't attempt to take control of the world or order the hapless beginner around.
>
> Second, people begin to see the versatility of computer technology. By experiencing games, simulations, and rudimentary BASIC programming, adult visitors . . . began to formulate their own answers to the question, 'How could I use a computer?'
>
> Third, by actually pressing keys and operating the machine themselves, people gain practical knowledge of how to use a computer. Once a minimal threshold of confidence and interest is crossed, many people choose to take short classes in computer programming or the use of application software or computer-assisted instruction.
>
> Fourth, in every real computer environment, people see some examples of machine failure and many examples of apparent machine failure which usually turn out to be user generated. Visitors discover that everyone makes mistakes, even computer experts; that machines are usually reliable but not infallible; and that each of us can learn to use computers if we keep an exploratory attitude and don't quit (Loop et al., 1983).

The spread of ComputerTowns from their original source in California is in itself an indication of public welcome for the strategy. The organizers have found, as have all other comparable projects, that entirely unresticted public access was not as effective as making separate provision for adults and children. And they have sometimes seen advantages in making special provision for older adults, who tend to be hesitant about exploring computers when in the presence of younger, apparently more knowledgeable people. Funding for the project ended in the autumn of 1984, however, and it does not look as if the idea will be resurrected in precisely the same form again.

In Scotland, the main purpose of the SCEMP public computer exhibitions was "to provide a gentle introduction to computers in a way that is not available anywhere else" (SCEMP, 1983). Throughout 1982 and 1983, SCEMP mounted major and minor public computer exhibitions throughout Scotland, with the help of local community organizations, in locations as varied as sports centers, public libraries, pubs, theaters, health centers, community centers, and voluntary organizations. Each exhibition contained at least one computer, and sometimes a bank of computers, with a variety of educational and educative programs, including several of those discussed earlier in this chapter.

The general evidence from the organizations which supported the exhibitions was that there seemed to be an enthusiastic public response to them. In most locations there were frequent queues behind the users, with crowd conditions prevailing at peak times (SCEMP, 1982b). An account by the community education service which organized the exhibitions in Fife is representative of the careful preparation that went into them and of the enthusiastic public response:

> The exhibiton was projected . . . as the 'Fife Friendly Computer Roadshow' and was widely advertised in local newspapers, through schools and colleges, by personal invitation to members of existing . . . computer appreciation classes and other persons and groups deemed to be interested. This was supported by an attractive poster/brochure. . . . News items appeared in various newspapers. . . . The use of computers was shown to be within the grasp of all and emphasised their elementary and useful applications including . . . learning. . . .
>
> The exhibition provided more than 345 hours of public access with daily sessions in the mornings, afternoons, and evenings. . . . During the sessions at least one person with elementary knowledge of computers was on duty to advise and guide.
>
> The support from the public was most encouraging as is shown by the total recorded attendance figure of persons who spent some time at a computer, . . . 5,825, a considerable proportion of which were adults of all ages. . . . More than 90% of those seeking information had not had any previous experience with computers and many indicated an interest in obtaining further experience by requesting details of vocational and non-vocational courses available. . . .

The Roadshow was a great success in focussing the attention of the public on the presence and possibilities of the compact computer in everyday life and a visit offered the opportunity as a taster, of 'hands-on' experience. In summary, it was well attended, interesting, educational and an extremely worthwhile event. The timing caught both the mood and need of the public, the great majority of whom have a real worry, even fear, of these instruments of technological change (Urquhart, 1983).

There has not, unfortunately, been any detailed assessment of the impact of the exhibitions on those who attended; attempts to persuade users to complete brief feedback forms met with little success. Observers reported generally, however, findings which confirmed the experience of ComputerTowns that young people responded differently to computers than did adults, and that women and older adults were the most reluctant users except where they were offered specific encouragement away from the presence of children and young men (SCEMP, 1982b).

Since the idea for the exhibitions in Scotland was first mooted in 1981, public experience of computers has expanded considerably in Britain, where at least a million miocrocomputers are being bought every year. SCEMP is, therefore, no longer mounting such substantial public exhibitions but is instead trying to meet the rather more specific needs which it has identified through the wider public exposure to computers. Here again, as in the provision of courses, the most effective strategy seems to be one of an initial broad introduction to the potential and the practicalities of using computers, followed by opportunities to pursue the interest in more specific and carefully defined ways.

How widely diverse the needs served by computer exhibitions are may be seen in a small sample of the questions asked at one ComputerTown event, which are characteristic of those also frequently encountered in the SCEMP exhibitions:

Do you have anything for sale?

Which of the small color computers should I get for my kid as an educational toy?

How many kinds of computers are there? How do I know which one to buy? . . .

What career opportunities would be facilitated by my knowing about computers? How do I go about exploring a career in the field?

What are computer languages and how do they work? What is the difference between BASIC, Pascal, and the other languages I hear about? Which would be most useful to learn?

What is the job of a program? How does it work? Would it be difficult for me to learn to program? . . .

What good is the machine beyond playing games? . . .

How does a machine store data? Where does it store it?

What is the difference between hardware and software? . . .

When do I know that I need to move something onto the computer that I have been doing by hand? . . .
How do I know I am getting good software?
Who sells software? . . .
Is there a beginner's magazine or book? . . .
If I have a complex problem in terms of putting hardware and software together, who can help me?
Should I plan on doing my own programming, or can I get by without knowing how to program? . . .
How often do microcomputers break down?
Can I get a broken machine fixed without difficulty? (Loop *et al.*, 1983)

The range of interests and needs represented by such questions is enormous and daunting. Full answers to all of them would require the combined skills of educational computing specialists, systems analysts, computer programmers, career advisers, and computer technicians, all of whom would need to be able to communicate their specialist knowledge without using jargon! But the vitality of the questions and the craving for knowledge and information which they express must represent one of the most exciting situations ever presented to community educators. ComputerTowns, the SCEMP exhibitions, and other experiences like them have shown that it is not possible to provide full answers to all of the questions. But such exhibitions do appear to offer a welcoming learning environment in which answers can be sought and in which potential learners can be directed to more specific ways of learning about computers. As such, public computer exhibitions appear to have played, and to continue to play, a valuable role in starting learners on the path toward computer literacy.

It also seems as if their effect may extend even beyond computer literacy. In Scotland, public libraries in particular found that the exhibitions attracted "a lot of people to the library, many of whom were either infrequent or first-time visitors. Many of these were later to return as library users" (Groark, 1984). Another library also found that as a result of the exhibitions, "people are more likely to think of visiting the library in the future. . . . [The exhibitions] got people into the library who had heard of the microcomputers and came to see them but who subsequently asked if they could join the library to borrow books and records" (SCEMP, 1982b). Both membership and book issues rose dramatically during the period of the exhibitions: the number of children joining one library during the time of the exhibition increased by over three times the number in the same period of the previous year (ibid). It appears, therefore, as if computer exhibitions do not merely serve as an introduction to computer literacy, but that they may provide a pathway to learning about other things as well.

Other Forms of Computer Literacy

By analogy with the growing provision of literacy and numeracy through public "learning shops" and drop in centers, some providers of computer literacy now offer a chance to the general public to drop in spontaneously for various computer experiences, including using the keyboards of computers, exploring computer applications, learning how to program, or simply asking for objective advice about which equipment and programs might be most useful for particular purposes. In London, Microsyster offers a variety of services of this sort, while other "shop fronts" have been set up in other parts of Britain as well, including elsewhere in London, Newcastle, and Edinburgh.

The main difficulty in trying to describe projects of this sort in any detail is that both their characteristics and sometimes their very existence are subject to rapid change. Nevertheless, the flavor of such a center can be suggested through a brief account of what is, as this book goes to press, the "Microbeacon Project" in Edinburgh. In its "shop-front" premises near the center of Edinburgh, the project offers what its leaflet refers to as a "drop-in computer literacy centre." An experimental primarily voluntary project which is seeking long-term funding, it aims to provide computer literacy for a wide range of people who find conventional courses in computing inaccessible, and it hopes to develop specific learning materials and specifically tailored learning opportunities for the adults who seek it out and who would not otherwise have access to computers or computer skills ("Microbeacon," 1984). In particular, the organizers are eager to help adult basic learners to recognize realistically the limitations of computers rather than seeing them in the glorified way in which they are often presented by advertising (MacDonald, 1984).

While organizations, such as "Microbeacon," attempt to answer some of the needs of those who would not otherwise have access to computers, there has also been an explosive growth in more commercial forms of providing computer literacy for both adults and children. One of the most striking developments here has been the dramatic increase in the numbers of "computer camps" on both sides of the Atlantic. As Houser (1984) has commented, "computer holidays have become a growth industry."

Particularly for many children, computing is a leisure activity on roughly the same level as skiing or abseiling. Perhaps the most interesting feature of the "computer camps," therefore, has not been the way in which they predictably combine computing with other leisure pursuits, but rather the extent to which they have created an environment in which parents and children often choose to learn together. The Computer College at Millfield School in England, for instance, has increasingly attracted entire families. Its director comments on the phenomenon: "Some parents . . . want to know a bit about what their kids are being taught, or, like some of the solicitors we get, think it will help their careers. Others merely like the idea of computing in a social atmosphere—we even get a few grandparents who want to try to understand what their grandchildren are doing" (Houser, 1984).

The demand for such courses almost always exceeds an ever-increasing supply. Never having tried such an experiment before, Tayside Regional

Figure 6. Encouraging people of different ages to use computers. Photograph reproduced by courtesy of Apple Computer Inc.

Council in Scotland decided to offer a single residential computing weekend for parents and children. Within ten days of the advertisement, they had enough applications for three camps (McCann and McKay, 1983). The same experience has been repeated many times throughout the developed world; Figure 6 illustrates the wide age range of people using computers for enjoyment.

Despite such public enthusiasm, however, the teaching of computer literacy simultaneously to parents and children appears often to present problems, not only because of the children's preference for games if they are available, but also because children are often considerably more familiar with computers than their parents. One participant in Tayside commented that "the pace was fine for him but too slow for his 12 year old son" (ibid). Moreover, as even a cursory glance through the pictures of happy campers on computer holidays will confirm, it appears that such camps are heavily male dominated. It is possible, then, that those female learners who do attend may feel excluded from the dominant ethos and, indeed, may be disadvantaged in ways analogous to those in which girls are disadvantaged in computer studies at school.

The model created by purely commercial provision for as many learners. as possible may not necessarily, then, be one which community educators wish to follow. But computer camps rightly build on the fact that learning to use computers is a source of pleasure. The same sense of the excitement and delight of learning about computers has permeated the BBC's highly successful computer project. Indeed, it is this very sense that also lies at the heart of some of the most exciting prospects for learning about computers that have been devised for children and may now start to be used for adults as well.

New Ways of Exploring Computers

There is a great deal of common ground between the principles in use in many current developments of computer languages and learning experiences for children, and the preferences of most adult educators. Yet most of the computer educational programs which have been described earlier in this chapter tend to be based on a model of programmed learning. They may, thus, tend to induce a passive learning style which makes learning an instrumental rather than a meaningful activity, and which militates against further exploration. Moreover, at least some adults find it boring or irritating to be confronted with a predetermined range of options; one evaluation of such programs has shown that they tend to hold the interest of children for much longer periods than they interest adults (Swinfield, 1984). And most adult educators would reject a model of learning which provides a high degree of external control over the activities of their students; they would prefer instead to aim at enabling students to be responsible as far as possible for their own learning. Even in computer programs for children, it has been argued that the greater the didactic control, the less meaningful is the teaching (O'Shea and Self, 1983).

One possible solution to this problem would be the development of computer programs which allowed a more natural dialogue between the user and the program, by analogy with the exploratory responsive dialogue which flows between a tutor and his or her students. A number of computer programs have been developed which have some ability to handle natural language within their own highly specialist subject area, such as SOPHIE (Brown, Burton, and Bell, 1975) and GUIDON (Clancey, 1979). Such programs are not commercially available, however; even if they were, their cost would be likely to make them inaccessible to adult education, because they are expensive both in the time taken to develop them and in the size of the computer system which they require.

Already in many schools and homes in Britain, France, and North America, however, there are examples of computer programs which encourage children to explore the possibilities of computer language, of how computers work, and to become more aware of their own thought processes. They are within the relatively modest price range of the kinds of programs which have been discussed earlier in this chapter, and their characteristics match to an encouraging degree the kinds of learning which most adult educators would desire for their students.

The general approach of such programs, which are primarily based on the use of LOGO, an interactive programming language derived from work in artificial intelligence, has been summarized by O'Shea and Self (1983):

> The main claim is that the learner can express his own problem-solving strategy as a computer program and then 'stand back' and watch himself, as embodied in the computer program, solve problems. Having stood back, he can then reflect on his way of doing things and remove faulty methods and improve components of his strategy. In general, then, there is an emphasis on the process (rather than the product) of problem-solving, and an aversion to the 'right or wrong' model of learning.

LOGO is a computer language which enables even young children quickly to master the rudiments of being able to command a computer to do as they wish—usually to be able to draw a wide variety of shapes—by way of a systematic and easily learned set of instructions. Primarily designed for children, according to Piaget's theories about the progression of children from the stage of concrete thinking to that of formal thinking, it has rarely been used in adult education, apart from teacher training; the Open University's

"Micros in Schools" pack for teachers, for example, teaches users the principles and practice of LOGO.

The main response which adults using LOGO have reported, and which I have found through my own use of it, is that it is enormous fun. It also provides an enhanced sense of one's ability to master a computer, while enforcing a need for highly rigorous, self-directed thinking. It appears, as well, to be helpful in refreshing one's mind about, or acquiring for the first time, an understanding of a number of fundamental mathematical ideas.

Large claims (Papert, 1980) have been made for the extent to which LOGO can liberate children's learning, and it is doubtful if such claims could be sustained for its possible use in the education of adults. Nevertheless, its approach offers positive ways ahead for the use of computers in adult education in the future. It accepts errors or misjudgments as easily correctable; its use conveys a sense of genuine achievement through developing one's own powers of thought, and it rewards careful systematic dealing with problems.

Gill (1984) has called for the funding of artificial intelligence work which would refer specifically to adult learners. Such a Utopia may be yet some way off: most governments in the developed world have put few or no resources toward the use of computers in adult or community education, and most work in artificial intelligence is directed toward possible industrial applications. Nevertheless, the advantages offered to children through the use of computer languages, such as LOGO, expand the possibilities of computer-based learning for adults. The onus now falls on community educators to explore further all the kinds of ways in which computers can be used throughout adult learning and to see how they can adapt to the needs of their students some of those forms of exploratory learning now being made available to children.

A SOBER LOOK AT COMPUTERS AND ADULT LEARNING

Throughout this chapter, I have been suggesting that learning by and about computers presents community educators with an enticing, fascinating, and challenging opportunity for development both now and in the next decades. But major obstacles are also likely to lie ahead for educators who try to respond wholeheartedly to this challenge, and it would be foolhardy and indeed dishonest not to recognize how formidable the task is.

The enormity of the task that lies ahead has been spelled out by Trudel and Belanger (1982):

> While it took 150 years to realise the industrial revolution, it will take only
> 20 years to make the micro-electronic revolution. Adults who have already had

to adapt themselves to many changes will have their capacity to adapt submitted
to a severe test. Consequently, adult education, one of whose most important roles
is to help give individuals the tools necessary to face the complexity and rapidity
of change, will have to multiply its efforts and energies. Only that way will adult
education serve these new needs.

In trying to achieve this new task, however, community education as a
whole, and adult education in particular, will face obstacles that are almost
as formidable as the task itself is essential. In its survey of "Microtechnology
and the Education of Adults," ACACE (1984) identified, in descending order
of importance, some of the major constraints on increasing the provision of
computer literacy to cope with the rising demand for learning about computers.
They are funding, tutors, machines, software, sharing of information, organization and development, and accommodation. Each of these will require
serious attention even before we start to look at the perhaps even more onerous
constraints on helping adults to learn by computers.

Funding for adult education throughout most of the developed world has
tended generally not to keep pace with rising costs. Where computer literacy
courses have been offered, it has often been at the expense of other forms of
provision or on a self-financing basis. While there is clearly a healthy demand
even for profit-making courses in this area, as we have seen in the computer
camps discussed above, many community educators will feel serious reservations about having to charge the kinds of sums that purely self-financing
courses might require. And, of course, self-financing courses by definition
exclude many people for whom computer literacy is not available in alternative
ways. The cost of financing the purchase of sufficient, good computer equipment for use in computer literacy classes is also usually well outside the
budget of most providers of informal adult education, although, as we shall
see below, it is often possible to acquire the equipment in other (legal!) ways.

The next major constraint is that of staffing. There is a shortage of
computer experts generally, and an even more dire shortage of computer
experts who have been trained in teaching adults. The problem is further
exacerbated by the fact that many communication practices within the computing industry are diametrically opposed to what would normally be accepted
as good practice in adult education. As Knowles (1983) reports:

> The computer industry doesn't understand how adults learn. . . . Software
> producers and manual writers . . . understand how the machine works but have
> no idea about how adults learn. Consequently, their software and manuals are
> geared to teaching us how the machine works rather than helping us learn how
> to use the machine to perform the real-life tasks we buy it to perform for us.

The problems created in England by using tutors who are specialists in computing but who are not trained and experienced in teaching adults have been studied by Banks (1984) in his investigation into students' responses to introductory evening classes in computing in Leeds. He found that 77% of the students thought that the tutors seemed to know a lot about the subject, but that "nearly half of the interviewed students did not consider the tutor to be a good teacher." In Surrey, interviews with students showed a much higher degree of satisfaction with the tutor, and Banks speculates that the greater concern with the selection, training, and monitoring of tutors at the adult education center in Surrey may be one explanation.

Paradoxically, in such an apparently highly technological field as computing, there is some evidence to suggest that the best tutors of adults may not be those who have an expert command of the field but rather those who are skilled in tutoring adults and who have acquired a knowledge of computers as amateurs. In the United States, many educators are now finding that "the best instructors are people who had to struggle to learn how to program or use software applications themselves, because they empathize with students and have the patience to work with computer neophytes" (Schmidt, 1985). In Britain, Salkeld (1983) has commented on the numbers of effective tutors who, trained as adult educators but not professionally trained in the use of computers, learned together with their students in computing courses to support the BBC's Computer Literacy Project.

The availability of equipment on which to teach computer literacy is not in itself a major problem; many projects seem readily to be able to get hold of as much equipment as they need by borrowing it from educational institutions and using students' own computers. But using appropriate equipment presents a more serious problem. In the first place, there are significant differences between the kinds of microcomputers which might be used at home and those which are for serious business purposes, so there may be difficulties in acquiring equipment specifically suited to the purpose. Secondly, there is the problem of the wide variety of equipment now available on the market. If a course attempts to introduce students to a variety of possibilities, difficulties may easily arise because of the slightly different ways of operating each machine.

According to ACACE, the problem of finding good computer programs for use in computer literacy courses comes fairly well down the list of difficulties. This assessment is not generally supported by the actual experience of most adult educators who have been involved in using computer programs. The very poor quality of most directly educational programs has already been commented on and will be considered again below. But even in the realm of programs written for commercial applications there are many gratuitous problems that can easily create difficulties for new learners.

The problem of sharing information among those adult educators who are concerned with computer literacy is often a real one. Most of the established ways of exchanging information about computer literacy are to be found within the organizations and journals devoted to educational computing for schools. Within individual countries, information sharing about computer literacy for adults seems often to be only one function among many of the agencies whose main interests lie in formal education, although in Scotland, SCEMP has been able to provide a national focus for such information sharing. In general, however, this constraint is likely to substantially diminish over the next few years, as the topic becomes more and more common as part of national and international conferences and journals of adult and community education.

Organization, development, and accommodation tend to present lesser, but still real constraints for some providers of computer literacy. As we have seen, the variety of the demand can create problems for organizers who have the facilities to offer only a few classes. Accommodating computers often makes the kind of demands on power points and for security which may not be needed for more traditional forms of provision. But the main problem here is simply the fact that offering computer literacy to adults is such a relatively new activity that organizers often find it difficult to see clearly the directions in which they should try to develop their provision.

Most of these constraints also apply, of course, to the use of computers as a tool rather than as a subject in adult learning. Here, however, the most serious problem is the fact that very many of the educational programs so far available tend to be questionable in their educational assumptions. Particularly in Britain, where amateur development has been encouraged, programs are sometimes technically defective and academically inaccurate as well. Walker (1983) cites a typical example: "I once asked a program designer about the source of his data in some published packages and discovered that they consisted of random numbers. Although he had intended to replace them with genuine data, somehow this crucial step was overlooked."

In 1984 in Britain, too, the Mathematical Association found serious mathematical deficiencies in four of the mathematics microcomputer programs produced by the main government-sponsored agency in the field in England, Wales, and Northern Ireland—the Microelectronics Education Programme. Among the examples cited are the assumptions in a program called "What Shape" that "all squares with four equal sides are squares and . . . that a triangle always has only one sloping side" (Fairhall, 1984).

In Scotland, unwitting evidence of the kinds of deficiencies that have been found in programs designed for community education is found in SCEMP's "Guidelines for the Design of Computer Programs for Community Use." The kinds of questions which the "Guidelines" suggest should be asked in checking programs are a damning testimony to the quality of much of the software available. The questions include: "Are the instructions to the user clear?" "Have mysterious system messages been . . . eliminated?" "Does it always assume that both sexes will use the program?" "Are all the sentences grammatical?" "Is the punctuation correct?" "Are the instructions to the user . . . clear?" "Are the instructions consistent?" (SCEMP, 1982c). That such questions need to be asked at all for any educational computer program intended for general community use implies that they could be answered with "No."

One important reason behind the prevalence of many poor educational computer programs is simply that it is so time-consuming to develop good programs, and even to learn, as a consumer, how to discriminate good programs from bad. Estimates about the length of skilled programming time required to produce and document a single computer package that could be worked through by a student in one hour range from 50 to 500 hours (Megarry, 1983). The Open University reports that "to produce thirty minutes of interesting activity for students at a terminal takes several persons months of activity. . . . The minimum required to produce this half-hour is one month of an academic's time and one month from a member of the Academic Computing Service" (Scanlon, Jones, O'Shea, Murphy, Whitelegg, and Vincent, 1982).

The development of educational computer programs for adults is likely to be economically viable only if there is a sufficiently large market for the final product. Clearly, community education, with its attempts to meet the specific needs of individual communities, is not likely to provide such a mass market apart, possibly, from programs which offer general introductions to computer literacy. This problem is perhaps the most serious constraint on developing the uses of computers in adult education, although, as we have seen earlier in this chapter, there are many ways of adapting for adults programs that have been prepared for other purposes.

Just as educational resources for promoting the use of computers in community education are scarce, so, also, there has been only meager funding of projects intended to harness the power of computers to the benefit of the community as a whole. One of the major tasks confronting community educators for the foreseeable future will be to find ways in which the power of computers can serve the whole community, and not just those members who can afford to pay for such empowerment; it is a task that acquires even greater urgency in those countries where it is government policy to withdraw the state as far as possible from providing social and economic benefits.

As with the uses of computers in adult learning, there is no panacea for action in using computers for community development, and there are serious constraints on how far it may be possible to do so. But there are a number of projects which take advantage for the wider community of what computers can now offer and which suggest possible models for future development, as well as contributing to the development of computer literacy for those people who take part in them. It is to these that we shall now turn.

4

USING COMPUTERS
IN THE
COMMUNITY

"A merely well-informed man is the most useless bore on God's earth"
A. N. Whitehead.

There are a number of reasons why organizations within community education in its widest sense have been exploring how computers can be used for the benefit of the communities which they serve. The ethos behind such developments has already been suggested in Chapter 1: it is that the use of computers in community education could play a part in ameliorating those social effects of computers which appear to be damaging. Computers are also potentially powerful tools which community educators could use in the day-to-day running of their organizations and in improving the services which they offer to the public. Moreover, as Chapter 3 has suggested, the use of computers in community organizations can be one way of providing computer literacy to members of staff and to the wider public who actually use the computers.

Another important reason, referred to throughout this book, is the widespread enthusiasm for using computers. Many people prefer to use computers for education and information, particularly in situations which seem to be emotionally sensitive, such as the fear of failure in learning basic skills or enquiries about drinking habits. We have already seen in Chapter 1 that people are more likely to tell the truth to computers than to other people. Ample evidence also exists of preferences for computers. In Britain, the Research Institute for Consumer Affairs found that 85% of those people whom it questioned found that computers were more informative than the staff of the Department of Health and Social Services, while 58% preferred computers to social workers (Schofield, 1984). In the United States, there is now a rapidly growing market for computer programs for psychological self-assessment and behavior modification (ibid).

Many community educators are likely to feel uneasy about exploiting a technology which people prefer to other people, and the light which such preferences throw on those who hold them, as well as on the actual practice of many professional staff, is often harsh. The moral and ethical assumptions built into many of the programs, particularly some of those marketed for behavior modification, are sometimes offensive. Nevertheless, using computers for specific purposes in community groups can provide one valuable way of helping groups of people to cohere and to be able to focus on their common aims. In Scotland, for example, the use of computers in the project, Computerized Information for the Disabled, has boosted confidence, improved employment skills, and given a chance, which the participants have seized eagerly, for social integration (Clark, 1984). Similarly, the use of computers in an educational project in a prison in Edinburgh has resulted in an impressive degree of cooperation among the men involved, who have gained useful skills, self-respect, and a constructive use of their time. The report concludes: "It is some time now since I have encountered such a high level of enthusiasm for a project at the prison" (Whyte and Fluendy, 1984).

The extent to which computers can provide an initial attraction for people who then go on to other learning experiences has also been amply demonstrated. In Scotland, there were noticeable increases in enrollments in educational courses and an increase in the use of libraries following computer exhibitions (Laidlaw, 1984). The impressive figures for enrollments in computer literacy courses in Britain and Canada, and the sales of microcomputer equipment and programs, provide irrefutable evidence on a wider scale of the extent of public enthusiasm for computers.

To some extent, however, the real test of the value of using computers in community organizations must be based on the responses of those organizations which have had a chance to use them. Here the experience of the Scottish Community Education Microelectronics Project (SCEMP) has provided important evidence about the extent to which community organizations want to use computers. Despite a lack of publicity about the fact that its computers could be loaned for short periods of experimenting with them, and despite the often highly disadvantageous terms on which the computers were offered, SCEMP had more applications than it had computer systems available (SCEMP, 1982b); indeed, from the inception of the project in 1981 to the time that this book goes to press, there has always been an excess of applications over systems available.

But it may be argued that the real test lies in what happened in the organizations after the computer loans had ceased. Nearly all of the organizations found that they were unable to secure funding from central or local government for the purchase of their own systems. Nevertheless, nearly all of them proceeded to acquire their own computers. The two exceptions to this general pattern did not do so because, in one case, there was no computer program available for their particular needs and, in the other case, they were unable to obtain sufficient funding; however, the first of these two organizations declared that they would be happy to use a computer, if a suitable program could be devised, and the second said that "because of apparent benefits to our service, our eventual aim is to acquire a computer" (ibid).

Throughout Britain, Canada, and the United States, the considerable growth in the numbers of community organizations and groups who use computers in their work is further evidence of how valuable community education has already found computers to be, despite the serious limitations of cost and the relative lack of programs that precisely meet their specific needs (Woods, 1984). But what are they using them for? And, equally important, what are they *not* using them for? Before answering such questions by looking at several case studies of the use of computers in community organizations in Britain and the United States, I should like briefly to consider what it is that computers offer to community organizations. After presenting the case studies, I shall try to draw some general conclusions about the factor to consider in deciding whether to computerize and I shall suggest some of the processes involved. Chapter 5 will then take a wider look at the more general issues involved by depicting detailed accounts of the actual experience of computerizing.

VARIETIES OF COMMUNITY COMPUTER APPLICATIONS

So far, community organizations and groups who use computers have been mainly concerned with using microcomputers for their own immediate purposes, and, to a considerably lesser extent, with using computer data bases available through systems such as videotex. The two main models for the use of computer applications have been most usefully characterized by Menzies

(1981), in an adaptation of terms originally used by Nora and Minc (1980), as *télématique* and by Lussato and Bounine (1979) as *privatique*.

Nora and Minc envisage *télématique* as a vast electronic highway accessible to anyone anywhere for virtually any conceivable purpose related to information; organizations using such a model would be likely to have all of their information functions integrated with one another and would have extensive electronic communications with other organizations as well. The cost of implementing such a model makes its adoption unlikely in community education. Its tendency toward centralization also tends to make it an undesirable path to follow; in any case, the needs of most community organizations rarely tend to be the size of those of multinational corporations!

The more likely model for community use is *privatique*, where each user of a computer system tends to be self-sufficient and has relatively little need for communication with central computers or large data bases. Such an approach enables computer equipment and programs to be used for the specific purposes of individual organizations and communities without the need to conform to centralized specifications.

In fact, the two approaches are by no means mutually exclusive. It is possible, for instance, while using a microcomputer in an office primarily for the specific purposes of that office, also to use it as a way of accessing larger data bases, such as those available through "The Source" in the United States, Prestel in Britain, and Telidon in Canada, or of communicating with microcomputers in other organizations. As discussions below will suggest, the amount of information which such sources currently provide, which is of potential value to community education, is still relatively scarce, although it is likely to grow considerably in Britain in 1985 with the introduction on Prestel of detailed information about formal educational opportunities.

Bearing in mind the potential of further developments in such *télématique* approaches, the practical reality in the mid 1980s appears to be that most community organizations will want to explore, at least initially, a *privatique* model for their own development of computer services. Apart from an account of the kind of information provided by large data bases later in this chapter, then, most of the discussion that follows is based on the *privatique* model.

The kinds of organizations who may want to make use of the variety of applications now available and continually being developed are indicated in the range covered by a competition in 1984 by *The Guardian* newspaper in Britain. *The Guardian* noted that microcomputers can be particularly useful and cost-effective in charity work and offered complete computer systems to charities who described the most interesting, innovative, and potentially beneficial uses of microcomputers in their work. The charities concerned included ones working in fields involving children, disabled and handicapped people, unemployed people, elderly people, medical research, youth work, community development, health, and housing (*The Guardian,* 1984). Other kinds of organizations which may find the use of computers helpful include pressure groups, who already use them widely in the United States for the keeping of records about specific groups of people and for the mailing of individualized letters to carefully selected target groups, among many other purposes. Woods (1984) also notes their use in tenants' associations, political groups, sports and hobby clubs, and women's groups.

As this book goes to press, the results of *The Guardian* competition have not yet been announced, but they will doubtless enlarge considerably the range of applications that are already in use. Meanwhile, there appear to be a range of activities within community organizations for which microcomputers are particularly well suited. Their main advantages appear to stem from their capacity to handle data which need to be altered in specific ways, to do repetitive work or work which varies in systematic ways, to sort large amounts of information under various headings, and to perform fast calculations. They are, thus, particularly useful in word processing, including the preparation of material that requires frequent alterations, and that needs to be of publishable quality, such as newsletters, or leaflets, or even books. They are also very useful for indexing and cataloging; maintaining mailing lists; addressing labels; keeping membership and subscription payments up-to-date and other forms of invoicing; analyzing the results of surveys; keeping detailed accounts; and preparing financial plans.

It is notoriously difficult to assess the differences that the use of computers might make to the amount of work that is carried out by an organization. A rough guide is suggested by McWilliams (1982): in a small organization: "a personal computer could allow two persons to do the work of three and three to do the work of five." As many community organizations tend to be relatively short of paid staff, there are obvious attractions in being able to increase both the quantity and the quality of the work done by introducing computerization. While it scarcely counts as a voluntary organization, the experience of the Greater London Council in Britain is promising here. It has calculated that 60% of the benefits from computerization have consisted of improvements in the quality of its information services, with 30% of benefits being found through staff savings, and 10% on the extra volume of activity made possible by computerization (Goodman, 1984).

Many of the same advantages for computerization have been claimed by community organizations participating in SCEMP. One participant reported that wordprocessing "is undoubtedly a great time-saver—in our case specifically for up-dating the monthly diary and also for the production of papers, training handbooks, and similar items which go to several drafts before the final copy. A recent example was when changes to the Constitution were made, which went to eight drafts before it was approved" (SCEMP, 1984). Another organization taking part in SCEMP concluded that use of the computer "has resulted in improved efficiency, is time-saving, and it is taking the drudgery out of the administration as well as the collection, co-ordination and dissemination of information, thus supporting neighbourhood workers in giving more time to the care and development of people and the community" (SCEMP, 1982b).

At the same time, however, there are many things which community organizations would like to do with computers that microcomputers cannot really deal with efficiently. In particular, the possibility of creating data bases of community information has attracted many organizations, but the result has generally been disappointing for a number of reasons. The first problem is that most of the commercially available data base programs tend to require a fairly high level of technical expertise, if they are to be used effectively. The second problem is that the amount of data that can be stored on most microcomputer systems is rarely large enough to enable the kinds of rapid searches which might be effective. In Scotland, for example, when information about the courses available in distance education was stored on disks for the most commonly available educational microcomputer in Britain, three different disks were required (Paine, 1984), thereby drastically reducing any convenience and value that the data base might have for the user. A third problem arises from the time involved in transferring the necessary information onto the computer from the various, often inconsistent, formats in which it already exists. For many smaller information data bases which are possible on microcomputers, "the file box with 3×5 cards will do just as well as a computer and cost . . . $2000 less" (McWilliams, 1982).

As these illustrations suggest, the "paperless office" is likely to remain a long way off for most community organizations! But the ways in which computers have already been successfully used in community organizations are sufficiently varied and productive to warrant a closer look at some specific projects before trying to tease out those factors which appear to have contributed to their success.

CASE STUDIES

Because of the existence in Scotland since 1981 of a government-sponsored project to encourage the uses of computers in community education, there are particularly rich Scottish examples of the very varied uses to which computers may be put by community organizations using the *privatique* model.

In the discussion which follows, I shall draw mainly upon these examples before ranging more widely in the next section on information data bases stored on large central computers, which share many characteristics of the *télématique* model.

The distance that has been measured in the use of computers in community education during the first three years of SCEMP has been summed up by the Chairman of the original SCEMP Management Committee: "The question that community workers are asking now is not 'What can we do with a computer?' but 'What resources do we need to do this task on a computer?' " (SCEMP, 1984). Throughout, the emphasis of SCEMP has lain on developing experimental uses for computers in community education. It is notable, however, that the immediate value of computers for use in administration, particularly in word processing, is so great that, once the computers actually went on loan to organizations who had requested them for experimental purposes, the "main interest often returned to administration" (Laidlaw, 1984).

The experimental uses of computers in community education in Scotland were encouraged through SCEMP by a series of "placements," or loans, of computers with a variety of community organizations who wanted to use them in innovative ways. The essential criteria for the placements were that acceptable proposals must:

1. Contribute to the development of community education;
2. *EITHER* develop further the achievement of earlier placements *OR* extend the range of achievement by providing variety of placement;
3. Allow for the appointment by SCEMP of an independent assessor to the placement; and ᴧ
4. Have the potential for success within constraints of time and support imposed by SCEMP (SCEMP, 1982b).

These constraints were so great that SCEMP warned participating organizations that placement of a computer with them might prove to be more of a hindrance than a help. Because of financial restrictions, SCEMP was able to offer only very limited support by way of advice and training, and organizations were largely thrown back on their own resources and those which they could generate from their own communities (SCEMP, 1982b). Despite these limitations, the numbers of requests for information about what SCEMP could offer so oversubscribed the equipment available that a report on the project commented that it was "as if the lid had been lifted off a pot that one supposed to have been full of cool water and discovered suddenly that it was already simmering" (SCEMP, 1982a). The range of projects which resulted was varied and promising, as the following accounts indicate.

On the island of Tiree on the West Coast of Scotland, the local community education service asked for a loan of a microcomputer "to examine the use which island communities could make of microcomputers and the implications which they may have in the day-to-day lives of the communities" (Finlay, 1984). In particular, they wanted to introduce the islanders to the basic application of such computers, to encourage people who were already interested in exploring wider uses of the equipment, and to promote computer literacy in general.

Tiree, with a population of 800, is a small, mainly agricultural island with no large industry. Here, unlike the experience on a much larger island on which a similar experiment was tried, the project was assessed as having:

> A tremendous influence on the development of computer use on the island. The Apple placement has led to the island acquiring an Apple computer to be based there permanently. This computer is used by the school and by a wide variety of community organisations. The most interesting development . . . is the use of the computer by local crofters and farm managers to enable them to keep track of their stock accounts, crop rotas, and animal prices. The project on Tiree proved that, regardless of the size of the community or its isolation, there is a use for computers (ibid).

On Tiree, the computer was based in the secondary school, where introductory sessions were provided to familiarize people with the uses and the potential uses of computers; since the school is the focal point of the community, nearly all groups meet there, so it provided a natural center for activity. In order to allow maximum access to the equipment, the janitor undertook computer training, and the machine was then based in the library attached to the school, so that people could use it whenever they wished. Because of the largely homogeneous nature of the community, it was possible to provide the farm management programs which many people wanted.

In Motherwell, an industrialized area in the west of Scotland, the loan of an Apple computer was made to the District Library for a project:

> To investigate the suitability of storing community information, in this case a local organization file, on computer . . . and to explore the impact of providing this information by means of a computer on the library staff, members of the public, and the community as a whole. . . . One of the main features of the project was that people were to be allowed to use the Apple themselves (Bennet, 1984).

The library wanted to create a data base of information about all of the organizations active within the local community—about 800 clubs, societies, and agencies. They wanted a program to enable them to do so which would fulfill certain requirements:

> Our main requirements were that it had to be simple to use, and provide the user with the name of the organisation, meeting place, meeting time, and contact person, supplemented where necessary by a short sentence explaining the aims

of the group. We also wanted a program that would be able to sort on . . . type
of organisation, place of meeting and time of meeting, allowing us to pinpoint,
for example, all self-defence groups meeting in Craigneuk on Tuesday evenings
(ibid).

As usually happens with such specific requirements, the library soon
found that it had to choose among them. The experience as reported by the
project is characteristic of the kinds of choices that community organizations
who want to use computers for public use frequently have to make:

> SCEMP provided us with a choice of three programs to choose from. The
> first, a standard commercial database package, could do all the things we required,
> but needed greater staff expertise than was available at the time. In addition, the
> computer jargon used to access the information made it unsuitable for public use,
> and as this was a major feature of the project, this program was ruled out. The
> second program considered led the user to the information he required through a
> tree structure similar to that used by Prestel. However, the program could only
> hold a limited amount of information on each organisation, and user reaction
> revealed that it involved 'pressing too many buttons.' The program we finally
> decided upon was created by SCEMP. Unfortunately, it could not sort, nor allow
> for supplements to the basic information, but it did avoid the use of jargon and
> was easy to use. The user simply selected the appropriate disc, inserted it into
> the disc drive, and typed in the kind of organisation he wanted information on,
> e.g. Tenants Association, Karate Clubs, etc. (ibid).

Assembling the information and entering it onto the computer took about
six months; for much of this time, four girls who had had computer experience
at school, were occupied in the actual work of entering the information. The
library felt, however, that the time expended had been worthwhile, although
there have been significant problems:

> From the start of the project, response from the general public and agencies
> within the District was very encouraging. . . . During the placement we received
> on average 30–40 enquiries a week for information on organisations. . . . This
> is the first time that the library service has attempted to list all organisations within
> the District, and this has further confirmed our position as a major information
> agency. . . . Having the file on computer has also meant that it can be accessed
> and updated quicker than traditional methods. This plus the facility to print off
> all, or part, of it efficiently and cheaply has confirmed that it is an ideal way to
> store information of this nature (ibid).

The problems, however, both in development and in use, have also been
notable. The impossibility of acquiring a single program that was able to meet
all of the requirements has already been noted. But there were other problems,
as well:

> The workload involved in setting it up, collecting the information, structuring
> it, staff training, publicity, etc., placed great burdens on already limited staff

resources. In addition, one particularly unfortunate incident resulted in the contents of one disc being wiped completely and because we hadn't made a back-up disc, the information had to be input again. Another problem was that as librarians we didn't know very much about computers or their application. I had never before encountered a floppy disc or disc drive and terminology, such as 'booting' and 'syntax error,' took some getting used to. We also, because of our policy of general use, had to contend with bogus clubs appearing every now and again. The Bash Street Kids, and worse, had to be erased on more than one occasion (ibid).

In the North of Scotland, in the small community of Inverurie, which has a population of about 5,000, a project for disabled people at the local community center illustrated "that microcomputers can be easily used by disabled people and can help them integrate more fully into society" (*SCAN*, 1984). The project was run through the local community education service and tried to "set up an information resource for the disabled and those working with the disabled and to integrate the able-bodied and the handicapped in a working situation" (Clark, 1984). They borrowed a SCEMP Apple computer to set up a data bank for the disabled of information about aids, organizations, employment rights, welfare rights, holidays, research, and signs and symptoms of disabilities. As a result of their experience in gathering together such information and entering it on the computer, they then decided to broaden their scope to offer bureau services, such as addressing, to local voluntary organizations, thereby varying the range of activities of the group and also giving them work experience which they could use in applying for employment.

In assessing the project, the organizer has reported that it has been of benefit to the group in many ways:

> Every member of the group has had their confidence boosted, so much so that one member has decided to try home studies via a specially adapted computer. We now have really good discussions at tea breaks, etc., whereas before they listened but rarely answered. They are now capable of deciding what should happen within the project without relying on my ideas. Some have even started to take an interest in their own appearance whereas before it was left to their parents to decide; others are making their own decisions on what they want to do now and in the future. . . .
>
> Over the last six months, each member has been given a skill that they can take into the job market and compete with everyone else. Computer operating is one of the few jobs that disabled people can do just as well as the able-bodied. . . .
>
> This aspect has become quite important to them, and they would like to cover more and more of the basic computer and word processing procedures. They hope to set up a small business using the skills they have learned, offering data base information, word processing, mailing lists, and finances. . . . Altogether this project has been a very worthwhile experience for all of us and has shown how valuable the computer can be to the disabled and the handicapped. It has proved that with a little time and effort the disabled/handicapped can operate and under-

stand computerised work and are capable of working alongside the able-bodied"
(ibid).

Another way in which computers may be used to draw people together was illustrated by a SCEMP placement of computers in Saughton Prison in Edinburgh. The intention was that a group of prisoners should be introduced to computer programming by a nearby college of further education, with the hope that they could then produce much-needed programs for use in adult literacy and numeracy. The project progressed slowly, because the men had many other commitments to fulfill as well. But it has had a dramatic effect both on the prisoners themselves and on the agencies involved. From the beginning, the group of prisoners agreed on a team approach to the writing of programs, and the report on the project commented that "the degree of cooperation amongst the programmers is impressive. . . . The heart of it is a group of men who can be and should be useful members of society—the SCEMP project is allowing this to happen, while at the same time the men gain useful skills, self-respect, and a constructive use of their time" (Whyte and Fluendy, 1984).

The agencies involved—the college, the prison, and SCEMP—have also been centripetally drawn by the use of computers into providing a "model of interagency cooperation to the benefit of all concerned. . . . The project has been something of a catalyst, drawing the College resources in to help, raising the general level of interest in computing in the education unit, and specifically stimulating the use of computers in the clerical administration of the unit" (ibid). Here, as at Inverurie, the use of computers has apparently created good working relationships among both individuals and agencies.

Another illustration of the many uses to which a computer may be put in a voluntary organization which already deals with a large amount of information may be seen in the placement of a SCEMP Cromenco computer in Network in Glasgow. As Network Scotland Limited, this organization is now relying increasingly on computerizing its administrative and some of its information work. When the SCEMP placement was originally made in 1981, however, Network, then part of the Scottish Institute of Adult Education, had no previous experience in using computers in its work of providing support services for educational broadcasting and offering a limited educational information and advisory service by telephone and post for adults in Scotland.

From the beginning, Network was committed to the possibilities of using the computer both for increasing its own internal efficiency by word processing and for up-dating public information to support its educational information services. Working together with other agencies, it created a computer file of all the information contained in a directory of opportunities in open learning in Scotland, which it was then able to up-date annually. Particularly in Scotland, with its large areas of relatively sparse population, courses in distance learning have grown dramatically in the 1980s, so computerization was an obvious way of coping with the need to make constant amendments in time for annual editions. It also used the computer to store and print out on request information about all the computer courses and clubs available in Scotland, again, an area in which constant changes are taking place. It also used the computer for cataloging educational resources held by other organizations (SCEMP, 1982b).

It was not, of course, possible for Network on its microcomputer to create the data base of the information that was most essential as a backup to its educational information and advisory service. The major need was for a data base of all the local educational opportunities available throughout Scotland, and Network had neither the staff time nor the computer storage space for the creation of such a data base. The other major difficulty which emerged was that of ensuring that the information about those educational opportunities which it did hold on its files was up-to-date and accurate. There was no standard format in which the providers of adult and continuing education presented information about their courses, and it was often difficult to obtain precise information about exactly which courses were in operation at any one time (ibid).

Despite the constraints imposed by a small staff and a relatively small computer, Network was clearly developing in promising directions that have since been strengthened, as we shall see below in the discussion about educational information. At the same time, another Scottish experiment was taking place in the provision of an equally promising kind of community information—that of welfare benefits.

Like many other voluntary organizations which offer information and advice about a wide range of matters to the general public, the Citizens Advice Bureau in Edinburgh was anxious to reduce, if possible, the often considerable amount of time that its voluntary workers had to spend just getting hold of the precise information which they needed to help their clients. They were, therefore, particularly interested in the possibilities offered by computerized sorting of information and, especially, the way in which a computer program could help in calculating an individual's entitlement to welfare benefits; this is an area where the very specific circumstances of each individual need to be matched with highly specialized information about entitlement to, and amount of, benefit. SCEMP, therefore, placed an Apple computer, together with a program on welfare benefits, intended for the general public, with the Bureau.

At that stage in Britain, the development of welfare benefits programs was still at a highly experimental stage, and there were obvious disadvantages to the particular program used: it had been developed for use in England and needed "fine-tuning" for Scotland; it would need constant up-dating; and it took a long time to work through. It, therefore, proved impossible to use for the accurate calculation of entitlement to welfare benefit. Nevertheless, it appeared to be valuable "as an educative tool by which potential claimants can assess their own position before proceeding to personal interview with an adviser" (SCEMP, 1982b). As in the case of educational information, there have been considerable developments in this field since the SCEMP placement (for a review of developments, see Ottley and Kempson, 1982). Problems remain, however, because of the complexity of the rules and regulations on the one hand and the uncertainty of clients on the other.

Another way in which communities can be helped by computer services is in the provision of unpaid or very inexpensive bureau services for voluntary organizations. A number of local authorities in Britain now provide free bureau computer services to voluntary community organizations, in an attempt to overcome the need for considerable expenditure by these organizations. There are also many analogous projects which try to bridge the gap between computers and community organizations who would like to use computers in their work but are simply not sure where to begin. Although its provisions are for women only, Microsyster, which will be considered further in Chapter 5, is a good example of such nonprofit-making projects, which have to charge for some of their services, but which offer help over a wide range of the interaction between people and computers.

The Newcastle Information Support Project (NISP) in the North-East of England forms another good example of such services. It is intended to offer "a bureau-style service, running the type of programs which its users want . . . word-processing, . . . mailing lists, simple financial management, . . . and various other forms of information storage and retrieval" (*Community Computing Network Newsletter,* 1984). The project aims to fill an unnecessary gap between community organizations and computerization, but recognizes realistically that computerization is not always the appropriate answer:

> The voluntary sector may be short on 'technical' computer expertise, but this need not be a bar to using software packages, which really do not require a specialist skill, but only a brief training and a creative interest in their uses. Project staff will be available to help people involved in project administration to develop computer programs for particular tasks, and appropriate training will also be given to those who actually type in data and use the programs. NISP will also be incorporating a more general service for voluntary organisations who either don't need to make use of the computer or don't have the staff resources available. It certainly isn't always more efficient to computerise! Often all that is necessary is

a review and reorganisation of an existing system. We therefore plan to offer
advice on improving the effectiveness of services and project management; for
example, streamlining procedures and paperwork, cataloguing reference materials
and directions to other sources of assistance (ibid).

The experiences of projects such as SCEMP, NISP, and Microsyster
consistently suggest that there is a greater demand for the services they provide
than they can hope to supply. Thus, Microsyster has had to cut back on the
visits paid by its staff to community organizations, while SCEMP has always
had far more requests for the placement of computers than it had equipment
available. There are, of course, rapidly growing numbers of profit-making
agencies which perform the same services, but there are such wide areas of
mismatch between what they offer and the needs of most voluntary organizations that they are, on the whole, irrelevant: their charges are high and their
advice is directed toward using computers to increase profit rather than for
the benefit of communities of people.

But the experiences of organizations which try to take part in the complex
interaction between people and computers also contain hints of the potentially
explosive mixture between people and computers which can bring communities and machines together but which can also drive them apart. The case
studies from SCEMP cited above illustrated the centripetal force of computers,
which drew together a group of prisoners and a local community of disabled
people. As we have seen in Chapter 3, computers, too, can draw in groups
of educationally disadvantaged adults.

Equally, computerization can seriously divide organizations against
themselves, particularly where there are unrealistically high expectations of
what a computer on the *privatique* model can achieve, where the wrong
programs are chosen, or where skill in using the computer is confined to only
a few of the staff. Voluntary organizations which computerize large portions
of their repetitive work simply because it is such an obvious use of a computer
may find that, unless handled carefully, there will be a loss in social contact
caused by the fact that fewer volunteers are needed to do many trivial tasks;
members may thus become alienated. Similarly, as has been suggested in
Chapter 2, there are dangers of creating a largely male preserve around the
computer, unless positive steps are taken to overcome the generally male bias
of the way in which the equipment is presented.

Serious work with computers requires a considerable investment of money
on the part of organizations who often find it difficult to purchase adequate
equipment. Even more importantly, it remains a substantial risk, because it
requires a considerable investment of time, in many cases the time of people
who are giving it voluntarily. To some extent, the centrifugal force of an ill-
chosen computer, poorly functioning programs, or unevenly spread expertise

in use can be counteracted by sheer commercial pressures in a profit-making body, although even there such problems can have disastrous consequences (Covvey and McAlister, 1982). But in a voluntary organization, the effects can be still more destructive, given the voluntary nature of participation in its activities. The question of how best to introduce computerization into community organizations is, therefore, a crucial one and will be considered later in this chapter.

Meanwhile, we need to consider some of the other ways in which communities can also make use of computers. Beyond the *privatique* model in which community organizations use computers within their own groups to improve the working conditions of their staff and members and to increase the quality and quantity of their public services, many organizations are turning also to the possibilities offered by the formation of large-scale data bases of information which are stored on a large central computer and are available to substantial numbers of people and organizations.

COMPUTERS AND SOCIAL INFORMATION

So far this book has been concerned largely with specific ways in which organizations involved in community education can help people in their communities to use the power of computers for education by and about computers, for easing the workload in voluntary organizations, and for enabling individuals and organizations to cooperate with one another more fully. The emphasis has lain almost entirely on the *privatique* model, in which individual microcomputers are used within particular organizations for educational, administrative, and social purposes.

But some of the purposes for which people want to use computers to serve their communities cannot be confined within that model. We have already seen how the resources available to a voluntary organization make it difficult for such a body to maintain a computer program which provides constantly up-dated information even about organizations in the local community. The need for information about educational opportunities available on a larger scale is clearly impossible to fill by individual microcomputers using the *privatique* model. Information about careers opportunities, about consumer affairs, and welfare benefits are other areas in which computerized information of a national kind is likely to be helpful.

However attractive it appears to be, the provision of social information of this kind, by way of a large central computer to which individuals and organizations have local access through the telephone system, is strewn with practical difficulties and theoretical pitfalls. Before taking a closer look at some of the many examples of publicly available computerized information systems, then, I should like to take a few exploratory steps around the perimeter of this rapidly developing territory.

The first obstacle is the practical one that it may be very helpful to groups and individuals to have certain kinds of social information, but it is in no one's commercial interest to provide such information. To cite an obvious example, people seeking information about their entitlement to welfare benefit are unlikely to be able to pay a commercial rate for such information. Unemployed poeple seeking information about careers opportunities are in a similar position. Many community educators find themselves unable to pay for the searches of literature about community education theory and practice, which could be conducted for them through data bases that already exist.

The next obstacle is that in practice many "people prefer to access their information through people rather than through machines" (Rushby, 1984). We have seen earlier that for sensitive matters perhaps even a majority of people prefer to communicate with computers rather than talking with other people. But for many forms of information, particularly information with educational implications, there is evidence that people prefer at least some access to people. In London, England, an information service about educational computing found that its enquirers overwhelmingly preferred information by way of personal visits or by letter, telephone, or published material rather than by using computers (Rushby, 1984). And, in the United States, a computerized information exchange for community organizations recognizes the need to offer help from people as well as by way of computers (*Community Computing Network Newsletter,* 1984).

There are, of course, many possible reasons for such a preference. One reason appears to be simply the fact that, failing any global *télématique* arrangement, people need a context in which they can make sense of information services: "Users need information about information services—what information services are there, what do they provide, and whom do they serve?" (Rushby, 1984). A related reason may be that computer data bases offer highly specific information which is likely to be of use only to someone who already has a precise idea of the information he or she wants. In England, one computerized information provider has found that there is "a direct correlation between the expertise and knowledge of the users . . . and the value of the final printout; the less knowledgeable the users, the less likely they are to get the information they really need" (Keel, 1984). As educational information guidance services have often found, too, there is a need for more information than can appear on a computerized data base. Even after they have acquired information about the range of provision of educational opportunities available, enquirers "need access to more detailed information and guidance based on the expertise and private knowledge of advisers" (Myers, 1983).

A further limitation in providing community information on large data bases is that, in many cases, the demand from users may be greatest for just those kinds of information which are not susceptible to handling on large computers. As Butler (1983) has found, it appears that more people who use libraries to enquire about education opportunities want information about local opportunities than about nationally available courses, although only the latter are available on a computerized data base in Britain. Similarly, Kania (1983) found that people using the computerized data bases of the Prestel system in Britain were more likely to obtain information of a light general nature rather than more specific serious information: users sought local information but were often disappointed in the result.

Nevertheless, as we have seen, there are often strong preferences for using computerized information. Kania (1983) found that 91% of users of Prestel for information said they would come back to use it again. Public response to an analogous system in Canada, Telidon, was also favorable (Wilson, 1984), while the growing number of subscribers to computerized data bases, such as "The Source" in the United States, provides further evidence of the preference for computerized information. Before concluding that such favorable responses auger well for extensive nationally available computerized data bases of social information, however, it might be worth having a closer look at exactly what information the users of such services are getting.

In the first place, some of the usage of computerized data bases consists of learning more about the specific technology itself; it can therefore be seen as one form of acquiring computer literacy, but may or may not result in gaining helpful information. In Canada, the Telidon terminal "was used mostly for learning about the technology, rather than to learn with it. Demonstrations of the system accounted for the most frequent use followed by casual exploration of the system" (Wilson, 1984). In a British study of the use of Prestel in public libraries, the type of information sought on Prestel, excluding the use of the set merely for demonstration purposes, is shown in Table 1 on page 122.

Of the information found useful, only business/financial/economic, travel/holidays, and careers/jobs rated mentions above 10%. In the United States, recent studies of the major uses of general computerized data bases, such as "The Source" and "CompuServe," also emphasize their advantages for managing financial matters, but rarely their use for educational purposes (Hawkridge, 1983).

Where services exist that allow users not merely to enquire from centralized data bases but also to be able to enter information by way of them,

TABLE 1. Information Sought on Prestel (Adapted from Yeates, 1982)

Type of information	Percent
Business/financial/economic	29
Travel/holidays	16
Employment/careers/jobs	12
News/weather/current affairs	8
Consumer information	5
Information about Prestel	5
Information about leisure activities	5
Sports results/news/events/information	4
Local information	3
Government services and publications	3
Social information and advice	3
Education	2
Scientific/technical	2
Bibliographical	2
Legal information	1

such "interactive" features clearly enlarge the possibilities considerably. Using a central computer as a way of processing information fed in by telecommunications offers the kinds of possibilities that are already being exploited by electronic mail services, computerized home shopping and banking, and so on. Here, there are considerable possibilities for community education, as electronic exchanges of information become more feasible and accessible.

One possibility here may be seen in the United States, where the Community Information Exchange uses computerized data bases and other computer services in order to help neighborhood organizations, minority enterprises, and other kinds of community organizations to find and to learn from each other and from the centralized information held by the Exchange. Because community organizations need help from people, as well as computerized forms of information, the yearly membership fee entitles users to a certain number of hours of time with the staff or with the computerized data bases or both (*Community Computing Network Newsletter*, 1984).

The main focus of the Exchange lies on networking—"people actively finding and talking to each other and learning from each other's experiences to avoid reinventing the wheel" (ibid). As well as providing computerized communications, the Exchange gives information about development projects and technical guidance on matters in demand by its members. It also acts as a clearing house for information about useful research and other reports, government programs, and so on. Such electronic exchanges have been slow to develop elsewhere, however, presumably because the cost of developing them tends to be prohibitive except where it is underwritten by external funding.

Computerized data bases are also being increasingly used to offer support for learners in community education by providing careers and educational information and advice. Here again, there is ample evidence that certain potential learners prefer such systems, at least as an initial approach. Gibbons and Simpson (1982) report that for many of the adult students using a computerized system of careers guidance, "to approach the computer seemed to be a much less threatening process than talking to a human being, at least initially. . . . You don't have to worry about your inadequacies, or the fact that you are taking up someone's valuable time." Keel (1984) cites, in detail, an example of how the use of computerized information about educational opportunities opened up possibilities that would otherwise probably have remained closed for at least one student:

> A recent example was the young man who asked for help in finding a suitable course to become a sound recordist. He was intelligent but inarticulate and profoundly suspicious of any help provided by a 'bureaucrat.' However, as soon as he saw the personal information he was being asked for was going to be processed by computer this attitude changed. The terminal gave credibility to the advice, and he became animated. His relationship with machines was better than with strangers.
>
> Between us, we processed his request . . . until at last we achieved a list of eight courses which interested him and for which he was qualified. It could otherwise have been a long, drawn-out process to have given him enough confidence to allow any adviser to point him in the right direction.

Most computerized data bases for careers advice have been prepared primarily with school-leavers in mind. These data bases offer useful ways of matching highly detailed information about the educational and training possibilities and the characteristics of various occupations with individual preferences and aptitudes. Adult educators have, therefore, experimented with adapting them for mature learners. The preference which some adults have for using such systems has already been noted. It appears that they are used most effectively, however, not on their own but as part of a process, including human advisers. What they really offer to students and potential learners is an opportunity to match their preferences with available opportunities; they cannot, and do not pretend to, assess how far each possibility is realistic for each individual. In Britain, ECCTIS, whose display on Prestel is shown in Figure 7, provides computerized information about all courses in higher education and about some courses in nonadvanced further education. But ECCTIS "as a computerised service . . . cannot aspire in any strictly defined sense to offer personal advice or counselling" (ECCTIS, 1984).

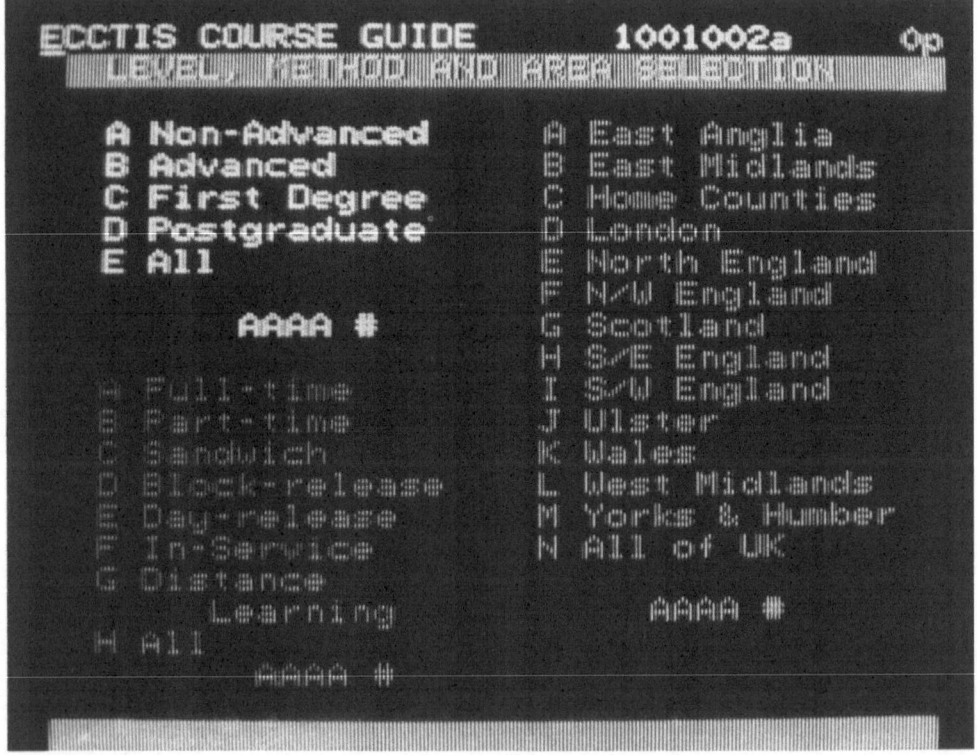

Figure 7. Computerized information about educational courses in Britain. Photographs reproduced by courtesy of Educational Counseling and Credit Transfer Information Service.

Despite the recognized need for such services to be placed within the context of human advisors, in each of these forms of potentially useful computerized community information, the emphasis on the part of the providing body or agency often seems to lie on the relative inexpensiveness of the service provided. Thus, the System of Interactive Guidance and Information (SIGI) in the United States is claimed to save "time and money for counselors and counseling offices. . . . SIGI is a cost-effective way to deliver a superior career counseling service" (SIGI, undated). In Britain, an argument for the use of ECCTIS is that is saves "quite a lot of time and energy—expensive commodities these days" (Keel, 1984).

It is important to place such claims in context. Where charges for the use of such systems are made—and they are not always made—they do not reflect the true cost of development. The development of large-scale computerized data bases costs a great deal of money and is usually funded by external agencies. In the case of ECCTIS, a large government grant was required to construct the data base, collect the information, and enter it. SIGI required the help of grants from the Carnegie Corporation, the National Science Foundation, and the W. K. Kellogg Foundation. The experimental uses of Telidon in Canada have required external funding from government, as well as a considerable expenditure of time from various institutions.

Where substantial funds are not available for development, the usual pattern is that reflected in an under-funded project for educational advisory services for adults in England. The advisory service:

> Was situated in the Central Library, occupying a small room on the 4th floor. It was sited next door to a computer terminal; and for a period of about eight months a computer clerk was employed by the library to put Educational Advice Services for Adults information onto the computer. This was a pilot scheme and because the information was never up-dated, by the time it was operational, it was of no use to the service (Midgley, 1983).

Even once the costs of development are met, the commercial viability of providing socially useful information is by no means assured. It is clear, then, that nationally available computerized data bases of socially useful information will either have to ride "piggy-back" upon more general information data bases, whose users rely primarily on financial information and transactions, or will have to receive public government or foundation funding. Current constraints on public expenditure in most of the developed world suggest that public funding of such computerized information is unlikely to expand, despite the fact that the support which can be offered to educational experiences by such information may be considerable. Funding for the *télématique* pathway for computerized community information is, therefore, uncertain.

At the same time, members of community organizations may also have reservations about the wisdom of moving along such a path. As we have seen earlier, there are already many ways in which computer systems can be maliciously entered and their contents altered, illegitimately distributed or even destroyed. The consequences of illegitimate interference in interlinking computer systems are even more devastating. There are also, as we have seen, severe limitations on the kinds of data bases that individual community organizations will be able to create for their own use: with a few exceptions, SCEMP experiments were least successful in their attempts to develop information data bases (Laidlaw, 1984). Woods (1984) has suggested that the only way of establishing a practical data base would be if a network of community computer users was developed. They could link up to a data center or could use each other's data bases for their own purposes; even here, he argues, local groups might feel that such a national network might detract from their responses to their own immediate local problems.

INTRODUCING COMPUTER SYSTEMS

At least for the present, then, it may be that community education has to explore the possibilities of the *privatique* model in its own communities, while making use, in a limited but still effective way, of the specific national data bases that already exist to provide social information. In pursuing such a path, community groups and organizations who want to develop their own uses for computers may find it helpful to note SCEMP's very practical list of the *dos* and *don'ts* of introducing computer systems into community organizations:

> *Do* have well-defined objectives within the capabilities of the machine and the programs that are available.
> *Don't* try to tackle too much and end up achieving little.
> *Do* identify a progression of steps, leading to objectives, which will be within the staff's computer expertise at the time.
> *Don't* raise expectations of early success. Disappointments are difficult to erase from people's memories.
> *Do* ensure that there is staff available to support the investment in equipment.
> *Don't* expect a computer to ease workloads initially.
> *Do* involve all members of staff in any changes.
> *Don't* allow an elite of computer-literates to emerge.
> *Do* match the calibre of the staff to the task.
> *Don't* abandon traditional methods until the computer solution is well tested
> (adapted from SCEMP, 1983).

Those community organizations who do explore the *privatique* way, at the least will have an opportunity to develop the computer literacy of their own members, as all of the organizations taking part in SCEMP found. At best they may find that they can serve their own communities better by finding nearer matches between need and provision, and by widening the scope of community education by attracting individuals who would normally not take part in community activities. Computers are no panacea for the threats to communities, but failure to take advantage of the real, if limited, opportunities which they provide is likely to make many people even more vulnerable to the antidemocratic and socially divisive tendencies in the world.

Because introducing computer systems can have a significant effect on organizations, however, it may be worth looking at examples of the actual processes involved, as well as at the ways in which community educators can support one another in such developments. Chapter 5 will pursue such practical considerations in greater detail.

5

COOPERATING
WITH COMPUTERS

*"It is in the area of cultivating cooperation that computers . . . offer us the
greatest educational possibilities"* Boyd, 1983.

During the past few years, groups of people in community organizations who
are knowledgeable about computers have found a wide variety of ways of
cooperating with each other and with their computers. The word which keeps
recurring in the accounts of their experiences is "networks." The term refers
predominantly to networks of people, but more and more often refers also to
networks of computer systems. So far, the main types of people and computer
networks which seem to have arisen are those of volunteers who give freely
of their professional or amateur computer expertise; voluntary organizations
which provide a mixture of paid and unpaid computer services to their local
communities; public bodies, such as libraries, which, despite tighter restrictions on public expenditure, are attempting to increase the computer-based
services which they offer to the community; short-term computer projects in
community education; and nonprofit-making organizations which attempt to
use computers to meet the specific needs of their members.

While any generalizations or predictions in the rapidly changing field of
computers in interaction with people are unreliable, it does seem as if some
of these models of marrying people with computers are stronger than others
and more likely to survive in an increasingly harsh financial world. The rapidly

changing responses to computers, and the shifting patterns of public expenditure mean that the categorization of the organizations discussed below may very well have changed between the time of writing and that of publication. Nevertheless, as the following case studies suggest, there appear to be a number of characteristic strengths, as well as common difficulties, which are shared by organizations who use computers for what they see as the good of the community rather than for commercial benefit.

CASE STUDIES

1. Voluntary Expertise

In developing computer literacy and in other forms of community work with computers, networks of volunteers who give freely of their time and computer expertise—whether professional or amateur—have been emerging since the late 1970s. In computer literacy, perhaps the most widely known of the networks were the linked groups which formed "Computertown USA" and "Computertown UK," which have already been briefly discussed in Chapter 3. In community work, the Community Computing Network in Britain provides a good example of the strengths and weaknesses of purely voluntary networking to humanize technology by using computers in community education.

The networks of ComputerTowns, which began in California in 1979, consisted of local, voluntary projects which aimed to provide:

> Learning opportunities for thousands of people who might otherwise be left behind in our society's rush to embrace computer technology. ComputerTown projects exist . . . as informal learning environments offering computer hardware, software, . . . print materials, and teacher intervention. They can be found in libraries, museums, Boys Clubs wherever there might be an extra table, an open door, and people who want to learn about computers and their uses (Loop and Anton, 1982).

The computer literacy which they aimed to teach was designed not only to enable people to become familiar with the new technology, but also to encourage them to move on to purchasing their own equipment:

> In ComputerTown, computer literacy implies knowing how to load and operate preprogrammed software appropriate to the age of the individual, a nodding acquaintance with computer programming, and understanding that the computer can be used as an educational, recreational, data processing, or computational tool with a small investment in independent study. Computer literacy is a pro-

gression from comfort with the technology, through skills and knowledge acquisition, to using the computer as a personal tool (ibid).

The ComputerTown concept of literacy was supported by the National Science Foundation, who awarded it a grant to develop a demonstration computer literacy project, to disseminate this model as widely as possible to libraries and other institutions, and to promote the formation of similar projects throughout the United States. The grant came to an end during 1984, however, and the voluntary groups who had been supported by the central link since that time have had to function on their own.

During the years in which the project was funded, staff were to identify a number of sometimes unexpected problems with the idea of using volunteers to promote computer literacy. In the first place, few of the first-time visitors to the initial events returned for more computing (ibid). Secondly, the computer classes, in which students played games, evaluated software, and learned to program in BASIC, "were not always successful due to the desire of adult students for more structure and direction than the ComputerTown teachers were prepared to provide" (ibid).

In Britain, an analogous scheme, ComputerTown UK!, was supported by the computer magazine, *Personal Computer World* until 1984. Its Guidelines describe it as:

> A network of volunteers who are prepared to give up their time to introduce members of the public to computing. They usually do this by making one or more computers freely available for 'hands-on' experience to anyone interested. . . . The most common approach is to take machines, games programs and self-teach programming courses to the local library, church hall, community centre, or even your own garage and allow all comers to 'have a go' at using a computer. Each person would be given 20 minutes or half an hour on the machine with someone qualified around to help if they need it. . . . The important thing is to have fun and not to force the technology down people's throats (Tebbutt, undated).

Similar enthusiasm for bringing high technology to the general public has also led many computer hobbyists' clubs to try as volunteers to fulfill what they see as a real need for the computer literacy that can be acquired by actual experience of computers. For a number of reasons, however, such enthusiasms have not generally resulted in ventures that could be sustained over a considerable period of time.

In the first place, computer hobbyists or other volunteers have tended not to be trained or skilled in community education, and there may be large and significant gaps between what they can offer and what adults may want in the field of computer literacy; potential learners may be made uneasy both by the concentration on the equipment itself, as well as by the hobbyists' possible lack of experience as tutors of adults. Secondly, there are serious problems involved in trying to sustain something as demanding as computer literacy purely on a spare time basis, where it necessarily has to occupy a low priority in any one person's life. Finally, the field of computing is one that requires a significant amount of serious training and study to master: one cannot volunteer to teach computer literacy with the same competence as one might undertake many of the unskilled volunteering tasks that are part of community organizations. In all these ways, then, the match between the need for computer literacy and the capacities of volunteers to provide it may not be as close as many had originally hoped.

Some of the same issues appear to arise in the use of volunteers to meet the needs of those individuals and organizations who wish to use computer applications to help in developing their own communities. We have already seen in Chapter 4 that the demands for such help which are made to funded agencies, such as Microsyster or SCEMP, quickly outstrip the resources available. Where help can be given solely by volunteers, who also have demanding professional commitments, the issues become still more complex.

"Sheffield Computers for People" in England is characteristic of many local discussion and action groups which have sprung up during the last few years. It was formed:

> To discuss issues connected with computers and new technology from a socialist standpoint, and to foster a greater awareness of how computers are used and how they could be used. . . . We try to forge links with people who work with or are affected by computers and new technology. We hope to increase their understanding of the social and political aspects of their work (Sheffield Computers for People, undated).

The activities of the group fall into two main branches. First, seeing the wide range of social, economic, and political needs relating to the new technologies, the group attempts to raise awareness of their undesirable social effects, such as the loss of jobs, diminution of the quality of work, and the possible loss of privacy; it also supports trade union interests in negotiations on new technology. It organizes demonstrations and exhibitions for local communities on new technology and its effects, where it demonstrates the use of computer-based games, data bases, and word processing. As all other public demonstrations of computers have also found, they have been impressed by the great variety of interests expressed by the visitors to the demonstrations: Parents have wanted to see what their children were doing with computers at school; owners of small businesses have wanted to explore the possibilities of using computers in their work; community groups have wanted help with using computers for their day-to-day administration.

Secondly, Sheffield Computers for People are concerned with promoting the use of computers and other new technologies in ways that benefit people, so they offer to produce computer programs for the use and benefit of community groups, such as publications lists, address systems, card-box indexes, and nonsexist, nonaggressive games. The possibilities for further developments in these areas abound, but the group is restricted by the fact that they do not receive any external funding, so there is rarely sufficient programming time available to be able to meet the many, highly specific needs that exist.

As Figure 8 suggests, however, they have been able to encourage community groups to think seriously about the implications of computerizing. They have pointed to the practical dangers of organizations becoming overly dependent on the computer expertise of a single individual, who may then leave. They are also concerned that the placing of account records on a computer system may limit the number of people who can voluntarily help with accounts. They fear that people who are computer-illiterate and who receive word-processed mail from voluntary organizations may react negatively. And they are very aware of the antisocial tendencies of computerization: Performing functions by computer rather than by using volunteers to do the work may inhibit the kind of social contact that has always played such an important part in the operation of community groups.

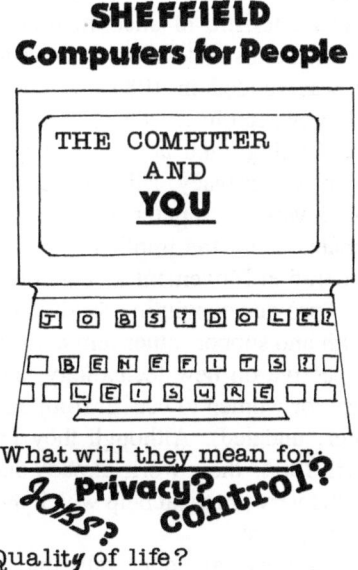

Figure 8. A voluntary organization expresses concern about the impact of computers on the community. Figure reproduced by courtesy of Sheffield Computers for People.

It may be, then, that the primary value of such voluntary groups as Sheffield Computers for People—and the many others like them—is to provide supporting "networks" both for the individuals involved in them, as well as for community groups who need advice and support as they try to work out the implications of computerization for their real aims and objectives. Funded voluntary bodies, on the other hand, are likely to find it somewhat easier to offer more specialist computer services to their local communities.

2. Funded Voluntary Agencies

Following the introduction of microcomputers in the late 1970s, a number of voluntary groups which offer computer services to their local communities have attracted support from local government and from foundations. Their remits tend to be more specifically directed toward serving particular groups in the community than are those of the purely volunteer organizations, and the services which they are able to offer to those groups tend also to be more precisely defined. Like the purely volunteer organizations, out of which many of them have grown, these agencies are primarily concerned to redress the balance of many contemporary developments in new technology which tend to militate against particular sections of the community.

One of the most characteristic of such funded voluntary agencies in Britain is Microsyster, which aims at developing ways to use microcomputers for women and which was funded in 1984–1985 by the Greater London Council. As we have already seen in Chapter 2, many women feel alienated and excluded by new technology and are worried by the very real threats posed to their employment and privacy. Microsyster therefore aims not only to provide positive ways in which computers can be made to work for women but also to open up debates about the implications of the new technologies within the Women's Liberation Movement as a whole.

Microsyster aims to "provide computing services to women and women's groups; make contact with and support other feminists working in computing; provide a feminist perspective on new technology; and introduce the skills and knowledge necessary for women to benefit from and critically assess new technology" (Microsyster, undated). Although they have been fully operationally only since April 1984, their work already indicates that there are substantial demands for the very practical help which they offer and enormous potential for further development.

So far the work which they have done falls into five main areas: introducing women to computers at conferences and seminars, providing a consultancy service, undertaking bureau work, writing specific programs, and analyzing surveys. They train women at conferences and workshops for women because they believe, as do many of the other organizations which have been discussed in Chapter 2, that women often prefer to be introduced to computers by other women who are sympathetic to the anxieties of novice users. They are particularly concerned with reaching three groups of women who might not otherwise be ready to learn about computers. "Women who are not in paid employment have little if any access to computers—while women who do work in offices have few opportunities to learn about the machines they spend most of their day in front of. There is also a demand by mothers to know a little about the computers that are the source of total distraction for their children" (Crowley, 1984).

Their greatest demand, however, appears to come from women's groups who believe that computerization could help them but are not sure exactly how. They have found serious over-estimation and under-estimation about the power of computers: "We have found that people either think that computers, at the press of a key, can do all their boring but essential work, or they are totally unaware of the potential of computers to ease their workload" (ibid). Women from Microsyster, therefore, talk with women's groups about whether computerization is or is not desirable for their specific work. If, after such discussion, they think that computerization would be helpful, they offer advice about the most appropriate equipment and programs. If the groups are unable to afford the necessary investment, Microsyster offers to help with the work on their own equipment, often by undertaking bureau work.

The bureau work which they undertake is mainly from feminist magazines and bookclubs, for whom they maintain membership lists and produce labels. This work tends to consist mainly of entering data on the computer, and is very time-consuming. Microsyster has tried to offer groups the option of coming in to do the data entry themselves, an arrangement which has had the added advantage of giving more women practical experience in operating computers. The heavy demand for such services, however, has meant that open access has had to be restricted, despite the fact that it has saved time and increased the efficiency of the operations of the organizations which have used it.

Microsyster also works with groups to provide specific programs for specific needs that cannot be met by the mass-market programs available. The requests for help in this area have been fewer than for consultancy, but it is, the group feels, "by far the most interesting work we undertake" (ibid). Finally, they are involved in survey analysis in order to "provide women's groups with resources to analyze the data they collect continually on the position of women in our society. The ability to produce relevant statistics greatly enhances our campaigning effectiveness, particularly when dealing with the media and official bodies" (ibid). While work in this area of development is barely underway at present, it is clearly another important area in which computers can be used to empower women.

The group also attempts to maintain contact with other women in the computer industry as part of the wider group, National Women and Computing Network, which has compiled a network of women in the industry which details their skills and work interests. They also attempt to monitor the media and government in the area of women and new technology and to respond when necessary from a feminist perspective.

Over time, as Microsyster introduces more women and women's groups to the new technologies, it may well be that the demand for its services will move from the present emphasis on consultancy to a greater concentration on specific bureau work, program development, and survey analysis, as women both as individuals and in groups become more familiar with the ways in which computers can empower them. Meanwhile, their work, together with that of similar agencies, has uncovered a substantial need for services that help to link specific groups of people with computers. Many professional bodies now include such services for their own members. There is clearly a need for analogous services to be made more widely available for voluntary community groups at little or no cost, so that both their own understanding of computers and the services which they offer to their local communities can be enhanced.

3. Public Bodies

During the 1980s, the severe restrictions on government expenditure on publicly accessible institutions, such as libraries and educational centers, have meant that they have been largely unable to meet the demand from their local communities for using computers both for general familiarization and for specific learning experiences. Even casual observation indicates the real demand. In Scotland, the short-term placement of computers in selected public libraries by the Scottish Community Education Microelectronics Project resulted in the equipment being in constant use; at peak time, queues formed. In Canada, at the Ontario Science Center in Toronto, the microcomputer systems available to the public appear to be in almost constant use, with eager children and adults often waiting for their turn. In the United States, the eager public response to the first ComputerTown USA! project in the Menlo Park Public Library appears to have been a major factor in the development of the ComputerTown USA! networks. And, as we have seen in Chapters 3 and 4, the same experience of eager public interest in using computers in the setting of a public library or education center has often been replicated in all three countries.

Increasingly, of course, public libraries are making use of computerized data bases for literature searches, and many other central library functions are also being computerized. So far, however, it appears as if the major developments in this area have been in easing the way to traditional printed material rather than in libraries being able to provide direct access to computers for their local communities.

Projects using Prestel in Britain and Telidon in Canada have already explored the potential for using computer-base videotex in public settings and have concluded that, despite the current drawbacks of both systems, there is an obvious public desire for such a service, with scope for further development. Even as early as 1981, when Prestel development in Britain offered only a very limited range of information, an experimental project on the use of Prestel in the public library concluded that library staff felt that Prestel has "enormous potential for conveying business and community information to the public" (Yeates, 1982).

Since that time, there have been other experiments in using Prestel for information in public settings, and the conclusions reported by Yeates have been generally confirmed elsewhere in Britain. During 1981–83, the "Prestel for People" project set up Prestel sets in 36 public sites including Citizens' Advice Bureaux, Head Post Offices, local government offices, shopping areas, and social security offices. The information available on these sets included a wide range of "social information" of the kind which has been discussed in Chapter 4, including information about education, consumer advice, local clinics, solicitors, and leisure centers, legal matters, such as divorce and consumer credit, employment, housing, and citizens' rights (Kania, 1983).

"Prestel for People" found an encouragingly high level of favorable public response, despite problems both with the equipment itself and with the depth of the information available: 91% of users of Prestel in public places said that they found Prestel information useful and would come back to use it again (ibid). This project also concluded that public libraries provided perhaps the most effective public access to Prestel and recommended that "every encouragement should be given by local authorities to provide special funding for the placing of public access Prestel terminals in libraries" (ibid).

In Canada, there have been a large number of experiments in the use of Telidon, and results have generally indicated favorable public response both to the information, as well as to the specifically educational programs provided (Wilson, 1984). These experiments have included both public settings, as well as home-based viewing, and the services provided have been heavily subsidized; as in Britain, there has been no satisfactory resolution of the problem of "who will be able to afford this service and how much access, if any, should be subsidized, and by whom, and through what mechanism" (ibid). Nevertheless, the results are promising. The range of information and education services in these experimental uses of Telidon has included information services for farmers; computer-aided courses on electricity, the mathematics of finance, and history; calculation programs to calculate interest on loans and savings; a bilingual travel game; the technology of early native Canadians; and an explanation of nuclear fission and nuclear reactors, among many other topics. Although, as with the uses of Prestel in public settings in Britain, a number of difficulties were encountered, users generally found the systems "informative," "useful," and "entertaining" (ibid).

Apart from such experiments with the use of computer-based videotex, a number of public libraries are investigating other ways in which they can support the individual learning that has traditionally formed such an important part of their role. In Britain, as this book goes to press, the Council for Educational Technology is investigating ways in which libraries can offer better support to independent learners, while a number of libraries are exploring ways in which they can make microcomputers available for independent learning by their users. On the whole, however, government and foundation financing for the use of microcomputers in public libraries has not been as generously available as it has been for the introduction of computers into formal education. Many librarians and others involved in public agencies now have well-developed ideas for ways of making microcomputers available for information and for independent learning, but they are unable, through lack of financial resources, to translate these ideas into reality.

4. Short-term Computer Projects

While microcomputers have been proliferating in formal education in Europe and North America, their use has been less widespread in community and adult education, where funding tends to be more precarious and less generous. Nevertheless, there has been a steady growth in short-term, experimental computer projects in community education, where a small amount of funding for equipment and skeletal staff has often been made to go a very long way.

One of the earliest of such projects was the Scottish Community Education Microelectronics Project, which was established in 1981 on a three-year experimental basis by the Scottish Council for Community Education. Chapters 3 and 4 have already discussed some of the ways in which SCEMP explored how computers could be used to create opportunities for individualized learning within community education and to provide information within a variety of community settings. For a number of reasons, it was possible to achieve these aims only by "networking" among people and institutions. It is worth exploring this method for the light which it throws on the efficacy and drawbacks of using networks as a way of cooperating with computers.

SCEMP was founded on the principle of working with national and local resources in order to help both individuals and community groups to become aware of some of the implications of computers in their own lives and in our society as a whole. Its very functioning presupposed a method of "networking," which it understood as follows:

> The word 'network' . . . describes a pattern, woven from many threads which sometimes cross over without touching, at other times run parallel but separate and which at points of intersection lead to new threads. The whole may appear one piece at first glance but a patient observer can trace its intricacies and distinguish individual threads. Some of these may be differently coloured or of a stronger material than others and so predominate in the weave; some may be broken or lead uselessly into a corner. The finished product . . . may have great strength despite the weakness of individual threads (Kirk, 1982).

A method of working through overlapping and interrelated structures and informal contact was implicit in SCEMP from the beginning. In the first place, the project was initially set up to build onto the experience and achievements of the Scottish Microelectronics Development Programme, a large Scottish program to develop educational applications of microelectronics largely in schools. Secondly, rather than imposing any preconceived lines of development on participating organizations, it was agreed that SCEMP should try to identify the ways in which groups and individuals themselves might wish to use computer facilities once they became aware of their potential. It was intended that it would build on local initiatives and networks, identifying local needs as they were mediated through already existing local groups and organizations (SCEMP, 1982a).

SCEMP was also seen as a means of exploring how formal and informal education agencies could work together with voluntary organizations and with government bodies in support of a project which could potentially benefit many different kinds of groups and individuals. There were a number of reasons—both of expediency and of principle—why this networking was seen as essential.

To begin with, there were then in Scotland few individuals who combined computer expertise with experience in community education. Most computer skills lay within formal education, while most of the experience of working directly with people in their own community lay with community groups and organizations, including the community education services of the local authorities, as well as voluntary organizations.

Moreover, in an experimental project, it made practical sense to work together with other agencies who were actively involved in projects and activities analogous to those of SCEMP. The project, therefore, sought and obtained active practical help from a wide variety of other organizations currently involved in computer familiarization. Information Technology 82 (the government-sponsored program to increase public awareness of information technology), the BBC Computer Literacy Project, the Scottish Council for Educational Technology, and the Open University were only a few of the many organizations which contributed equipment, materials, and advice to the early development of SCEMP.

But mere expediency also played an important role in choosing to network. SCEMP had been provided with an ambitious remit and only two full-time members of staff, together with additional part-time secretarial, administrative, and technical support. The basic difficulty was that SCEMP had banks of computers but no programs; it was like having a television set in a country where there is no broadcasting. Because the ideas of programming for general community use were at that time so little developed, there were no obvious programs which could be borrowed or even bought for immediate use. Nor were there any resources for commissioning programs. Yet SCEMP had to develop within the first year a bank of computer programs suitable for use by adults at public exhibitions. It was, thus, essential to seek out additional sources of help and support from virtually anyone who was willing to help.

SCEMP, therefore, started to tempt computer experts, both those working on their own and those within educational and other institutions, with a scheme whereby each could have the personal loan of a microcomputer for several months on condition that he should create programs for use in the proposed computer exhibitions; as a result, five programs were produced from the loan of eight machines. In addition to bartering equipment for programming time, SCEMP also approached organizations with programming capacity, such as banks and educational institutions, to ask them to create or adapt programs for use in the wider community; three Scottish clearing banks, and schools, colleges, and universities were persuaded to contribute significant amounts of programming time to the development of sample programs. A computing student-trainee who asked to be placed with SCEMP for the element of practical experience in her course, contributed an additional program and helped to amend others.

SCEMP also made many approaches for help to profit-making organizations, particularly to commercial software agents. The project was, however, rarely successful in securing programs in this way. Such persuasion is a very time-consuming activity and, therefore, could not be carried out in any comprehensive way. In any case, there appeared to be few commercially available programs which had potential educational value for the community as a whole, as differentiated from the numerous programs intended primarily for children.

The programs, then, were nearly all developed by a network of professionals who volunteered their expertise over a period of time. The exhibitions at which the programs were demonstrated were less heavily dependent on purely voluntary help, but nevertheless found that it was essential to use volunteers on a rota basis to oversee public use of the equipment and programs, as the latter at least were still experimental. Each of the early public exhibitions was coordinated by one main local organization, such as a district council responsible for libraries and leisure, a regional community education service, and an umbrella voluntary organization which included all the major local voluntary organizations in one part of the country. The amount of voluntary help varied considerably, but often included students from schools and colleges who helped users at the exhibitions with any problems encountered in using the equipment and programs.

Did this heavy reliance on "networking" work? An evaluation of SCEMP three years after it began concluded that such a "process works well when resources are scarce" (Laidlaw, 1984), and all SCEMP resources apart from the computers themselves were very scarce indeed. The financial effectiveness of the approach was estimated by the management committee in 1981–82 as providing the equivalent of £70,000 annual budget at a time when the actual budget was well under £20,000 (ibid). This figure was reached by taking into account the estimated contribution of programming time, equipment and materials, as well as an element in the salaries of the project director (seconded from an educational institution), the student-trainee, and the staff time allocated by those organizations taking part in the various parts of the projects.

The evaluation of SCEMP commented that "whether this networking has 'worked' should be judged against results achieved that can be said to contribute to community education in a general sense" (ibid). Unfortunately, the evaluation then considered only that part of the scheme which placed computers in community organizations and not public exhibitions, which were the major locus of networking. There has been no detailed examination of the experiences of participants in the exhibitions, and there is thus insufficient evidence on which to conclude whether the networking did or did not make a contribution to community education.

The programs that were created as the result of the networking, however, were evaluated as part of a process that resulted in SCEMP's producing a set of "Guidelines for the Design of Computer Programs for Community Use"

(SCEMP, 1982c). As has already been noted in Chapter 3, these programs bore unwitting testimony to the difficulties created in trying to create educational computer programs on a purely voluntary basis. While they were often imaginative and well-designed, the lack of time available for creating them sometimes resulted in their needing additional work before they were ready for use by computer novices.

The problem is that creation of programs for general community use requires even greater time than writing programs designed for experienced computer users, which, as we have seen in Chapter 3, is time-consuming in itself. As ever in much of community and adult education, the resources to produce materials, however, are almost invariably less than those in formal education. SCEMP, therefore, finally evolved a method whereby programs were initially developed by volunteers, evaluated, and then amended where necessary by professional educational computer programmers before being released for public use. This mix of voluntary effort with professional help seems to have been effective and has enabled SCEMP to draw on the ideas of a wider variety of people experienced in different facets of community education than it would otherwise have been able to do.

Meanwhile, other indices of whether the "networking" has worked also seems to be positive: as Chapter 3 has noted, the figures for attendance at many of the exhibitions which used the programs were high, and in 1984 the project was given a further three years of life. As with much other educational work with computers, however, there is no answer to many of the questions one would like to ask.

5. Nonprofit-making Computer Organizations

The nonprofit-making use of computers for cooperative networking among individuals and groups who share specific interests is well illustrated in the United States by the "National Women's Mailing List." This organization describes itself as:

> A national feminist communications network which is available *at cost* to grassroots women's organizations, so that they can mail to people who are interested in their projects. In this way, individual feminists can get mail from a wide variety of women's organizations that are working in the areas specific to their interests. At the same time, it enables grassroots feminist organizations to reach out to large numbers of interested people who they would otherwise not be able to contact (National Women's Mailing List, undated).

The organization began in 1980 with a mailing of 5,000 brochures which offered women and men a chance to register and receive mail in chosen areas of interest. Since then, with the help of many women's groups, it has become a self-sufficient organization operating without grants or subsidies. Near the end of 1984, there were 40,000 individuals and 10,000 organizations registered with the list, a Canadian Women's Mailing List was operating, and feminist mailing lists were under serious discussion in France and England (Feen, 1984).

The eventual goal is to create a "network of one million North American feminists who can unite around common interests and concerns. A large communications resource will provide the women's movement with an effective response to the mail-based networks of antifeminist groups" (National Women's Mailing List, undated). Registration on the mailing list offers subscribers a number of important options. They can specify precisely the subjects in which they are interested within the general areas of women's culture, sports, legal and political issues, health, education, violence against women, and work, among others; and they can choose, among other options, whether they do or do not wish to receive mail from political candidates.

Throughout its activities, the organization believes that it is using computers in ways that are acceptable to feminists. Thus, the privacy of individuals and organizations is protected; subscribers are offered a wide range of topics; feedback is encouraged rather than a system being imposed on subscribers; and applicants are not turned away merely because they do not have the very modest fee requested to cover processing costs.

As a way of providing national links among specific interest groups and individuals, such computerized mailing lists have already proved their efficacy in political lobbying, particularly among neoconservative organizations in the United States. The National Women's Mailing List has shown the viability of a nonprofit-making computer-based service not merely for immediate political ends but also as a means of offering support to those enrolled in it. The expansion of the idea into Canada and the current interest in France and England strongly suggest that the model is ripe for replication in other countries and among other interest groups and individuals, who wish to maintain contact on a national basis with others who share their interests and concerns.

6. General Features

These case studies suggest that there are certain circumstances in which individuals and groups can successfully cooperate with computers for community rather than personal or corporate benefit. As Chapters 3 and 4 have already discussed, there are also a number of important ways in which using computers in community groups strengthens the motivation and development of those groups themselves. The Janus-faced nature of computers, however, means that at times there may be a clash between those computer benefits which are of greatest use to the community and those which are of greatest value to the group which provides them. Microsyster has found that the greatest need from the community appears to be in consultancy; on the other hand, the greatest satisfactions for the group itself appear to lie in the development of programs, an activity which they find most interesting and which allows them to work together as a group. Analogously, some of the program development undertaken by the Scottish Community Education Microelectronics Project appears to have resulted in more group activity and cohesion than viable computer programs.

The criteria on which one might try to assess the efficacy of cooperating with computers, then, are likely to be mixed. The case studies considered above are all ones which would, I think, choose to be evaluated on the grounds of the value of the service which they provide to the community. Nevertheless, all of them would probably see the means by which they provide such services as equally important; thus, the "National Women's Mailing List" uses feminist criteria in its methods as well as offering a service for feminists, while the public libraries are concerned with maintaining their high professional standards in whatever form of information they provide for the public, whether it is computerized or not.

Using what appear to be the criteria of the organizations themselves, then, the most successful examples of cooperation between people and computers appear to arise when professional computer specialists or other professionals, such as educators or librarians, commit themselves to offering a nonprofit-making specific public service in an area in which they have clearly identified needs and aims. The fact that the network of ComputerTowns in both Britain and the United States is apparently diminishing highlights the fragility of the amateur, purely voluntary approach. Virtually all of the other projects and organizations above have a solid core of professional expertise on which voluntary effort is often built.

At the same time, however, professionally trained computer specialists are often hard to get and tend to be expensive. And, although the power that they provide increases as their price decreases, computers cost money. Most successful projects have received some form of external funding. Yet, throughout most of the developed world, less and less money is being made available for such funding. Community groups may, therefore, have to turn instead to developing computer applications which can be financially self-sustaining, where services are offered as inexpensively as possible to those who can pay and are subsidized for those who cannot. With such a model, there will be many potentially beneficial community computer applications which will never exist. Nevert'ieless, in a time of increasing divisions between the economically rich and poor, and between the information-rich and the information-poor, such a model of nonprofit-making cooperation between people and computers can at least not exacerbate the divisions.

But the discussion has so far focused only on the larger vision of co-operation between people and computer for community benefit. In the day-to-day life of organizations which serve the community, introducing computers may have many unexpected, unpredictable, and even damaging results. In order to try to determine the effect of computerization on the people in those community organizations which use computers, let us look over the shoulder of two real-life diarists during the period when they were involved in introducing computers to, respectively, a primary school and a voluntary organization in adult education.

INTRODUCING COMPUTERS: TWO DIARIES

1. A Computer in Formal Education

In 1983, Michael Shaw, headmaster of a primary school in England, reported on the following details of his experience as he introduced a computer into his school:

"I welcomed with open arms the Department of Industry's initiative to introduce micro-computers into primary schools. My application to have a BBC Micro-Computer went in the same day that the form arrived on my desk. After about three months, one of my staff and I were summoned to our initial course run by the local education authority. This was a part of the package and was designed to give us some ideas about how we could use the micro and to give us 'hands-on' experience. It was a very interesting day and one which we both enjoyed.

"I should have known that there was something wrong when one of the tapes refused to load for the second time, having performed perfectly the first time. But a spare copy was given to me, and all was well. At the end of the day, the computer and its bits went into the back of my car so that I could try the programs out at home, and my children could see what they could make of the programs developed by the Microelectronics Education Programme (a government-funded project to promote and support the use of computers in schools in England, Wales, and Northern Ireland).

"The 'Welcome' tape was the first one to be tried. The first time through it all worked, but gradually fewer and fewer of the programs ran. Strange words appeared on the screen: 'data', 'block.' What did they mean? Was this what I had committed £350 of capitation to? I suppose I am lucky in that I had the advice of a neighbour who diagnosed a faulty tape recorder. This was put right, and a new one was ordered. But the damage was done, and two tapes had to be replaced. Worse was to follow.

"I had managed to make use of an old recorder of my own which was kinder to the remaining tapes, and I had been lent a couple of games, so all looked fair for the Easter holiday. My son, aged 10, called me down one morning, 'Dad, what does this mean?' The computer said 'language.' I asked my neighbour. The language ROM had gone wrong, and there was no way in which I could do anything at home. What can you say to a frustrated and angry son who had seen the tapes being damaged, and who wanted to play 'Swoop'? And what could I say to the other member of staff who was going to have the machine after the holiday?

"Back at school, I phoned Acorn Computers (manufacturers of the BBC Computer) who went to a great deal of trouble to get the problem sorted out. A very calm, sympathetic voice at the end of the telephone said, 'Yes, sir, you undo the four screws showing, and the top comes off; you won't hurt the computer.' But it was no use; back it went for repair. Frustration all round.

"The replacement tape recorder arrived and was tried out with an audio tape to check the head alignment. The entire machine locked solid. There was no way in which anything could be made to happen; back it went. A third one followed, and, after adjustment, it works perfectly.

"But several staff members who had been lightly resistant to the idea of a computer were now positively hostile. After all, it had taken a great chunk of the school's allowance, which could have been used for other things. Others were sympathetic: tape recorders go wrong, so all technology was suspect!

"Soon after this the repaired computer arrived, and I was able to start the long-term staff training that had been promised. People started taking an interest in what the computer had to offer. All was going well except for the occasional loading problems, and they were solved by the introduction of a disk drive. That took a little while to master; finally, the elder brother of a pupil explained the correct way to use it.

"By now the computer had been in the school for a month, and my earliest fears were slowly fading. I should have known better. A call from one of the staff: the word 'language' was on screen again. Once more the computer went back to Acorn, and the staff training programme stopped, and the staff started muttering. So did the parents, who had decided to raise money to pay for the computer and the disk drive.

"This time the repair seemed to work. For the rest of the summer term, the computer was in use in as many classes as possible. Staff took it home, and all was well. The summer holiday saw it being shared, transported around Luton and St. Albans. Most of the staff were getting interested. Even one of the most ardent anti-computer members of staff became involved when she realized that the children were quite capable of setting it up and that the disk system made loading very easy.

"A school computer club started, and we used games which two of us had bought for our own children. Then trouble again: the terrible word 'language' was seen. This time, in anger, I took it to our computer centre and borrowed a spare machine, while they examined it carefully.

"A few days later I was asked to collect it. The fault had been traced to a loose ROM, and all that was needed was a gentle push of the right bit. Two days on, no amount of gentle pushing, shaking or more would make it go. By now, I admit to being more than just angry. I was prepared to visit Vector Marketing and demand a replacement. A phone call elicited the following information:

'Yes, you do have cause for complaint.'

'Return the computer and we will replace it.'

'The only problem is that at present we do not have any in stock.'

"Much to my amazement, three days later a large parcel came to school with a brand new computer. This is one of the latest models and certainly seems much better; the keyboard has a smoother feel to it. At the moment, it is being used by my colleague, who is very pleased with it. I just hope that this one does not let us down.

"If I were the only person to experience these problems, then I could accept that we had got a 'Friday Computer.' However, my experience has been met in other schools in the area. And, as the organizer of a local self-help group, I am aware of others with similar problems.

"On the negative side, there is the frustration and anger felt by the staff. Local advisers are saying that the curriculum needs to be changed to accommodate the new technology, and yet the new technology is not reliable. On the positive side, I have made a lot of new friends in the area discussing the computer. I have learnt how to take the lid off. I have also discovered that big business does have a kind face.

"I am looking forward to computing in 1984, especially as I have got a place on a computer training course. Hopefully, the machine will continue to perform well, and the children can start to benefit from the spin-off ideas that are starting to come from the staff. I might even consider buying a computer in the next couple of years for myself. Where did I put the screwdriver?"

2. A Computer in a Voluntary Organization

My own experiences in introducing a computer system into a voluntary organization in adult education were recorded in diary form during 1983–84.

August, 1983: During the interview for the post of director, emphasized what I saw as the need for the organization to take account of the implications of the new information technologies for adult and continuing education. Suggested to the interviewing panel that the organization should provide a forum for discussion of current developments and their implications. Also mentioned in passing that, on the surface, the organization seemed to be a reasonable candidate for computerization of some of its work: there was extensive paperwork, much of it repetitive; there were large mailings of papers to members; much information was collected and stored; new accounting procedures would need to be set up following radical changes in the organization. Did not mention own selfish predilection for composing on a word processor!

Offered the post, so assumed that these possibilities were at least tolerated.

Only clue, so far, is that the present director has noted the possibility of sending the new administrative assistant on a computer training or awareness course.

September: Decided to keep a record of the actual events leading to eventual introduction of a computer system in a voluntary organization. Made rough notes about purpose, criteria, specifications, and potential difficulties of computerizing.

Purpose: computer could be used for (1) word processing of papers and publications, thereby saving the time and cost of retyping and type-setting; (2) keeping financial accounts; (3) indexing records, such as subscriptions to periodicals; (4) managing membership and mailing lists; (5) demonstrating use of computers at seminars or other events.

Criteria: computerization must not threaten employment of current staff or de-skill them; programs should be reasonably easy to use; the possibility of computerization should be presented realistically, without raising expectations unduly.

Specifications: ideally, each member of staff should have a personal computer, with networking among the four of us, with at least one letter-quality printer; the system should be compatible with those in use in allied organizations with whom we might eventually want to establish computer communication; best of all, would be the possibility of preparing documents at home on my own computer and bringing in the disks to be amended and printed in the office.

Potential difficulties: computerizing would initially be so expensive that the organization could not sustain the full capital cost; the running costs, including maintenance, would be greater than present office running costs; other than the fact that the administrative assistant recently expressed her interest in computerization, the attitudes of the other members of staff are unknown; introduction of a computing system would place a considerable burden on an organization where staff are already very pressed for time.

Despite potential difficulties, determined to raise the possibility of computerization with office-bearers during initial meetings. Am also determined, however, not to attempt too much too soon! 1986 would probably be sufficient time.

October: Take month's leave in between former post and new one to write book on computers and adult learning on my word processor at home. Fears of computer breakdown at crucial moments remain unrealized, despite bitter memories of previous failure of system when it was needed for an earlier publication. Only problems are a recurring but sporadic fault which formats pages badly, difficulty in getting printer ribbons to function properly, and headaches and eye-strain caused by staring at a screen for many hours a day. Enjoy the luxury of being at home for a month, but fail to meet the diary deadline optimistically headed "Post book; start new post."

November: Start new post—and post new book shortly afterwards. Possibility of computerization pushed to back of mind by more immediate concerns of becoming familiar with new post.

December: Am very busy and start to prepare some papers (agendas, minutes, policy papers, notes for office-bearers) at home on my own computer because of ease of alterations and speed of typing. Have fantasies about being able to send such material directly to office, if we had a computing system there, and if home and work were linked by modems. But also feel need to be in office more often. Budget projected for next financial year has no scope for purchase of computer system but does require more in-house production of publications and greater increase of sales income.

January, 1984: Visit organization in Glasgow where the director has a new computer system which he lovingly demonstrates; they plan to use it for word processing, accounting, and for keeping and searching file records. But they have considerably more cash than we do. Storm-bound for two days at home, work steadily preparing papers on the computer. Feel more strongly than ever the need for computerization in the office. Discuss with a colleague, who is head of an educational institution, the possibility of our using their computer on a regular basis until we can afford our own system.

February: Pressure of paper work makes computerization more and more attractive. Plan to bring my computer from home to work in order to introduce staff to some of its possibilities, but more immediate priorities keep intruding. Hear about possibility of applying for a government grant for purchase of a system, but am a little reluctant, because any final purchase would have to be completed before the end of March, so any application would have to be ready in about a week's time. Feel the need of more time to discuss with staff and evaluate possible systems and suppliers. Want to avoid sequence of technological determinism, where machine is supplied first, the programs come second, and the people last.

On the other hand, given our need and the possibility of financial support, feel I am being overly scrupulous. Spend intensive few days consulting with staff, colleagues, office bearers; investigate possible suppliers and, under pressure to be as economical as possible, decide to place order with the supplier offering the lowest price. Submit application for funds and receive immediate confirmation of offer of 100% grant for a computer system linked to the printer recommended by the supplier as being the best for our needs. Intention, discussed both with funder and with supplier, is to start with word processing, then move on to keeping records in a data base, and finally to transfer our accounting system to the computer.

March: Continue discussions with staff about computerization, and agree timetable for training with them. Computing system and invoice arrive simultaneously on the 16th, and the invoice is taken by hand to the appropriate government office to meet their deadline for submission. Supplier installs and tests computing system, pronounces it to be working perfectly. My son drops by to check it and explores the computer functions, all of which seem in perfect order.

First training session scheduled for the 26th, but no one turns up; supplier explains apologetically that, due to pressure of work in their office, the message about the arrangement did not reach the trainer. Rearrange first training session at some inconvenience, as days are already fairly full.

April: Training sessions begin. Trainer very enthusiastic, assures us we can't really damage the computer, discusses what computers are and how they do what they do, and introduces all of us to all the things the computer can do. Glazed looks appear part-way through the session. He keeps saying that "it's unlikely you will want to use this" about many of the facilities available, but then demonstrates what they are and how to use them without asking whether we would like to know or not. He also demonstrates a bewilderingly wide range of technical vocabulary, which is particularly confusing where ordinary English words are used in very specific ways. He allows each of us to practice on the keyboard (all of us are familiar with typewriter keyboards), but does not explain what we are doing and why.

Finally, there is a sudden renewal of interest when, near the end of the session, he moves on to what we really want—how to use the word processing program and the printer. But there is time for only a brief, tantalizing glimpse of the possibilities, and the session ends. Because of difficulties in arranging the rest of the training sessions at times which would suit all of us and because the session took up so much time for such an apparently minimal result, we agree that the administrative assistant should undertake the rest of the training and then teach the rest of us.

After several more hours of training, she and I tackle the first piece of real work that needs to be done on the system, as a preliminary to the extensive work scheduled for several weeks away. It is a flop. The printer does things that we are sure we have not commanded it to do. The trainer from the supplier promises by telephone to sort the problem at the next session.

Several days later that session runs into a technical quagmire, as the printer performs equally badly for the trainer. Despite maintenance agreement that faults should be repaired within 24 hours or the equipment replaced, supplier attempts over a couple of weeks to test each part of the equipment, but is unable to discover any fault in the individual pieces. The problem with printing continues. We are now in trouble, as, during May, a lengthy piece of work will have to be prepared as camera-ready copy for an outside printing firm; we are also into our busiest time of year as we prepare for our annual conference.

May: Fault persists, and supplier is still unable to diagnose the problem. We are often unable to reach specific people at the suppliers because of their apparently over-stretched staff. Meanwhile, have to hire additional temporary staff to cope with the backlog of paperwork created by the days that have by now been spent fruitlessly with the computer. Printer's deadline for camera-ready copy looms larger. After trying various alternatives, finally in desperation, bring own computer to office, and administrative assistant and I type in the entire camera-ready copy over one intensive weekend. Write letter to supplier, with copy to manufacturer, saying that we are seeking legal advice about the fact that, having chosen the printer on their recommendation, many weeks after delivery, we still do not have a workable system and have been involved in considerable expense.

June: Supplier finally diagnoses problem as fundamental incompatibility between computer and printer and claims that manufacturer's specifications for computer did not indicate such incompatibility. Supplier installs new, even better, printer, which works perfectly. Finally, two months after the equipment was delivered, we have a working system. On legal advice, decide to withhold from the final payment for the system the amount of the expenditure we incurred through the problem of the printer.

July and onwards: System continues to work smoothly. The administrative assistant becomes highly proficient on it, and trains the secretary and me how to use it. By late autumn, most paper work is done on it. In-house publications start to expand dramatically; membership lists, the constitution, and other documents requiring up-dating are held on disk; form letters are adapted to specific purposes and even individuals by computerizing them; and so on. The supplier and the manufacturer have still not informed us where they believe that the fault for the incompatibility of printer and computer lies, and the supplier has still not produced an additional piece of important equipment. We are wholly convinced of the value of computerization, however, and the three of us who know how to use it are now vying for the keyboard. Our only problem is how to get funding for the final system of four computers, linked to computers in analogous organizations, which we need for full computerization.

THE MARRIAGE OF PEOPLE AND COMPUTERS

These two tragicomedies of the adoption of computer systems for educational purposes and for administration are not exceptional. The availability of funding for the equipment itself—whether such funds come from government, from voluntary fund-raising, from grants from external bodies, or from donations of the equipment—is frequently the determining factor in the speed of the marriage between people and computers. The hastily arranged unions which result are potent sources of frustration and misunderstanding between people and uncooperative computers.

The morals of the tragicomedies are self-evident. It may, however, be worth noting that, however frustrating and exasperating the experience, the institutions and individuals involved have become convinced of the value of computerization. It is notable, too, that virtually all of the organizations in community education with which computers were placed experimentally by the Scottish Community Education Microelectronics Project were determined to acquire their own computers after the placement had ceased, as we have seen in Chapter 4.

Deciding whether and how to computerize in community education should be a lengthy process which includes the seeking of professional advice for the specific purposes envisaged. But organizations may also want to take into account those general features of the interaction between computers and people in community education, which SCEMP has uncovered in its many loans of computers to community organizations and which are confirmed by the experience of other organizations.

The most fundamental and elementary question to ask is, of course, whether computerization is likely to be useful at all. "A computer should be considered only if it can perform a task which has to be done more efficiently and accurately" (SCEMP 1982b). For many tasks undertaken by organizations, as for many tasks in people's homes, as Chapter 1 has suggested, using a computer may merely produce more elegant or more sophisticated results where more mundane, nonelectronic methods would have been entirely adequate. The paperless office may be fashionable but is unlikely to be a feasible or even desirable goal for most organizations.

The assessment of whether computerization would actually be more efficient has to include taking into account the usually limited budgets on which most community organizations operate. Where there is only one computer keyboard, for example, it might be faster to store and retrieve most information on paper rather than run the risk of discovering that essential information cannot be retrieved exactly when it is needed because the only computer is being used for another purpose at the time. And, just as it is generally faster to use a pocket paper diary for organizing one's life or index cards for organizing one's recipes, so also it is usually faster to store small chunks of information in traditional, noncomputerized ways.

Secondly, community organizations need to assess precisely the main functions for which they will initially use a computer. There will always be later, creative, unexpected tasks to which computerization can be applied, but, in the beginning, it is crucial to determine whether the functions which one wants to perform can all be performed on the same computer or whether there will have to be "trade-offs" of one desirable characteristic against another. Computers which handle graphics well, for instance, tend not to be as effective at word processing, while programs which are very easy to use tend not to leave as much available memory in the computer for the actual task at hand. One of the main "trade-offs," however, is likely to arise not in the choice of the equipment itself but rather in the programs which are chosen for it. Most voluntary organizations may well find themselves in a situation in which the mass-market version of a program which they need does not quite meet their purposes, but they are unable to pay the considerable sums needed to meet their precise specifications.

A third consideration is whether any computer which a community organization can afford to buy will be able to cope with the real volume of the information which it will be used for. We have seen earlier that the price of computers is steadily decreasing as their capacity for information increases. Nevertheless, the less expensive systems—particularly those which are sold primarily for home use—process too little information too slowly for many of the tasks for which voluntary organizations may wish to use them. Chapter 4 has already discussed the limitations of such systems for storing the volume of community information which many organizations might wish to store on a computer.

An example of the practical limitations imposed by current microcomputer systems may be seen in an experience in Scotland in 1984. An experimental data base of courses in distance learning was designed to be run on a particular microcomputer which was widely available in Britain, so that people seeking information about particular courses could get the precise facts which they needed without having to work their way through a large number of entries in a directory. The capacity of the computer, however, requires that a number of different disks have to be searched slowly before the user can feel assured that he or she has the full information available (Paine, 1984). It would probably be faster—if less elegant—merely to thumb through the relevant pages of the original directory.

Fourthly, community organizations will want to look carefully at whether they want the computer and its programs to be used by staff or their members or the general public or all three. Here again, there are many accounts of the need to choose among a number of ideal goals. In Britain, for example, the first experimental programs for determining people's eligibility for welfare benefits, differed considerably depending on whether they were for use by trained members of staff or the general public: those intended primarily for staff use required detailed training in their use and provided information more quickly than did those intended for the general public, which were both easier and slower to use. In many fields, programs are now being developed which allow trained users to take short-cuts through the introductory and helpful material presented to new users. However, there are few, if any, programs which adequately meet the competing needs of both trained staff and untrained users.

Finally, there are a host of practical details to be resolved before attempting to computerize. Where the computer will be placed, for instance, sounds like a trivial decision, but actually raises a number of questions which have to be answered: while computers are generally not prone to accidental damage, for example, the consequences of spilling any liquid over a computer keyboard are almost inevitably disastrous. Arrangements for maintenance also have to be worked out with some care. It is now generally accepted computer lore that anything that is likely to go wrong will do so in the first hours of use, and that, afterwards, the equipment will tend to be trouble free. On the other hand, the consequences of not being able to retrieve information or documents because the computer has broken down can be not merely embarrassing but seriously damaging to the efficient working of an organization.

As in any marriage, the careful preparation of both partners for the realities of cooperating with each other helps to minimize the divorce rate. Already, some microcomputers have joined the programmed learning machines which educationalists espoused and then divorced some years ago. But with realistic, informed expectations, and with tolerance of the initial difficulties of the honeymoon, most organizations in community education appear to have worked out a productive and even enjoyable relationship cooperating with their computers.

6

PROMISES AND PITFALLS

"There are no simple technological fixes for complex social problems"
Norman, 1981.

Much of this book has focused on the Janus-face of computers and has emphasized the contrast between their promises and their practical realities. As Chapter 1 suggested, the possibilities offered by computer power for increasing the choices available to people and communities are overshadowed by the economically and socially divisive effects of computers where they are introduced into a competitive world. Chapter 2 then considered both the current antifemale bias of the world of computing, and the fact that, in certain respects, women may be more effective than men in exploiting a computer as the powerful slave it is. Chapter 3 discussed the educational opportunities that can be opened up by learning both by and about computers, but it also recognized the bizarre extent to which the realities of computer courses and computer learning programs often fail to meet the needs of learners.

In Chapter 4, there were many examples of how community organizations could use computers to help in the services which they provide to the public, but there were also many illustrations of the kind of constraints which hamper such developments. Chapter 5 looked at the practical realities of computerization, contrasting the face of cooperation and collaboration with that of the often damaging realities of the highly commercialized world of computer suppliers. I should now like to look at whether such apparent contradictions may form an inherent feature of the contact between people and computers, and how it may be possible for community educators to cross the technological quagmire with some assurance that they will get safe passage, and that the journey is worth making.

In making this assessment, I shall look first at the claim by many writers that computers have an immense potential for opening up learning experiences and, indeed, perhaps for achieving many of the traditional goals of adult education. I shall also consider whether there may not be even more pitfalls in using computers than the practical, social, and economic ones which have already been discussed. But pragmatism will finally defeat theory, and I shall conclude with the argument that community education can use computers to strengthten its collaborative and cooperative approaches. For anyone who is sufficiently convinced by the arguments so far and wants to pursue further the possibilities offered by computers in community education, the Appendices outline the factors to consider in buying a computer for use in a community organization, suggest further reading to follow each chapter, and provide a glossary of the terms which have been used with specific technical meanings in the text.

NEW MODELS OF LEARNING?

Even a brief glance at the literature of educational computing presents an enticing prospect of using computers to enhance adult learning. The visions of the future look ahead to a golden time when all learning will become open in the fullest sense of being always accessible to everyone in the form in which each individual chooses to have it, and in which the present strictures of knowledge will be demolished by the power of the computer to make universal expertise available to everyone.

Taking together the predictions for the golden future of learning as they appear in Martin (1978), Evans (1979), Papert (1980), Toffler (1980), and Naisbitt (1982), among many others, certain characteristics seem to be generally agreed on. In the first place, the analytical linear approach that presently characterizes much learning will change to a reiterative, recursive model of exploring possibilities, of seeing what happens when you try something, and then when you try something else instead. As more and more people learn programming, particularly in the programming languages derived from work in artificial intelligence, attitudes of embarrassment or shame at wrong answers will change to a belief that errors can always be corrected by trying and then trying again. And, as more and more data bases of information become available, learning will increasingly consist of exploring various kinds of information in a mode of discovery rather than attempting to grapple with entire bodies of organized knowledge. Learning, thus, will be more creative, inventive, and democratic.

Secondly, the nature of the student-educator relationship will change. Where students do still gather together with a tutor, in many respects the students will know as much about the subjects they are studying as do their tutors; a "family" style of learning will emerge, in which all participants will work together, each contributing on equal terms. Such a situation will come about partly because the mastery of facts will no longer be so important when computer systems can be so much better at holding facts than people can ever be. It will also come about partly because, at least as far as computers are concerned, children will in many respects be more knowledgeable than their parents, thereby reversing traditional and conventional expectations.

More usually, however, self-learning will become the major form of learning, with each individual able to choose educational forms tailored to his or her specific needs. It will no longer be important, other than perhaps for social reasons, for people to have to gather together to learn, and the existence of traditional educational institutions will no longer be necessary as learning will take place wherever an individual learner happens to be. And, unconstrained by artificial institutional boundaries, individuals will assume the responsibility for their own learning. Current educational disadvantages created by distance, or time constraints, or by physical disability will no longer matter.

Finally, with the rapid changes in the kinds of work that people do, and with a great increase in leisure time, learning will become a lifelong activity, in which people move in and out of training and education with great ease, in response to needs as they arise in their own lives. People will increasingly expect in their own learning experiences the kind of "modular" approach to knowledge that they already know from their experiences of computer programming.

A few bits of this picture of how computers can revolutionize our educational experience are already in place. In the light of recent developments in the use of computers in American higher education, Van Gelder (1984) has painted a highly plausible picture of new ways of studying on a university campus:

> Imagine yourself on a typical evening in the dorm. You sit down at your computer to start research on a paper on the influence of the Women's Movement

on the television industry. You log onto a data base that contains abstracts of thousands of magazine articles and professional papers that have been published in the last five years. You key in the phrases 'women' and 'television,' and the computer performs a lightning-quick search for articles that deal with both topics. As you read the abstracts, you reject several articles about who the most popular women on television are, but you arrange to download copies of numerous articles which do relate to your topic. (You can scan these articles at your leisure on your computer screen or you can print them out on your printer.) Then you log off the data base and log onto your campus mailbox. There's a note from your biology professor, who has the flu and is canceling tomorrow's class. You're glad, because you hadn't finished the assignment anyway—it involved using your computer to dissect a simulated rat—and you're now free tonight! But you really don't feel like going out. No problem—you call up the campus entertainment network and find three other poeple who want a fourth for on-line bridge.

Van Gelder might realistically have added that on the following night you sit down at your computer, and use the word processing facilities to draft the essay, amend it until you are reasonably happy with it, and then send the final version for marking by your professor at his or her leisure. Details, such as when the library is open, or arriving at a class in time to hand in your essay, have ceased to matter.

Both in North America and in Britain over the past few years, there have been enormous increases in the numbers of "open learning" opportunities available. In Scotland, where there are powerful geographical reasons for providing learning opportunities at a distance, the numbers of such courses rose from 47 in 1981 to well over 200 in 1984 (SCET, 1981 and 1984); this figure did not include the many additional courses offered nationally in Britain as a whole, such as the degree and post-graduate work offered by the Open University. In Canada, most universities and many community colleges offer courses at a distance, and increasing numbers of institutions are making use of computers as one mode of presenting their learning opportunities (Burge *et al.,* 1984). In the United States, there is already a long tradition of open learning, and the Electronic University is likely to spawn many analogous developments.

Meanwhile, at both primary and secondary school, children are learning to program in at least one computer language. The programs currently operating in Britain and France to provide schools with microcomputers will mean that, as adults, our children are likely to have acquired at least some of the learning stances mentioned above; they are particularly likely to believe in the relative ease of making corrections and to assume that learning takes place in modules, many of which are interchangeable.

ALTERNATIVE SCENARIOS

Based as they are on the impact of technological developments, the golden pictures of a future of open learning for all tend to rely perhaps too readily on the assumption that what is technologically feasible will necessarily happen. But as Hurly (1984) comments, "the mere application of the new information technologies will not guarantee the emergence of a progressive learning environment." There are, indeed, a number of assumptions underlying the golden vision of the future which may cause uneasy doubts among many community educators.

To begin with, the very assumption that what is technologically feasible is what will happen is itself a form of technological determinism. Rather than accept such a stance, most community educators probably believe that people should determine how machines are used, and that they should not have their experiences determined by those machines, even if the learning Utopia offered seems particularly attractive. The frequently heard comment that computers in education are "a solution looking for a problem" (see, for example, Skues, 1983; Wilson, 1984) is unlikely to encourage such educators. Nor are adult and community educators likely to warm to an approach which starts from the availability of the equipment and then tries to find uses for it, a technique illustrated by Figure 9. Yet such approaches are by far those most frequently found in the literature of educational computing; one educational technologist characteristically asks, "Which are the devices and systems that belong to new information technology? What can we do with each" (Hawkridge, 1983)?

Secondly, the context in which it is expected that computers will be used to create more open learning remains one in which there is an increasing divide between two parts of society—those who can afford investment in the advantages offered by computers, and who are often already educationally equipped to be able to learn easily how to deal with them, and those who do not have the initial resources either of money or of education. Where computers are used for open learning in such a divided society, they may well open learning to certain individuals. However, if no steps are taken to counteract the tendency of computers to reinforce the status quo, the creation of more open learning opportunities for some will almost certainly destroy such possibilities for many of the others.

In the golden future of open learning made possible by computers, other assumptions are embedded which also warrant futher examination. For instance, do we necessarily want always to encourage people to think in ways analogous to those of computers? Certainly, a belief in the relative ease of

"Wallace is making great use of his computer. He can tell you what the Bolivian tin exports will be for the next . . . what is it, Wallace, 67? . . . for the next 67 years."

Figure 9. Cartoon reproduced by courtesy of Sidney Harris.

correcting errors is helpful in freeing the learner from certain kinds of lack of confidence. But what might be the consequences of encouraging learners generally to adopt the kinds of "operational thinking" (Weizenbaum, 1976) which are characteristic of computers? Eason (1982) has depicted the issue with great clarity:

Computer systems are excellent vehicles for handling data which can be unambiguously catergorised or quantified. It is more difficult for them to cope with feelings, motives, aesthetic qualities, . . . ambiguities, uncertainties, etc. Many tasks . . . involve both kinds of data. The original hope of man-computer interaction was that the computer could deal with the formal data leaving man free to deal with the informal. However, experience teaches that man tends to be drawn into the computer model's rational way of interpreting a task, and the less quantifiable aspects are not given appropriate emphasis.

It is also possible that too great an emphasis on the availability of the technology of open learning will make it more difficult to recognize the real practical obstacles that stand in the way between many adults and the learning experiences they might wish to undertake. Merely having a computer terminal at home is not much help as a way of providing learning opportunities for a woman with full-time responsibilities for young children. Nor does having access to a world of information at the touch of a keyboard provide many learning experiences for someone who is unfamiliar with general knowledge structures or, at the most elementary level, with the layout of a keyboard.

Finally, the assumption that individualized, self-directed learning is an ideal form for all adults needs more evidence to support it than yet exists. As Smith (1983) notes:

Current pressures towards so-called self-directed learning and fostering self-directed learners are well intentioned and potentially useful but also simplistic. . . . Interdependence and even dependence can be as functional as independence and autonomy . . . and . . . there is potential danger in confronting learners with the responsibility for exercising more autonomy than experience or training have prepared them to exercise.

As we have already seen in Chapter 3, learners tend to have very favorable or very unfavorable reactions to using the new information technologies as a learning medium. In Canada, TV Ontario, with its remit to develop educational technologies, advises caution in assuming that all learners will be equally happy in open learning with computers. Reporting on the use of computers in adult literacy and numeracy in a project in Toronto, Sharon (1984) finds that "the learners who progress most easily with the self-directed learning materials often remain in the program for a longer time. . . . Some students, however, are unable to learn in this setting." Analogously, Wilson (1984) notes the "individual differences among learners that predict the degree to which they learn seccessfully" from computer-based systems.

It appears that, as yet, there has been relatively little investigation into why people dislike learning and teaching by computers; most studies seem to focus on the reasons for positive responses. But there have been high dropout rates in TICCIT trials of computerized learning in the United States

(Alderman, 1979) and low take-up rates for computer-assisted learning options in some Open University courses in Britain (Jones and Scanlon, 1981). The apparent dislike of using computers, which is suggested by such figures, makes it impossible to advocate computerized open learning as a medium suited to all students.

But perhaps the most dubious of all the assumptions underlying the fostering of individualized self-directed learning is the apparent belief that other people simply are not needed, that learning is better accomplished on one's own than in the more social forms in which it has traditionally taken place. In its more extreme forms, this approach tends to deny the contribution that can be made by knowledgeable, sensitive tutoring and that is made by other learners. The implicit assumption is that learning is best achieved in an atomistic fashion by individuals in their own homes, but such approaches rarely examine the implications of such a situation for all the social bonds that draw people together. Even leaving such general reservations to one side, most community educators will probably find arrogant and unjustified any assumption that individualized learning should be adopted as a general model, when there is ample evidence that many students place a high value on learning together with other people.

In the end, it may be that the atomistic model of individualized self-directed learning will be rejected by community educators for reasons such as these. If computers are to contribute significantly to community education, therefore, it will be essential to show how they can form part of a collaborative, cooperative model of learning and interaction that draws participants toward one another rather than encouraging centrifugal flight.

COMPUTERS AS A CENTRIPETAL FORCE

We have already seen in Chapters 3, 4, and 5 how, depending on the context and purposes of their use, computers can form a powerful centripetal force. They can draw into learning experiences both individuals and groups who might otherwise feel alienated from education; they can create a focus for the activities of community groups; the processes of computer programming can encourage team-work; the desire for computer literacy can bring people together for exhibitions or classes; even the need to seek support with often unfriendly computer systems can encourage collaboration among people who might otherwise not have worked together.

We have also seen, especially in the discussion of the use of large computerized data bases of information in Chapter 4, that computers seem most effective when used within the context of help and advice from other people rather than on their own. The dichotomy which is sometimes presented between computers and adult educators, therefore, seems to me inappropriate. I do not accept the assumption implicit in Hurd's (1982) comment that "with the price of teachers going up and the price of computers going down it [computer-assisted instruction] clearly will play an increasing role in education in the days to come."

Rather, the experience of organizations, such as SCEMP in Britain and the Community Information Exchange in the United States, points toward a model of collaboration among institutions and individuals as the most fruitful way of advancing the uses of computers in the education of the community as a whole. Indeed, as Burge *et al.* (1984) recognize, any viable future development of open learning demands that institutions move toward such a model: "The degree to which institutions can supplant a competitive ethos with a collaborative one will determine the future effectiveness of distance education."

Formal educational institutions have moved quickly to establish such collaborative networks. In Canada, for example, the working mandate of the Office of Educational Communications which links universities in the Association of Atlantic Universities, stresses the need to "coordinate the sharing of resources and the collective exploration of new technologies" (ibid). Similarly, the Council of Ontario Universities has established a Committee on Distance Education to reduce the operating costs of their distance programs by sharing resources, exchanging information about each others' activities, coordinating program planning, and developing other mechanisms for cooperation (ibid).

It is obviously more complicated and difficult for local community organizations to follow such highly cooperative models, especially where they often have to respond to highly specific local needs. In the development of computerized services, however, it may well be that it is only by working collaboratively that they will succeed. They will never have behind them the immense forces of the commercial world that so far have developed computers largely in their own competitive image, nor are they likely to have the large-scale resources of major educational institutions.

As SCEMP has shown, however, cooperation among organizations in community education and also between community organizations and educational institutions is a viable model for using computers to serve the needs of communities, It does not begin to bridge the desperate gap between the developed and the developing world in the use of computer power, nor does

APPENDIX A:
BUYING A
COMPUTER FOR
COMMUNITY USE

This Appendix is *not* intended as a buyer's guide. There are numerous guides of that kind; of the books mentioned in other sections, Deakin (1984) and Covvey and McAlister (1982) both have many useful suggestions to offer. Moreover, any community educator who is thinking of investing in a computer should seek objective professional advice before he or she actually tries to confront a computer supplier. All this Appendix does is to pose a few of the elementary questions that a community educator will want to ask about the equipment he or she is considering. Here, as elsewhere, I have tried to avoid the use of specialist language, but some jargon is unavoidable; all words in inverted commas are fully explained in the Glossary in Appendix C.

1. WHAT WILL IT BE USED FOR?

The purpose for which a computer is bought crucially affects the choice of equipment. Community educators are unlikely to be in the market for a "mainframe" (very large) computer or for a "minicomputer" (medium-sized).

Rather, they will probably choose a kind of "microcomputer," also known as a "personal computer." The main distinctions here are between those relatively inexpensive microcomputers which are intended primarily for home use (often mainly for playing games), and those more expensive machines which are intended for serious educational and business applications.

The main differences are that "home computers" tend to have less available "memory" (working capacity), often plug into a television set so that games can be played in glorious color, and tend to use audio-cassette tapes to store programs. They also tend to be machines which, in general, do not link to other computers or to a printer. "Business computers" tend to have a substantially larger memory and to have their own screen to provide a clearer image than a television screen. They also almost invariably use "disks" to store programs, thereby enabling them to deal with a great deal more information than home computers; those which use " hard disks" (also known as "Winchesters") can store much more information than those which use the more common, and much cheaper, "floppy disks." They also tend to be of a type which can link up at least with a printer and often with other computers too, either within the same office or by telephone.

The next crucial distinction is between printers. Most community organizations are likely to want to use their computers for word processing, often for producing material which needs a wider audience. For such work, the cheapest printer, a "dot-matrix," is simply not suitable, as its print composed of tiny dots is much harder to read than ordinary typescript. A "daisy-wheel" printer, which costs more, produces even in its cheapest versions the kind of high quality typeface which one associates with typed material, and at its most elaborate can perform many functions similar to those carried out by a typesetter.

2. WHAT PROGRAMS WILL I WANT TO USE ON IT?

This is probably the most important question of all, as the choice of a computer should be governed by the programs that can be run on it and which determine whether one can do with it what one wants to do. Here the wisest option is probably to choose the kind of microcomputer which is most widely used among other organizations who have roughly the same purposes as one's own. In Britain in 1985, for example, the BBC Computer is frequently chosen for community education use, as it is the most widely used microcomputer in schools and, therefore, has the largest range of educational programs available for it. In the United States and Canada, a similar choice might be one or another of the computers made by Apple.

3. HOW MUCH WILL IT COST?

It is a truism that the price of computers is constantly coming down: every year one can buy more computer power for less money. One can also, as a general rule, buy the equipment more cheaply in the United States than in Canada and more cheaply in Canada than in Britain. Regardless of where it is bought, however, a serious business or educational computer, together with the essential additional bits and pieces, is likely to cost at least one or two thousand dollars or pounds rather than the much smaller sums for which one can buy home computers.

But the full cost of a computing system consists of much more than merely the purchase price. Indeed, the final cost may well be at least double or even quadruple the original investment. It will be essential to allow for the time involved in making the choice and for the time of all the staff as they are trained to use the equipment and then as they become accustomed to it. In addition, a considerable sum of money will be required to buy the appropriate programs, which can cost nearly as much as the equipment itself— and that is merely for programs which are already available, let alone the cost of having ones specially developed if necessary. Money will also be needed for paying the trainers, for maintenance and insurance, and for the additional costs involved in the bits and pieces, such as special paper to feed through the printer in a continuous sheet, for disks, and so on.

4. WHO ELSE HAS ONE?

This question matters not just for the reasons suggested above but also because any community educator venturing into using computers will probably want to be able to call on informed and informal help. As comments throughout the book have implied, the help given by computer manuals and trainers is rarely sufficient to enable a new user to move forward without problems. Because so many organizations in community education now make use of computers both for education and for other ways of serving their local communities, however, such sources of informal help are daily becoming more available.

APPENDIX B: FURTHER READING

The following books and other materials explore the major ideas discussed in each chapter in language that is generally free from computer jargon.

1. THE PARADOX OF COMPUTERS

BBC TV. *The Computer Programme,* 1982—. A series of ten programs which aims to explain the fundamentals of computing at a practical and theoretical level and is illustrated by diverse examples of the use of computers in the real world; it is available on video from BBC Enterprises Limited, Educational and Training Sales, Woodlands, 80 Wood Lane, London W12 OTT.

Burkitt, Alan, and Williams, Elaine. *The Silicon Civilisation.* London: W. H. Allen, 1981. A very readable account of the development of the microchip and its social implications.

Dertouzos, Michael, and Moses, Joel (Eds.). *The Computer Age: A Twenty Year View.* Cambridge, Mass: MIT Press, 1979. A collection of essays which presents overall a balanced account of the complex effects of computerization, including individual use of computers, trends in traditional computer uses, social and economic effects, and expectations of computerization, underlying technological trends, and a sample of the major attitudes toward the development of artificial intelligence.

Evans, Chris. *The Mighty Micro.* London: Victor Gollancz, 1979. An entertaining, popular forecast of the effects of the microelectronics revolution on many facets of our lives, including educational experiences.

Jones, Barry. *Sleepers, Wake! Technology and the Future of Work*. Brighton: Wheatsheaf Books, 1982. A sober look at the economic implications of extensive computerization, illustrated by examples drawn from many countries.

Laver, Murray. *Computers and Social Change*. Cambridge: Cambridge University Press, 1980. An excellent general introduction to the social, economic, and political implications of computerization written by a computer specialist who avoids jargon.

Sieghart, Paul (Ed.). *Micro-Chips with Everything: The Consequences of Information Technology*. London: Comedia Publishing Group in association with the Institute of Contemporary Arts, 1982. A collection of contributions on the often contradictory effects of information technology on our lives, including the impact on the third world, implications of computerization for work and leisure, the issue of privacy, and significant changes in the mass media.

Toffler, Alvin. *The Third Wave*. New York: William Morrow, 1981. A widely read discussion of the implications of computerization on society, including how and if we may work in the future.

2. COMPUTERS AND GENDER

Deakin, Rose. *Women and Computing: The Golden Opportunity*. London: Macmillan Publishers, 1984. A popular account of why women are not well-represented in computing, with many ideas and practical examples of how women can launch themselves into careers in the field.

Gerver, Elisabeth, and Lewis, Linda. "Women, computers and adult education: liberation or oppression?" *Convergence*, 1984, *17*, 4. An investigation of the extent of the under-representation of women in learning about computers, together with an analysis of the factors involved and suggestions about how to improve the situation.

Menzies, Heather. *Women and the Chip: Case Studies of the Effects of Informatices on Employment in Canada*. Montreal: Institute for Research on Public Policy, 1981. A balanced study of the present and foreseeable impacts of office automation on the extent, and the nature, of women's employment in Canada; the findings seem likely to be replicated in most developed countries.

Simons, G. L. *Women in Computing*. Manchester: National Computing Center, 1981. A detailed investigation of the underrepresentation of women in the field of computing, including substantial statistical evidence together with case studies of women who have succeeded in the field.

Women's National Commission. "The other half of our future: report of the WMN's Ad-Hoc Working Group on Training Opportunities for Women." London: Cabinet Office, 1984. A very readable set of proposals for improving educational and training standards for women, including detailed discussion of issues related to women and the new technology.

3. COMPUTERS AND INFORMAL LEARNING

ACACE (Advisory Council for Adult Continuing Education). "Microtechnology and the education of adults." Leicester: ACACE, 1984. A brief account of approaches to computer literacy and other facets of using computers in adult education in England and Wales; many of the findings from a survey of providers would probably be replicated in other countries.

Adams, Anthony, and Jones, Esmor. *Teaching Humanities in the Microelectronic Age.* Milton Keynes: Open University Press, 1983. An account which, while intended primarily for school teachers, discusses present developments in computer programs for the humanities, many of which have direct or analogous applications in teaching adults; it includes a useful appendix on how to evaluate educational software.

Coburn, P., and Kelman, P., Roberts, N., Snyder. T. F. F., Watt, D. H., and Weiner, C. *Practical Guide to Computers in Education.* Reading, Mass: Addison-Wesley, 1982. A practical handbook which, while intended primarily for school teachers, is also useful as a general introduction to the potential of computers in education.

Gerver, Elisabeth. *Computers and Adult Learning.* Milton Keynes: Open University Press, 1984. Explores existing developments in using computers in adult education, including learning by and about computers.

Hawkridge, David. *New Information Technology in Education.* London: Croom Helm, 1983. Surveys most of the important developments in the field, and contains many useful suggestions for further reading.

Megarry, Jacquetta, Walker, David, Nisbet, Stanley, and Hoyle, Eric (Eds.). *Computers and Education* (World Yearbook of Education 1982–83). London: Kogan Page, 1983. A wide-ranging international collection of essays, which gives a good overview of most of the current developments in using computers in education, although it has little to say about computers and adult education; it includes a useful annotated bibliography.

Papert, Seymour. *Mindstorms: Children, Computers and Powerful Ideas.* Brighton: Harvester Press, 1980. Seminal book for those who believe that artificial intelligence can transform children's learning; while sometimes hard to follow for a nonmathematician, it has many implications particularly for adult basic education.

Radcliffe, John, and Salkeld, Roberts. *Towards Computer Literacy: The BBC Computer Literacy Project 1979–1983.* London: British Broadcasting Corporation, 1983. The story of the thinking behind, and the development of, this highly effective and influential multimedia project on computer literacy for adults.

Rushby, Nicholas. *An Introduction to Educational Computing.* London: Croom Helm, 1979. An excellent introduction to the subject, which makes useful distinctions among different types of learning and how computers might enrich them; the glossary of terms used in educational computing is particularly helpful.

SCEMP (Scottish Community Education Microelectronics Project). "Guidelines for the design of computer programs for community use." Glasgow: Scottish Microelectronics Development Programme, 1982. Based on research into early programs designed for SCEMP, a useful set of guidelines for community educators who are developing programs for novice computer users.

4. USING COMPUTERS IN THE COMMUNITY

BBC TV. *The Electronic Office*, 1984—. A series of six programs which explains and explores the revolution in office technology, including the detailed characteristics and effects of many contemporary computer applications.

Kania, Helena. "Prestel for People . . ." London: Council for Educational Technology, 1983. Contains a very useful discussion of the nature of "social information" and the difficulties in providing it cost effectively.

Legge, Derek. "Development of information, guidance, and counselling services." Amersfoort, the Netherlands: European Bureau of Adult Education, 1981. While not about using computers in this field, nevertheless offers a helpful account of the ideal and actual characteristics of such services.

5. COOPERATING WITH COMPUTERS

Covvey, H. Dominic, and McAlister, Harding Neil. *Computer Choices: Beware of Conspicuous Computing*. Reading, Mass: Addison-Wesley, 1982. A realistic look at what computers really have to offer organizations, and how people can best choose a system for their own needs.

Farrow, H. F. *Computerisation Guidelines*. Manchester: National Computing Center, 1979. A detailed practical guide to the stages involved in computerizing an organization; although some of the guidelines are more applicable to large-scale computerization, even small community organizations would find it helpful.

6. PROMISES AND PITFALLS

Brookfield, Stephen. *Adult Learners, Adult Education and the Community*. Milton Keynes: Open University Press, 1983. While not dealing with computers, a useful study of the field which argues the need for social learning.

Knowles, Malcolm. "Malcolm Knowles finds a worm in his Apple." *Training and Development Journal*, May, 1983. A forthright account of the experience of learning to use a computer system, which puts inflated claims for computerized learning in perspective.

Smith, Robert M. *Learning How to Learn: Applied Theory for Adults*. Milton Keynes: Open University Press, 1983. A detailed study of how adults learn, which again sets inflated claims for computerized learning in a realistic and humane perspective.

Weizenbaum, Joseph. *Computer Power and Human Reason*. San Francisco: Freeman, 1976. The classic attack on the overenthusiastic promotion of artificial intelligence, reminding us of the human purposes which lie behind the use of computers.

APPENDIX C: GLOSSARY

The words and phrases below have appeared in this book and are described below in fairly rough and ready terms. Explanations of other words which are often encountered in educational computing and in introductory guides to computers may be found in Rushby (1979), O'Shea and Self (1983), Deakin (1984), and Gerver (1984).

Address ● A specific location within a computer program, to which information is sent.

Applications ● A term referring to the uses to which a computer program is put; word-processing is one example of an application.

Artificial intelligence ● The area of computer science concerned with computer programs which attempt to emulate the processes of human thinking.

Assembly language ● A programming language which uses mnemonics rather than words to make a computer carry out tasks. It is nearer to the language of the computer itself and, therefore, more difficult to write than high-level languages.

BASIC ● Currently the most widely used programing language for microcomputers; the initials stand for "Beginner's All-purpose Symbolic Instruction Code."

Binary ● Refers to a choice of only two alternatives, such as on-off or 1-0. It is the basic operating principle of all computers.

Block ● A term often associated with a computer error.

Boot ● Refers to the process of getting a computer program to start working.

Bug ● An error in a computer program.

Bus ● A route within the computer along which signals from one of several sources travel to one of several destinations.

Business Computer ● Term often used for a sophisticated microcomputer intended for serious business applications, such as word processing, accounting, or data bases; also known as a "desktop computer."

Computer ● An electronic machine that stores and manipulates data by following detailed instructions.

Computer aided learning ● One of many terms referring to the use of computers for educational purposes, with the implication that other methods are used as well.

Computer architecture ● The structure of a computer system.

Computer assisted learning ● Another term for using computers for educational purposes, with the implication that other methods are also used.

Computer assisted instruction ● Using a computer for teaching purposes; in Britain the term often implies a highly pedagogical approach.

Computer based education ● Another term for using computers for educational purposes.

Computer based learning ● Yet another term for using computers for educational purposes.

Computer conferencing ● Refers to communication among two or more people by way of computers linked to one another, often by telecommunications.

Computer literacy ● A term, discussed at length in the text, which has a wide range of meanings. It generally includes familiarity with the uses and abuses of computers and the ability to use a computer keyboard.

Computer operator ● Someone who enters pre-prepared data into a computer.

Computer supported learning ● Still another term for using computers in education.

Computer system ● Term used for the interrelating or interacting components of one or more computers

Computer technician ● Someone who is trained to service and repair computers.

Computing ● Refers to the process of interacting with computers.

Console ● Term used for a way of communicating manually with a computer, generally by way of a keyboard and terminal.

Cursor • A mark that appears on the screen of a computer to show the user where the next character will appear once he or she enters it on the keyboard.

Daisy-wheel printer • The kind of computer printer which produces a high quality, typewriter-like print, so-called because of the way in which the letters in it are bunched together on a stalk.

Data • Any numbers, words, or other precisely specified symbols that are manipulated by a computer.

Data base • A highly organized collection of data that can be searched to yield specific information.

Data processing • The manipulation of symbols by a computer.

Desk-top computer • See "business computer."

Disk • A thin magnetic device that holds a large amount of data for use by a computer. A floppy disk is generally used with a relatively small computer and holds much less data than a hard disk, which is generally used with a mainframe or a minicomputer.

Disk drive • A piece of equipment which holds a disk and transmits the data on it to and from a computer very quickly.

Documentation • Notes about the content and purposes of a computer program.

Dot matrix printer • A computer printer which produces print made up of little dots which, depending on how fine the dots are, can be considerably more difficult to read than the print of a "daisy-wheel" printer.

Download • The process of transferring data from one computer directly into the memory of another.

Drill and practice • An instructional program in which the learner is given a highly structured sequence of exercises.

Echo • The return of data to the point from which it was sent.

Educational technology • Term used to refer to all of the technological means by which learning can be supported, including computers.

Electronic blackboard • Term used in the text to refer to Cyclops, a system developed by the Open University to allow telephone transmission of diagrams and other figures by way of a computer system.

Electronic journal • Term used to refer to "publication" of a journal by way of a computer; articles are submitted and distributed by computers communicating with one another.

Electronic mail • Term used to refer to communication between individuals via computers which are generally at a distance from one another.

Feedback ● The use of information produced at one stage for another stage.

Field ● A unit of information within a larger amount of computer data.

Floppy disk ● See "disk."

Graphics ● The visual material (other than text) that appears on the screen of a computer; it can include drawings, lines, graphs, charts, maps, and moving images.

Hands-on ● A popular term for practical experience of a computer.

Hard disk ● See "disk."

Hardware ● The various pieces of equipment used in computing.

High-level language ● A programming language which more nearly resembles natural language or mathematical notation than does assembly language.

High technology ● An umbrella term which often includes sophisticated uses of computers.

Home computer ● A term for a nonbusiness microcomputer, often particularly well adapted for playing games and usually relatively easy to operate.

Informatics ● Another term for information technology.

Information ● Meaningful data or symbols.

Information retrieval ● The process of getting useful information by searching a large amount of data.

Information technology ● An umbrella term which usually refers to the use of computers and/or telecommunication systems. The terms "new technologies" and "new information technologies" both tend to be used in the same sense.

Interactive ● Refers to the situation in which a user gives information to a computer which then gives a rapid response.

Keyboard ● A device by which data is entered into computers. Microcomputers almost invariably have a QWERTY keyboard.

Keypuncher ● Term used for the person who carried out the now largely old-fashioned function of using a keyboard to punch data into cards or paper tape.

Language ● Refers to the code to communicate with a computer. The term often appears on the screen, if there is a serious malfunction of a particular part of a microcomputer.

Load ● The process in which information is fed into the computer from an external source, such as a tape recorder or a disk drive.

Log on ● The process of starting to interact with a computer system.

LOGO • A programing language derived from work in artificial intelligence, which is widely used in teaching children how to program.

Mainframe computer • The largest kind of computer.

Memory • Where a computer finds its instructions and its data and stores its results; the working capacity of a computer.

Micro • Term often used casually to refer to a microcomputer.

Microcomputer • The smallest kind of computer, also known as a "personal computer," or simply as a "micro."

Microelectronics • A term usually used in connection with the technology of silicon chips; the word itself refers to that branch of electronics which deals with very small voltages and currents. See "microprocessor."

Microprocessor • A silicon chip which contains the components needed to carry out the operations determined by a program.

Microtechnology • Refers to the technology built on applications of the microprocessor.

Minicomputer • A medium sized computer.

Model • An analog of a real-life situation or system which can be used to elicit information about the likely behavior of the real situation or system.

Modem • A device which enables computers to communicate over telephone wires.

Monitor • A term frequently used to refer to the television-like screen by which many computers display information.

Mouse • A device which enables a computer user to dispense with the keyboard for certain functions.

Network • A system in which computers communicate with one another.

Operating system • Refers to the program used by a computer to enable it to load a high-level language and to communicate with the user and with printers and disk drives, etc.

Pack • To put more than one unit of information into a single storage space on a computer.

Pascal • A programing language.

Personal computer • See "microcomputer."

Port • That part of a computer from which certain specific kinds of information are fed in and out.

Printer • Equipment that prints out information from the computer line by line.

Print-out ● The information printed out by the computer printer.

Privatique ● Term defined at some length in the text. Refers to use of freestanding computer systems.

Program ● The instructions that tell a computer what to do.

Programmed learning ● Term referring to highly structured, regimented, predetermined learning, now often used in derogatory fashion.

Programmer ● A person who writes computer programs.

Programming language ● A symbolic code which allows a programmer to communicate with a computer; there are many different programming languages, which bear variable relationships to English.

Queue ● Refers to information waiting to be processed within a computer.

QWERTY ● Refers to the layout of a standard typewriter, which is used for most computer keyboards; the letters represent the first six letters of the keyboard.

Read ● A term for obtaining data from one form of storage and transferring it into another.

Remote work ● Refers to work undertaken, often at home, at a distance from a central computer, with which the worker communicates.

ROM ● Stands for Read-Only Memory. Refers to that part of a computer's memory which contains a fixed pattern of data which cannot be altered.

Simulation ● An analog of a real-life situation or system which can be used to elicit information about the real system.

Software ● Computer programs.

Software package ● Term used to refer to an entire program together with its documentation and other materials associated with it.

Sort ● To arrange computerized information into related groups.

Stack ● A storage area on the computer which is used for temporary storage of data.

String ● A term used in programming to refer to a set of items arranged in a particular kind of sequence.

Syntax error ● Term that often appears on the screen of microcomputers, referring to a mistake made in the form in which data is entered.

Systems analyst ● Someone who analyses how best to put computers to work in specific situations.

Tape ● Used here to refer to ordinary audio-cassette tape, which is used for loading programs into certain home computers.

Télématique ● Term discussed at length in the text. Refers to an interlocking system of computer communications.

Terminal ● A device for communicating with a computer, usually consisting of a keyboard, a monitor, and perhaps a printer.

Touch-sensitive ● Refers generally to a computer monitor which receives commands from pressure placed on it, thereby reducing the need for use of a keyboard.

Trace ● A way of using a computer program to check and locate errors in other programs.

Track ● A channel on a disk.

Tree ● Used here to refer to a computer structure of information in which one begins at a common starting point and then branches out for more specific information.

Turtle ● Term used for a computer-controlled "animal" which either moves on the computer screen or exists as a physical object which can move around. Used in programing in LOGO.

Up-date ● To change the information in a program so that it is up-to-date.

User friendly ● Refers to a computer and/or programs which are supposed to be easy for beginners to use.

VDU ● Stands for visual display unit; an alternative term for a monitor.

Videotex ● Refers to computer-generated information displayed at a distance by a television screen. Also sometimes appears as "videotext."

Winchester ● A term often used to refer to a "hard disk."

Word processing ● Refers to computerized manipulation of words usually by way of a keyboard.

Write ● To transfer data from one form of store onto another, as, for instance, from a disk to the main memory of a computer.

REFERENCES

ACACE. *A Strategy for the Basic Education of Adults: a Report Commissioned by the Secretary of State for Education and Science*. Leicester: Advisory Council for Adult and Continuing Education, 1979.

ACACE. *Adults: their Educational Experience and Needs*. Leicester: Advisory Council for Adult and Continuing Education, 1982.

ACACE. Microtechnology and the education of adults. Leicester: Advisory Council for Adult and Continuing Education, 1984.

Adams, Anthony, and Jones, Esmor. *Teaching Humanities in the Microelectronic Age*. Milton Keynes: Open University Press, 1983.

ALBSU. The use of microcomputers in basic education. London: Adult Literacy and Basic Skills Unit, 1982.

Alderman, D.L. Evaluation of the TICCIT computer-assisted instructional system in the community college. *SIGCUE Bulletin*, 1979, *13*, 3, 5–17.

Alderman, D.L., Appel, L.R., and Murphy, R.T. PLATO and TICCIT: an evaluation of CAI in the community college. *Education Technology*, 1978, *18*, 4, 40–45.

Argyll and Clyde Health Board. Alcohol and Health. Computer program developed for Scottish Community Education Microelectronics Projects, Glasgow, 1983.

Banks, David. Adult classes in computing: a survey. *Adult Education*, 1983, *56*, 1.

Banks, David. The effectiveness of introductory computing evening classes. *Adult Education*, 1984, *57*, 3, 255–261.

Barrett, Kristen. Written communication to the author at the Scottish Community Education Microelectronics Project, Glasgow, August 25, 1982.

Basic Education and Computer Course Interim Report: Basic Education in Numeracy and New Technology. Brighton, Sussex: Friends Centre and Brighton Polytechnic, 1984.

BBC. The computer literacy project. Unpublished BBC Broadcasting Research Special Report. London: British Broadcasting Corporation, 1981.

BBC. BBC's computer literacy project: an evaluation. Unpublished BBC Broadcasting Research Special Report. London: British Broadcasting Corporation, 1983.

Beer, Donald. Cited in Jane Adams, The high tech personality. *New England Business*, November 21, 1983, 12–15.

Bennet, Charles. Motherwell District Library Services. In Scottish Community Education Microelectronics Project, SCEMP: another view, 1984.

Bernstein, Danielle. The invisible woman. *Practical Computing*, January, 1984, 189.

Beyers, Charlotte. Growing sex gap shows up in computer tastes. *The Times Educational Supplement*, November 18, 1983, 15.

Boden, Margaret. *Artificial Intelligence and Natural Man*. Hassocks: Harvester Press, 1977.

Bostock, Stephen, and Seifert, Roger. Introducing a microcomputer into adult education classes. *Adult Education*, 1983, *55*, 4.

Bostock, Stephen, and Seifert, Roger. Computer integraton and computer literacy. In Microtechnology and the education of adults. Leicester: Advisory Council for Adult and Continuing Education, 1984.

Bown, Lalage. The challenge of adult basic education: its status and its role with lifelong education. In Ron South (Ed.), *Adult Basic Education Conference, University of St Andrews, June 26–July 1, 1983*. Amersfoort: Bureau Europeen de l'Education Populaire, 1983.

Boyd, Gary. Education and miseducation by computer. In Jacquetta Megarry *et al.* (Eds.), *Computers and Education*, 1983.

Bradbeer, Robin, DeBono, Peter, and Laurie, Peter. *The Computer Book: An Introduction to Computers and Computing*. London: British Broadcasting Corporation, 1982.

Brookfield, Stephen. *Adult Learning, Adult Education and the Community*. Milton Keynes: Open University Press, 1983.

Brown, J.S., Burton, R.R., and Bell, A.G. SOPHIE: a step towards creating a reactive learning environment. *International Journal of Man-Machine Studies*, 1975, *7*, 675–96.

Burge, Elizabeth, Wilson, Joy, and Mehler, Audrey. Communications and information technologies and distance education in Canada. New Technologies in Canadian Education Paper 5. Toronto: TV Ontario, 1984.

Burkitt, Alan, and Williams, Elaine. *The Silicon Civilisation*. London: W.H. Allen, 1980.

Butler, Linda. Educational information for adults: the public library user viewpoint. Paper presented at the Open University (Yorkshire Region), Leeds, June 19, 1983.

Champine, C.A. What makes a system reliable? *Datamation*, 1978, *24*, 9, 194.

Chandler, Daniel. *Young Learners and the Microcomputer*. Milton Keynes: Open University Press, 1983.

Chivers, G.E. A comparative international study of intervention studies to reduce girls' disadvantages in science and technology education and vocational training. Paper presented to Conference on Interests in Science and Technology Education, 12th IPN Symposium in cooperation with UNESCO, Kiel, West Germany, April 2–6, 1984.

Clancey, W.J. Tutoring rules for guiding a case method dialogue. *International Journal of Man-Machine Studies*, 1979, *11*, 25–49.

Clark, Alison. SCEMP computer placement and the disabled project at Inverurie. In Scottish Community Education Microelectronics Project, SCEMP: another view, 1984.

Coburn, P., Kelman, P., Roberts, N., Snyder, T.F.F., Watt, D.H., and Weiner, C. *Practical Guide to Computers in Education*. Reading, Mass: Addison-Wesley, 1982.

Community Computing Network Newsletter. Newcastle Information Support Project. October, 1984a, 6. Published by Community Computing Network, Whitehaven, Cumbria.

Community Computing Network Newsletter. Community Information USA. October, 1984b, *6*, 10–11.

Computerfax: A Guide to BBC and Open University Resources in Computing 1984–85. London and Milton Keynes: British Broadcasting Corporation and the Open University, 1984.

Control Data. Basic skills learning system. Leaflet, Control Data, P.O. Box O, Minneapolis, Minnesota 55440, 1980.

Control Data. PLATO: computer-assisted education. Leaflet, Control Data, P.O. Box O, Minneapolis, Minnesota, 55440, 1981.

Covvey, H. Dominic, and McAlister, Neil Harding. *Computer Choices: Beware of Conspicuous Computing*. Reading, Mass: Addison-Wesley, 1982.

CRASH. Some experimental research on computer-assisted distance education. 1984a, *2*, 2. Published by Scottish Adult Basic Education Unit, Dalkeith.

CRASH. Have a go. 1984b, *2*, 1. Published by Scottish Adult Basic Education Unit, Dalkeith.

Crowley, June. Microsyster: current work and future projects. London: Microsyster, August, 1984.

Deakin, Rose. *Women and Computing: the Golden Opportunity*. London: Macmillan Publishers, 1984.

Dean, Christopher, and Whitlock, Quintin. *A Handbook of Computer Based Training*. London: Kogan Page, 1983.

Dertouzos, Michael, and Moses, Joel (Eds.). *The Computer Age: A Twenty Year View*. Cambridge, Mass: MIT Press, 1979.

Eason, Ken. Human factors in information technology. HUSAT Memo No. 252, University of Loughborough, 1982.

ECCTIS. *ECCTIS Information*. Milton Keynes: Educational Counselling and Credit Transfer Information Service, September, 1984.

Elling, M. Remote work. Paper presented to Conference on Women, Work, and Computerization, International Federation for Information Processing, Riva del Sole, Italy, September 17–21, 1984.

Ellis, Lynda. Health Awareness Games. Computer program adapted by Michael Hendry for Scottish Community Education Microelectronics Project, Glasgow, 1981.

Else, Anne. Written communication to the author from Wellington, New Zealand, August 31, 1984a.

Else, Anne. Written communication to the author from Wellington, New Zealand, November 29, 1984b.

EOC. Information technology in schools: guidelines of good practice for teachers of IT. Produced by the London Borough of Croydon for the Equal Opportunities Commission, Manchester, 1983.

EOC. Attract more girls to information technology. News release, Manchester, January 19, 1984.

Evans, Chris. *The Mighty Micro*. London: Victor Gollancz, 1979.

Ezard, John. More than just words on paper. *The Guardian*, November 15, 1984, 17.

Fairhall, John. Experts uncover 'serious errors' in schools computer pack. *The Guardian*, April 4, 1984.

Farrow, H.F. *Computerisation Guidelines: Guidelines for Managers, other Employees and Trade Unions Involved in the Introduction and Use of Computer-based Systems*. Manchester: National Computing Center, 1979.

Feen, Frieda. Written communication to the author from San Francisco, November 29, 1984.

Feldberg, Roslyn, and Glenn, Evelyn. Technology and work degradation: effects of office automation on women clerical workers. In Joan Rothschild (Ed.), *Machina ex Dea: Feminist Perspectives on Technology*. New York: Pergamon Press, 1982.

Finlay, Aileen. Strathclyde Regional Council: Argyll and Bute Division Community Education Service. In Scottish Community Education Microelectronics Project, SCEMP: another view, 1984.

Forester, Tom (Ed.). *The Microelectronics Revolution: The Complete Guide to the New Technology and its Impact on Society*. Oxford: Basil Blackwell, 1980.

Freeman, Richard, Personal communication to the author at the National Extension College, June 25, 1983.

Gartside, Peter. Six courses linked to BBC Computer Literacy Project. Glasgow: Scottish Council for Educational Technology, May , 1982.

Geoffrion, Leo. Computer-based approaches to overcoming language handicap. In Jacquetta Megarry *et al.*, (Eds.), *Computers and Education*, 1983.

Gerver, Elisabeth. *Computers and Adult Learning*. Milton Keynes: Open University Press, 1984.

Gerver, Elisabeth, and Lewis, Linda. Women, computers, and adult education: liberation or oppression? *Convergence*, 1984, *17*, 4.

Gibbons, Sue, and Simpson, Ormond. Let the computer take the strain. *Teaching at a Distance*, 1982, *22*, 59–63.

Gill, Karamjit. Research work. In Basic Education and Computer Course Interim Report, 1984.

Gilligan, C., *In a Different Voice*. Cambridge, Mass: Harvard University Press, 1983.

Glyn-Jones, Anne. Job skills in the computer age. Exeter: Devon County Council and the University of Exeter, 1984.

Goldenberg, E.P. *Special Technology for Special Children: Computers to Serve Communication and Autonomy in the Education of the Handicapped*. Baltimore: University Park Press, 1979.

Goodman, Candice. We have all the technology, who's got all the money? *The Guardian*, November 15, 1984, 26.

Grace, Rosemary. Microelectronics, Electronics, Computing and Information Technology Courses in Scotland 1984–85. Paisley, Scotland: Microelectronics Educational Development Center, 1984.

Grant Johnson, F. Der computer und die Technologisierung des Inneren. *Psyche*, 1980, *34*, 790–811.

Greater Glasgow Health Board Education Department. Planning a Well-Woman Centre. Computer program developed for Scottish Community Education Microelectronics Project, Glasgow, 1983.

Groark, Dennis. Angus District Library Services. In Scottish Community Education Microelectronics Project, SCEMP: another view, 1984.

The Guardian. Society tomorrow: digital computer competition. October 17, 1984, 7.

Hammond, J., Cited in Ezard, More than just words on paper, 1984.

Harris, Ben. I have seen the future and it is down at the moment. Lecture in the series "Being Human in a Technological Age," Vassar College, November, 1983.

Harris, S. *What's so Funny about Computers?* Los Altos, Calif: William Kaufmann, 1982.

Hawkridge, David. *New Information Technology in Education*. London: Croom Helm, 1983.

Hebenstreit, Jacques. The '10,000 micocomputers plan' in France. In Jacquetta Megarry *et al.* (Eds.), *Computers in Education*, 1983.

Hetherington, Tony, Guys' games. *The Times Educational Supplement*, December 12, 1984, 40.

Home Office. An evaluation of the use of PLATO in Aylesbuy Prison. Unpublished internal report, London, 1983.

Houser, Michael. Computer college. *The Times Educational Supplement*, March 2, 1984.

Hurd, John. From computer to student: flexibility in program design. *Options*, 1982, *13*, 1–3. Published by University of Toronto.

Hurly, Paul. Continuing education, metamedia and the ghost shirt society insurrection. *Canadian Journal of University Continuing Education*, 1984, *10*, 2, 5–19.

Jones, Ann, and Eileen Scanlon (Eds.). A review of research in the CAL Group: a report of the first annual conference, November, 1981. CAL Research Group Technical Report 27. Published by the Open University, Milton Keynes.

Jones, Barry. *Sleepers, Wake! Technology and the Future of Work*. Brighton: Wheatsheaf Books, 1982.

Kania, Helena. *Prestel for People*. London: Council for Educational Technology, 1983.

Keel, Bridget. Avon calling. In Educational Counselling and Credit Transfer Information Service, *ECCTIS Information*, 1984.

Kidder, Tracy. *The Soul of a New Machine*. London: Allen Lane, 1982.

Kirk, Pauline. Local support services in continuing education: new opportunities? *Teaching at a Distance*, 1982, *21*.

Knowles, Malcolm. Malcolm Knowles finds a worm in his Apple. *Training and Development Journal*, May, 1983, 12–14.

Kulik, J.A., Kulik, C-L.C., and Cohen, P.A. Effectiveness of computer-based college teaching: a meta-analysis of findings. *Review of Educational Research*, 1980, *50*, 524–544.

Laidlaw, George. The identification of the scope of micros as a community resource: an evaluation of the Scottish Community Education Microelectronics Project. Dundee: Dundee College of Education, 1984.

Lally, Mike, and MacLeod, Iain. The promise of microcomputers in developing basic skills. In Jacquetta Megarry *et al.* (Eds.), *Computers and Education*, 1983.

Laver, Murray. *Computers and Social Change*. Cambridge: University Press, 1980.

Lean, Elizabeth. Byting back: the industry responds. *Training and Development Journal*, May, 1983, 18–20.

Legge, Derek. Development of information, guidance, and counselling services. Amersfoort: European Bureau of Adult Education, 1981.

Lewis, R., and Tagg, E.D. (Eds.). *Computers in Education*. Amsterdam: North Holland, 1981.

Loop, Liza, and Anton, Julia. Bringing computers to the people. *Classroom Computer News*, 1982, *3*, 1, 29–30, 86.

Loop, Liza, Anton, Julia, and Zamora, Ramon. *ComputerTown: Bringing Computer Literacy to your Community*. Reston, Virginia: Reston Publishing Co., 1983.

Loyer, Dennis. Alberta College Hearing Impaired Education Centre PLATO Project. Edmonton: Alberta College, July, 1983.

Luchins, E.H., and Luchins, A.S. Female mathematicians: a contemporary appraisal. In L.H. Fox, L. Brody, and D. Tobin (Eds.) *Women and the Mathematical Mystique*. Baltimore: John Hopkins University Press, 1980.

Lussato, Bruno, and Bounine, Jean. *Télématique . . . ou Pîvatique? Questions à Simon Nora et Alain Minc*. Paris: Editions d'Informatique, 1979.

Maccoby, E., and Jacklin, C., *The Psychology of Sex Differences*. Stanford, California: Stanford Unversity Press, 1974.

MacDonald, Gus. Personal communication to the author at Microbeacon, Edinburgh, October 16, 1984.

Marohn, Stephanie. Computer age feminists. *Woman News*, San Francisco, California, undated.

Martin, John. *The Wired Society: A Challenge for Tomorrow*. Englewood Cliffs, New Jersey: Prentice-Hall, 1978.

Matas, Robert. Failed predictions. *Globe and Mail*, August 18, 1983, 5.

McCann, John, and McKay, Martin. The family meets the machine: computer camps in Angus. *Mirror*, 1983, *6*. Published by Network, Glasgow.

McClain, E. Do women resist computers? *Popular Computing*, January, 1983.

McLean, Les. Taking the mystery out of microcomputers. *The Times Educational Supplement*, December 21, 1984.

McWilliams, Peter. *The Personal Computer Book*. Los Angeles: Prelude Press, 1983.

Megarry, Jacquetta, 1983. Thinking, learning and educating: the role of the computer. In Jacquetta Megarry *et al.* (Eds.), *Computers and Education*, 1983.

Megarry, Jacquetta, Walker, David, Nisbet, Stanley and Hoyle, Eric (Eds.). *Computers and Education* (World Yearbook of Education 1982/83). London: Kogan Page, 1983.

Menzies, Heather. *Women and the Chip: Case Studies of the Effects of Informatics on Employment in Canada.* Montreal: Institute for Research on Public Policy, 1981.

Menzies, Heather. *Computers on the Job: Surviving Canada's Microcomputer Revolution.* Toronto: James Lorimer and Co., 1982.

Metcalfe, George. Written communication to the author from Dunfermline, Fife, December 27, 1984.

Microbeacon. The Microbeacon Project. Leaflet, Edinburgh, 1984.

Microsyster. Microsyster. Leaflet, Wesley House, Wild Court, Off Kingsway, London WC2, undated.

Microsyster. Written communication to the author from London, November 13, 1984.

Microwave Band, 1984, *9.* Published by the Computers in Adult Basic Education Group, Liverpool.

Midgley, Judy. Educational information for adults: the educational advisory service—user viewpoint. Paper presented at the Open University (Yorkshire Region), Leeds, June 19, 1983.

Miller, Wendy. Personal communication to the author at Women's Technology Training Workshop, Sheffield, May 8, 1984a.

Miller, Wendy. Women's Technology Training Workshop—Progress Report. Report to Board of Directors, City Center Training Limited, October 24, 1984b.

Myers, C. Providing educational information for adults: the consumer viewpoint—the impact of inadequate information on the client. Paper presented at the Open University (Yorkshire Region), Leeds, June 19, 1983.

NA'AMAT. Working women and technology. Leaflet produced by the Status of Women Division, Movement of Working Women and Volunteers, Tel Aviv, undated.

Naisbitt, John. *Megatrends.* New York: Warner Books, 1982.

Nash, Vicki, The microspecial starter pack. Glasgow: Scottish Microelectronics Development Programme, June, 1984.

National Science Foundation. Science and engineering education: data and information. Prepared for the National Science Board Commission on Pre-College Education in Mathematics, Science and Technology by the Office of Scientific and Engineering Personnel and Education, Washington, D.C., undated.

National Women's Mailing List. National Women's Mailing List. Leaflet, San Francisco, undated.

NEC. Printout of "Micro-Aided Learning," produced by the National Extension College, dated 12.03.83. Distributed at the National Institute of Adult Continuing Education Annual Study Conference, Bangor, April 10–12, 1984.

New Literacy, The. The new literacy: an introduction to computers. Booklet produced for the Southern California Consortium for Community College Television, Cypress, California, 1983.

Noor. Managing adult literacy training. Cited in Lalage Bown, The challenge of adult basic education: its status and role with lifelong education, 1983. In Ron South (Ed.). *Adult Basic Education Conference, University of St. Andrews, June 26–July 1, 1983.* Amersfoort: Bureau Europeen de l'Education Populaire, 1983.

Nora, Simon, and Minc, Alain. *The Computerization of Society.* Cambridge, Mass: MIT Press, 1980.

Norman, Colin. *The God that Limps: Science and Technology in the Eighties*. London: Norton Publishers, 1981.

OECD. *The Challenge of Unemployment*. Paris: Organization for European Cooperation and Development, 1982.

OU. Study guide to micros in schools: an awareness pack for teachers (Apple edition). Milton Keynes: Open University, 1984.

O'Shea, Tim. Intelligent computer tutors. *The Times Higher Education Supplement*, March 23, 1984.

O'Shea, Tim, and Self, John. *Learning and Teaching with Computers: Artificial Intelligence in Education*. Brighton: Harvester Press, 1983.

Osin, L. Computer assisted instruction in arithmetic in Israeli disadvantaged elementary schools. In R. Lewis and E.D. Tagg (Eds.), *Computers in Education*, 1981.

Ottley, Penny, and Kempson, Elaine. Computer benefits? London: National Consumer Council, 1982.

Paine, Nigel. Personal communication at Dundee College of Education, November 20, 1984.

Papert, Seymour. *Mindstorms: Children, Computers and Powerful Ideas*. Brighton: Harvester Press, 1980.

PEER. Microcomputers in the classroom: are girls getting an even break? Washington, D.C.: Project on Equal Education Rights for the NOW Legal Defense and Education Fund, 1983.

Perkins, W.J. (Ed.). *High Technology Aids for the Disabled*. London: Butterworth, 1983.

Pollak, S., and Gilligan, C. Images of violence in thematic apperception test stories. *Journal of Personality and Social Psychology*, 1982, *42*, 1.

Poore, J.H. Jr., Qualls, J.E., and Brown, B.L. FSU PLATO Project: basic skills in math for Florida high schools (final report). Florida: Computing Center, Florida State University, 1979.

Preece, Jenny, and Jones, Ann. Training teachers to select educational computer software: results of a formative evaluation of a Open University Pack P541. Milton Keynes: Open University CAL Research Group Technical Report, 1984.

Quillan, Viv. *Women's Work*. London: Hamish Hamilton, 1984.

Radcliffe, John. BBC Computer literacy project progress report, June 1983. Unpublished report. London: British Broadcasting Corporation.

Radcliffe, John, and Salkeld, Roberts. *Towards Computer Literacy: The BBC Computer Literacy Project 1979–1983*. London: British Broadcasting Corporation, 1983.

Rogers, Rick. Pick a winning combination. *The Guardian*, August 16, 1983.

Rossen, P. Do schools teach computer anxiety? *Ms. Magazine*, December, 1982.

Rothschild, Joan (Ed.). *Women, Technology, and Innovation*. Oxford: Pergamon Press, 1982.

Rushby, Nick. *An Introduction to Educational Computing*. London: Croom Helm, 1979.

Rushby, Nick. The future of CEDAR. *CAL News*, July 25, 1984. Published by Imperial College, London.

Safran, C. Hidden lessons. *New York Daily News*, October 9, 1983.

Salkeld, Roberts. Personal communication at the British Broadcasting Corporation, London, on June 7, 1983.

SCAN. Disabled learn quickly at the Garioch. March, 1984, 10. Published by Scottish Community Education Council, Edinburgh.

Scanlon, Eileen, Jones, Ann, O'Shea, Tim, Murphy, Pat, Whitelegg, Elizabeth, Vincent, Tom. Computer assisted learning. *Institutional Research Review*, 1982, *1*, 59–79.

SCEMP (Scottish Community Education Microelectronics Project). Computers for all: report on work in progress. Edinburgh: Scottish Council for Community Education, 1982a.

SCEMP. Computers for all: report on work in progress, 2nd ed. Glasgow: Scottish Community Education Microelectronics Project, 1982b.

SCEMP. Guidelines for the design of computer programs for community use. Glasgow: Scottish Community Education Microelectronics Project, 1982c.

SCEMP. Report on work in progress, 3rd ed. Glasgow: Scottish Community Education Microelectronics Project, 1983.

SCEMP. SCEMP: another view. Glasgow: Scottish Community Education Microelectronics Project, 1984.

SCET. Guide to open learning opportunities in Scotland. Glasgow: Scottish Council for Educational Technology, 1981.

SCET. A directory of open learning opportunities in Scotland 1984. Glasgow: Scottish Council for Educational Technology, 1984.

Schmidt, Peggy. Custom fit in computer courses. *New York Times Education Consumer*. January 6, 1985, 7–8.

Schofield, Jack. How to bend your mind to suggestive proposals. *The Guardian*, October 11, 1984, 17.

Scotsman, The. FBI Inquiry into computer bank raids. August 13, 1983.

SED. Social implications of computer technology. 16–18 Module Descriptor 01–105. Edinburgh: Scottish Education Department, Spring, 1984.

Sharon, Donna. Applications of new technologies in nonformal adult education in Canada: two examples. New Technologies in Canadian Education Paper 9. Toronto: TV Ontario, 1984.

Sharpe, Tom. Cited in John Ezard, More than just words on paper, 1984. *The Guardian*, November 15, 1984, 17.

Sharples, Mike. A computer-based teaching scheme for creative writing. In R. Lewis and E.D. Tagg (Eds.), *Computers in Education*, 1981.

Sharples, M. and McConnell, D. Distance teaching by Cyclops: an educational evaluation of the Open University's Telewriting system. IET Paper 202. Milton Keynes: Open University, undated.

Shaw, Michael. Cause for complaint. *The Times Educational Supplement*. March 2, 1984, 58.

Sheffield City Council. Report of the employment coordinator, Women's Technology Training Workshop. Unpublished report for the Employment Program Committee, March 26, 1984.

Sheffield Computers for People. Leaflet, 118 Broomspring Lane, Sheffield S10, 2FO, undated.

Shotton, Margaret. Personal communication at the University of Loughborough, June 15, 1984.

Sieghart, Paul (Ed.). *Micro-chips with Everything: the Consequences of Information Technology*. London: Comedia Publishing Group in association with the Institute of Contemporary Arts, 1982.

SIGI (System of Interactive Guidance and Information). Leaflet, Educational Testing Service, Princeton, New Jersey 08541, undated.

Simons, G.L. *Women in Computing*. Manchester: National Computing Centre Limited, 1981.

Sims, D., VonFelt, J., Dowaliby, F., Hutchison, K., and Myers, T. A pilot experiment in computer-assisted speechreading instruction utilizing the Data Analysis Video Interactive Device (DAVID). *American Annals of the Deaf*, 1979, *124*, 616 and 618–623.

Skues, Nicky, New Horizons. *The Times Educational Supplement*, May 27, 1983, 41.

SMDP. List of microspecial software. Scottish Microelectronics Development Programme, June, 1984.

Smith, Robert. *Learning How to learn: Applied Theory for Adults*. Milton Keynes: Open University Press, 1983.

Smith, Stuart, Single-sex setting. In Rosemary Deem (Ed.), *Co-education Reconsidered*. Milton Keynes: Open University Press, 1984.

Smoker, Paul. In 1983, there were two false alarms of impending nuclear war every three days. *The Guardian*, August 2, 1984, 13.

Stanley, J.C. Comparison of men's and women's behaviors in high school math classes. California: SRI International, 1973.

Stevenson, Bob. Computer assisted learning. *CRASH*, 1983, *1*, 1.

Stevenson, Jim. In the piracy of their own homes. *The Times Education Supplement*, November 9, 1984, viii.

Sutherland, Margaret. Personal communication at Scottish Community Education Microelectronics Project, Glasgow, on September 20, 1984.

Swinfield, Ray. A software review of the computer-aided learning packages in numeracy/maths. In Basic Education and Computer Courses Interim Report, 1984.

Tebbutt, David. Computertown UK! Guidelines. Leaflet, London, undated.

TECS. Happenings. Computer program published by Teachers' Experience-Based Classroom Software, Liverpool, 1984.

Thompson, Henry. Always another moonrise. *The Scotsman*, October 17, 1984, 11.

Toffler, Alvin. *The Third Wave*. New York: William Morrow, 1980.

Traxler, John. Computers in basic education. *Viewpoints*, 1984a, *1*, 8–14.

Traxler, John. Computing. In Basic Education and Computer Course Interim Report, 1984b.

Trudel, Lina, and Belanger, Paul. Computerization: for better and for worse. Paper prepared for International Council of Adult Education Conference, Paris, October, 1982.

Turkle, Sherry. The subjective computer: a study in the psychology of personal computation. *Social Studies of Science*, 1982, *12*, 173–205.

Twyman, Jennifer. The use of computers in adult basic education: notes from a one-day EARAC/ALBSU Conference held on 5th December, 1983, at Robinson College, Cambridge. Norfolk: Norwich: Norfolk County Council Education Department, Adult Education Service, 1983.

Urquhart, Mary. Fife community education service. In Scottish Community Education Microelectronics Project, SCEMP: another view, 1983.

Van Gelder, Lindsy. The electronic campus. *Ms. Magazine*. October, 1984, 69–70.

Vincent, Tom. Home computing for the visually handicapped. *Teaching at a Distance*, 1983, *23*, 24–29.

Wagner, Ina. The acquisition of technical competence: do women workers' experiences with technical equipment contribute to a model of technology education? Paper presented to Conference on Interests in Science and Technology Education, 12th IPN Symposium in cooperation with UNESCO, Kiel, West Germany, April 2–6, 1984.

Walker, David. The evaluation of computer-assisted learning. In Jacquetta Megarry *et al.* (Eds.), *Computers and Education*, 1983.

Weizenbaum, Joseph. *Computer Power and Human Reason*. San Francisco: Freeman, 1976.

Weizman, Lenore. Sex-role socialization. In Jo Freedman (Ed.), *Women: A Feminist Perspective*. Palo Alto, Calif: Mayfield Publishing, 1975.

Werneke, Diane. *Microelectronics and Office Jobs: The Impact of the Chip on Women's Employment*. Geneva: International Labour Office, 1983.

Whiteside, T. *Computer Capers: Tales of Electronic Thievery, Embezzlement, and Fraud*. Scranton, Pa: T.Y. Crowell, 1978.

Whiting, B., and Pope, C. A cross cultural analysis of sex differences in the behavior of children age three to eleven. *Journal of Social Psychology*, 1973, *91*.

Whyte, Angus, and Fluendy, Annette. H.M. Prison, Saughton, Edinburgh: A Progress Report. In Scottish Community Education Microelectronics Project, SCEMP: another view, 1984.

Wider Opportunities for Women. Bridging the skills gap: women and jobs in a high tech world. Washington, D.C.: Wider Opportunities for Women, April, 1983.

Wilson, Joy. Educational applications of videotex: Telidon in Canada. New Technologies in Canadian Education Paper 11. Toronto: TV Ontario, 1984.

WISE (Women into Science and Engineering). "When I chose engineering, my friends thought it was a joke . . ." Equal Opportunities Commission leaflet, Manchester, 1984.

Women and Computing. Are computers feminist? London, 1981.

Women's National Commission. The other half of our future: report of the WNC's Ad-Hoc Working Group on training opportunities for women. Lòndon: Cabinet Office, 1984.

Woods, Howard. Community Computing. Unpublished project report for the B.Sc. Degree in Computer Studies, Sheffield City Polytechnic, March, 1984.

Wright, Peter, and MacLeod, Hamish. Breast or bottle? Experimental computer program developed for Scottish Community Education Microelectronics Project, Glasgow, 1981.

Yeates, Robin. *Prestel in the public library: reaction of the general public to Prestel and its potential for conveying local information.* Library and Information Research Report 2. London: British Library, 1982.

Zimmerman, Jan. Cited in Charlotte Beyers, Growing sex gap shows up in computer tastes, 1983.

INDEX